Indonesian & Javanese f
(Business, Military, Government

www.panduindonesia.com

www.aseanchameleon.com

Contributions by various people (see Author's Note)

Edited by Monique Van Der Harst, Galang Lufityanto, and Don Hobbs

English translations by Don Hobbs

Cover Art & Design by Katha Chareonpong and Don Hobbs

First Trial Edition published 25 December, 2011 (no ISBN)

E-Edition published 11 July, 2013

Current paperback ISBN 978-0-9897118-1-4
by Asian Lizard Languages

About the Book - Author's Note

This book came about because of a lack of quality Indonesian and especially Javanese language texts for foreigners, and my own desire to make sense of the years I spent in Indonesia. I have tried to make a text that is as versatile as possible –so that it can be used by teachers in a classroom, by individuals pursuing self-study, and as a handy reference guide.

My hope is that the text will prove useful for several groups of people: 1) those of you who already know some Indonesian and with the help of friends or a tutor want to learn more, 2) those of you who know Indonesian and want to learn Javanese, and 3) those of you who belong to professional organizations like the military, government, or an NGO, and whose particular technical language needs have so far been neglected by the Indonesian texts currently on the market.

Some features of this text make it different from most academic language texts. It does not contain a phonetic alphabet, undecipherable accent marks, or symbols that try to reproduce the intonation and flow of the language. I am not an academic linguist and feel that such features only make any language text less useful and impractical for most learners. Nor does this text make language more polite than it typically is (a common shortcoming of language texts). In short, it's a practical book for real language users in the real world.

Now, about the organization of the book, which is organized by topic. Each unit covers a single distinct topic. Naturally, many units complement one another (like Military and Environment), but each stands on its own and can be studied without having mastered a previous unit. Units 1 – 15 are meant to be generally useful to a wide range of individuals, while units 16 – 23 are more specialized.

This book assumes you have a basic knowledge of some Indonesian. It is not for beginners. At a minimum, you should know the Indonesian alphabet, pronunciation, numbers, and a few simple phrases and greetings before using this text, and have a vocabulary of several hundred words in Indonesian.

Finally, without the help of Indonesian friends who helped make some of the conversations, answered difficult questions about vocabulary and usage, and corrected my many mistakes in Indonesian, this book could not have been written. You know who you are: Mbak Mega, Heni, Desi, Jo-Jo, and Yusti. Bu Yeti and Andras. Mas Agus and Hendri. And of course, Monique and Galang for proofreading and editing all of the English language/culture notes and Indonesian/Javanese conversations, respectively. I thank all of you from the bottom of my heart.

Despite all of our hard work, I am sure this book (available in both print and e -pdf versions) will have a number of shortcomings, and would appreciate your help in improving it so that an enhanced 2nd edition can be published in a few years. Make suggestions, and check for new products at www.aseanchameleon.com

TABLE OF CONTENTS

Appendixes

Maps

CONVERSATIONS BY TOPIC
(Listed alphabetically. The Indonesian precedes the Javanese.)

READING SAMPLES BY TOPIC

Spellings & Markings Used in this Book

1. The letter 'e' in Indonesian can be pronounced one of two ways — as a short/soft 'e' found in words like bed, red, special. Or, as a schwa/short 'u' sound in words like problem, taken, listen. Sometimes, as in English, one word may contain a soft 'e' and a schwa 'e,' as in the word sentence or enemy. As normally written in bahasa Indonesia without any accent marks, the pronunciation of unknown words with the letter 'e' is not always apparent to non-native speakers. **In the vocabulary section** of each unit I have spelled words with an é (with an accent mark) whenever the 'e' is pronounced as a soft 'e' (red, bed). Wherever the 'e' is unaccented, it can be pronounced as the schwa. Additionally, an accent mark has been added throughout the text to words that might be troublesome to readers whose proficiency in Indonesian is limited.

2. 'e' in Javanese can make 3 sounds: (1) schwa, (2) soft 'e', or (3) long 'a' sound found in words such as *toupee* or *fiancé*. As a final 'e', which so often occurs, it makes this same sound (3) and has not been given an accent mark. I have simplified matters and used é with accent mark to denote sounds (2) or (3) in troublesome words. **Readers using the Javanese portions of the text need to read Unit 4: Javanese Pronunciation, for details on the pronunciation and marking of 'e' in this text.**

3. Javanese spelling: Words like *basa, Jawa,* and *lunga* are normally spelled with the letter 'a', but are pronounced as a long 'o' (boso, Jowo, lungo). To assist non-Javanese speakers, I have tried to spell such words correctly, but with the letter 'a' underlined: it appears as a wherever it should be pronounced as long 'o.' In cases other than the 'a' , I have occasionally used parentheses to assist with a particular word in which pronunciation is tricky and not apparent from its spelling. For example, uwis (already) is pronounced more like uwés; it appears in the text for the first time like this: uwis (uwés). The 'k' in Javanese is usually pronounced whenever it is added as a suffix to a root, but silent when it is considered part of the word itself. I have used parentheses to tell the reader when 'k' is not pronounced, so that the word déwéké (silent k) will appear like this: déwé(k)é But, the word uripké appears simply as: uripké .

4. Organization of each unit: Each of the main units (not grammar or appendices) is organized in the same way and may contain up to six sections. First, *Vocabulary*, followed by *Language and Culture Notes*, then by *Indonesian Conversations*, then *Reading Selections* if any, then *Javanese Conversations*, and finally, *English Translations of Conversations*. The Javanese conversations are the same as the Indonesian conversations in each unit.

5. In the vocabulary section of each unit, I have used the letter '**s**' in the Javanese column, to note when a word is the same (*sama*) in Javanese as it is in Indonesian.

6. In the vocabulary section of each unit, I have used a * to denote any word which has a related comment in the Language & Cultural Notes section, which follows the vocabulary.

1. WORDS YOU KNOW

These are all common words which come from English (or Dutch) roots that you will recognize. Familiarize yourself with them so that you can use them in everyday situations.

Electric & Household

(English)	*(Indonesian)*	*(Javanese)*
television	télevisi	—
TV	tivi	s
telephone	télépon	s
electric	listrik	s
radio	radio	s
lamp	lampu	s
neon	néon	s
dvd	dvd	s
cd	cd	s
computer	komputer	s
wi-fi	wifi	s
wi-fi access spot	hotspot	s
disk	disk	s
camera	kamera	tustel
photo	foto	poto
table	méja (think Sp: 'mesa')	s
dispenser	dispénser	s
tank	tangki	tandhon
gas (cooking)	élpiji (LPG-liquified petroleum gas)	
detergent	déterjén	s
capacity	kapasitas	s
volt	volt	s
amp	ampér	s
conversion	konvérsi	ganti/owah
installation	instalasi	s
wire	kabel	s
tape	tape (pron. same)	s
drill	bor	s
tissue (TP/Kleenex)	tissu	s
book	buku	s
shelves/rack	rak	s
drawer	laci (think 'latch')	s
calendar	kalender	tanggalan
envelope	amplop	s
rug	karpét	s

| pipe | pipa | s |
| perfume | parfum | minyak wangi |

Transportation & Mechanical

baggage	bagasi	s
bus	bus	bis
car	mobil	s
clutch, gears	kopling (coupling)	s
diameter	diaméter	s
diesel	disel	s
engine	mesin	s
gas/petrol	bénsin	s
gas station	pom bénsin (pump bensin)	s
helmet	hélm	s
hotel	hotél	s
kilometer	kilo/kilometer	s
license plate	plat	s
liter	liter	s
motorcycle	motor, sepéda motor	montor
oil	oli	s
passport	paspor	s
pedicap	bécak (silent k)	s
reservation	réservasi	pesenan
service/tune-up	servis	s
station	stasiun	s
taxi	taksi	s
terminal	terminal	s
traffic signal/lamp	lampu	bangjo
truck	truk	trek
visa	visa	s
wheel	roda (think 'road')	s

Food & Drink

alcohol	alkohol	s
apple	apel	s
avocado	apokad, alpokat	sapukad
beer	bir	s
bottle	botol	gendhul
bottled water	aqua (a-ku-wa, think Spanish for water)*	
burger	burger	s
buffet	buffet*	s
cafeteria/canteen	kantin	s
cheese	keju (think Spanish queso)	s
chocolate	cokelat	s
coffee	kopi	s
durian	durian	duren
fork	garpu	porok
glass	gelas	s
hot dog, sausage	sosis	s
ice	és	s
ice cream	és krim	s
ketchup	saus tomat*	s
mango	mangga	pelem
mayonnaise	mayonés	s
mineral	mineral	s
packet/package set	pakét	s
pear	pir, pér	s
pizza	pizza	s
rambutan	rambutan	s
satay	saté	s
sauce	saus	saos
soup	sop	s
soy sauce/teriyaki sauce	kécap*	s
sushi	sushi	s
syrup (for drinks)	sirup	stroop
tea	téh	s
tomato	tomat	s
vitamin	vitamin	s

Economic, Business, News

bank	bank (bang)	s
bankrupt	bangkrut	s
cashier	kasir	s
criminal	kriminal	s
crisis	krisis	s
deficit	défisit	rugi
devaluation	dévaluasi	s
engineer	insinyur	s
economy	ékonomi	s
export	éxpor	s
extreme	ékstrim	s
facilities	fasilitas	s
factory	pabrik (think fabric)	s
import	impor	s
information	informasi	kabar
infrastructure	infrastruktur, prasarana	sarana
international	internasional	s
nuclear	nuklir	s
patrol	patroli	s
police	polisi	s
president	presidén	s
the press/media	pérs	s
production	produksi	s
routine	rutin	s
tariff/duty tax	tarif	rega

Academic - School

teacher	guru	s
secretary	sékretaris	s
school	sekolah	s
university	universitas	s
Faculty/School (of Law..)	fakultas	s
department	departemén	s
thesis	skripsi (think script), tésis*	s
astronomy	astronomi	s
biology	biologi	s
gene	gén	s
chemistry	kimia	s
engineering	téknik	s
geology	géologi	s

11

novel	novél	s
physics	fisika	s
psychology	psikologi	s
politics	politik	s
demonstration	démonstrasi/démo	s
revolution	révolusi	s
implementation	impleméntasi	s
certification	sertifikasi	s
competency	kompéténsi	kabisan
inspiration	inspiras	ilham
attraction	atraksi	s
camp, program	outbound*	s

Countries

America (U.S.)	Amérika (A.S.)	s
Australia	Australia (pron: Ostrali)	s
Canada	Kanada	s
China	Cina	s
England	Inggris	s
Europe	Éropa	s
France	Perancis	s
Holland	Belanda	Landa
Israel	Israel	s
Italy	Italia	s
Japan	Jepang	s
Mexico	Méksiko	s
Palestine	Palestina	s

*The notable exceptions are Egypt – Mesir, New Zealand – Selandia Baru, and Greece – Yunani.

Months

January	Januari	s
February	Fébruari	s
March	Marét	s
April	April	s
May	Méi	s
June	Juni	s
July	Juli	s
August	Agustus	s

12

September	Séptémber	s
October	Oktober	s
November	Novémber	s
December	Desémber	s

Military - Political

attaché	atasé	s
military	militér	s
intelligence/intel	intelijénsi/intél	s
location	lokasi	s
compass	kompas	s
coordinates	koordinat	s
position (location)	posisi	s
detect	détéksi	s
camp	kamp (pron: often with silent p, kam)	
detachment	détasemén	s
tent	ténda	s
canteen, mess	kantin	s
general	jénderal	jéndral
colonel	kolonél	s
major	mayor	s
lieutenant	létnan	s
sergeant	sersan	s
commander	komandan	s
cadre	kader	s
retirement/retired	pénsiun *	s
marine	marinir	s
pilot	pilot	s
helicopter	hélikopter	s
tank	tank (pron: téng)	s
ammunition	amunisi	s
artillery	artileri	s
destruction	déstruksi	s
cargo	kargo	s
mortar	mortir	s
pistol	pistol (pronounce: péstol)	bedil
invade	(meng)invasi	s
tattoo	tato	rajah

Medical

AIDS	AIDS (same pronunciation)	s
alcohol	alkohol	s
analgesic	analgésik	s
anti-	anti-	s
antibiotic	antibiotik	s
antiseptic	antiséptik	s
asthma	asma	mengi
aspirin	aspirin (as pi rin' each syl. pronounced clearly)	
bandaids	pléster (from Brit. Eng.)	tensoplast
block	blok	s
cancer	kanker	s
compress	komprés	s
diabetes	diabétes	lara gula
diarrhea	diaré	mencret
doctor	dokter	s
dysenteri	diséntri (accent 2nd syllable)	s
form	formulir	isian
formaldahyde	formalin	s
HIV	HIV (ha i vé)	s
ibuprofen	ibuprofen	s
incision	insisi, iris	iris
insurance	asuransi	s
Iodine	Betadine (brand name)*	yodium
lotion	lotion (pron: losien)	s
medic	médis	s
mineral	minéral	s
narcotic	narkotika	s
nurse	suster (think 'sister,' at a Catholic hospital)	
pharmacy	apotik	s
pincers	péngser	s
sport cream (icy hot)	Counter Pain (brand name)*	s
stethoscope	stétoskop	s
tourniquet	turnikét	s
tweezers	pinsét (think pincers)	s
vitamin	vitamin	s
zinc	séng	s

Activities, Games, Sports

ball	bola	bal
balloon	balon	s
band	band	s
basketball	baskét	s
blackjack/21	blackjack	s
bridge (card game)	bridge	s
chat (online/on mobile phone)	chatting, cét	omong-omong
exhibition	eksibisi (for 'exhibition game')	s
fitness center/gym	fitness	s
guitar	gitar	s
lottery	loteré	lotré
marching band	drum band	s
mic(rophone)	mik(ropon)	s
mobile phone	hp (ha pé, think handphone)	s
monopoly	monopoli	s
piano	piano	s
pool/billiards	biliard/bilyar	s
poker	poker	s
racket	rakét	s
stadium	stadion	s
tennis	ténis	s
trumpet	terompét	s
violin	biola	s
volleyball	voli	s

Others

ashtray	asbak (ash bag)	s
audition	audisi	s
blinker/turn signal	réting (think 'right thing')	s
boss	bos*	s
Buddhist	budha	s
castle	kastil	s
Catholic	katolik	s
cement	semén	s
Christian	kristén	s
complaint	kritik* /komplain	s
Confucius	kong hu cu	s
credibility	krédibilitas	s
free	gratis	s
giraffe	jerapah	s

15

grand opening/premiere	launching* /perdana	perd<u>an</u>a
Hindu	hindu	s
jacket/coat	jakét	s
must	musti	mesti
obsession	obsési	s
particle board	bb/*block b*oard	triplék
porch (outside house)	téras (from terrace)	émpér
promotion/promo (sale)	promosi/promo	t<u>aw</u>a
quality	kualitas	mutu
romantic	romantis	s
sandals/flip-flops	sandal	s
sarong	sarung	s
sex	séks	s
sexy	séksi	semog
shoes	sepatu (like Spanish zapatos)	s
stamp	stémpel*	cap
sticker	stiker	s
typhoon	topan	lésus
run amok	mengamuk (amok)*	s

Language & Culture Notes

1. *Aqua* is not technically the correct term for bottled water, but rather the established most popular brand name, as well as the easiest and most common way to ask for it. Technically, it should be called *air mineral* or *air minuman*. (This is like asking for a 'kleenex' in the States, which will get you what you want, versus asking for 'tissue,' which might result in some confusion). Just ask for *aqua*.

2. The English word 'buffet' is used most commonly at mid-range or more expensive hotels popular with Indonesian and western tourists. Since breakfast at Indonesian hotels is usually included in the room price, they will often have a buffet breakfast that typically includes fried rice, noodles, eggs, some type of Indonesian potatoes or curry, toast, jams, coffee, and tea. The Indonesian word for buffet is *prasmanan*, but it is strictly a pay-by-the-plate affair, rather than a Western, all-you-can-eat one. Many Indonesians still do not know the word buffet, and some will pronounce it incorrectly, such as 'bupét'.

3. *Saus tomat* (lit. 'tomato sauce') is (American) ketchup. And, *kecap* is sweet soy/terikayi sauce, which is easy to remember since the Indonesian word is almost identical to the word 'ketchup' in American English.

4. The word *skripsi* is used to mean a thesis that undergraduates write to complete their degree, while *tesis* is used to mean one that graduate students have to write.

5. The word outbound (from the English) is used by Indonesians for special outings that would be called a 'camp,' 'program,' 'outing,' 'seminar,' or 'workshop' in English. For example, a church group's outing or Bible camp, band camp, summer camp, a teacher's training seminar, or day-long teacher's training program/workshop. Most Indonesians will assume that since the word 'outbound' is English, any Westerner will know what they are talking about when they describe some event as 'outbound.' Like many words borrowed from English, they do not realize the way in which the word is used has been changed by them, and is no longer the same as the original word in English.

6. *Pensiun* obviously comes from 'pension' in English. It is used the same way: *Menurut aturan militer AS, setelah 20 tahun, seseorang bisa dapat pensiun.* (In accordance with U.S. military regulations , after 20 years, one can receive a retirement/pensiun). Or more simply, *Dia sudah pensiun* (He's already retired).

7. *Betadine* is a brand name, but asking for iodine will only cause confusion.

8. *Counter pain* is a brand name, but the most common sports cream, easy to remember, and easier than trying to explain 'cream for sore muscles' in Indonesian.

9. I have included the word '*bos*' in this list, only because it has become widely known and fashionable to use, although in an extremely annoying and incorrect way by anyone who would be considered subservient to you (such as a parking attendant or a driver, or someone trying to sell you something). The response '*Ya, bos*' has unfortunately, become quite a cool, trendy thing to say in Indonesia; hopefully it falls out of fashion soon.

10. The word *kritik* is used only in a special context for 'complain,' either in restaurants or on TV shows. There is a *kotak kritik dan saran* (complaint/suggestion box) at some restaurants where you can fill out a form or write a note in order to complain, praise, or make a suggestion to management. And, after TV shows when the credits roll, the viewing audience is asked to 'send any kritik/complaints to ...' (some an address, phone, or email). In usage, the word *kritik* is like the noun critique in English - it is not used as the general verb 'to complain.' (Complaint is a better translation than critique, however, since we wouldn't say a 'critique box' or 'send a critique about a TV show to ...' Culturally, in Indonesia (especially in Javanese culture), it is considered ill-mannered to complain about things in public. So, one does not complain to a waitress, for example, even though the service is terrible and the food is cold. Nor does one ask for and complain to a store manager because the cashier doesn't know anything about the inventory and the store is out of some item it should have (common problems in Indonesia). You get the picture. Generally, people suffer through annoyances, inconveniences, and incompetence in situations where Westerners would complain.

11. Launching is the (English) word used in place of premiere or grand opening. For example, *besok ada launching untuk buku barunya.* (Tomorrow there's a grand opening event for the new book).

12. In Indonesian, *stempél* applies to standard stamps that go on envelopes; another word for this is *perangko*. Javanese tend to use *cap*. In both languages, the stamp + inkpad that businesses use is *cap* and for the official stamp that goes on documents, available from the post office for around 6000 rupiah, the word is *materai*. Indonesians love stamps.

13. The word amok and subsequent term 'run amok' in English actually come from the Malay/Indonesian word, and the tendency of crowds/mobs in the islands to do exactly that (as recorded by early colonial observers).

18

Recommended Self-Study Activities

Memory/Concentration:

(1) Use card paper to make a set of cards with all the vocabulary words from this unit on them, one with the English word and one with the Indonesian to form a matching pair. To make it more difficult, make the Indonesian cards without words – using pictures only. Alternatively, to make it easier, use cards of one color for the English, cards of another color for the Indonesian.

(2) Play the following 'concentration' or 'memory' game, with one or two other players, or in pairs:

(3) Place all cards face down in rows and columns. In turn, players turn two cards over with the object being to get a matching pair. Matching pairs go again, not matching = turn passes to next player. The winner is the player/team with the most matching pairs at game's end.

(4) Say each word as you turn over the cards. For all matching pairs, make a simple sentence using the word on the cards. Say it aloud. For example, 'Is there a computer here?' then, the same in Indonesian 'Apa(kah) ada komputer di sini?' or 'Do you have a computer? 'Apakah Anda punya komputer?' or 'Are you a teacher?' 'Apakah <u>title + name</u> (Pak Ronni) guru?' or 'Is this a _____?' Keep the sentences simple but vary them according to your existing level of Indonesian.

(5) If the other players catch a player making a mistake with the Indonesian, that player loses his/her turn and does not get the matching pair.

'Go Fish' card game 2-7 players:

(1) Use the same set of cards as above, deal 4-7 cards to each player (more cards for fewer players, fewer cards if there are more players).

(2) This is your hand. Do not let the other players see the cards in your hand.

(3) Spread out all the remaining cards face-down, to make a 'fish pond'/draw pile.

Rules for 'Go Fish' (cont.)

(4) The objective is to get matching pairs by asking other players for cards already in your hand. In turn, ask any of the other players if they have a card you need: '*Ada antibiotik?*'

(5) If the other player has the card in his hand, he hands (gives) it over, and you go again.

(6) If not, he replies: 'Tidak/nggak ada. Go Fish!' and you take any card you want from the fish pond. Turn goes to the next player.

(7) As you get matching pairs, lay them down, face-up in front of you.

(8) Play stops when one player has no more cards in his hand.

(9) The player with the most pairs at the end of the game is the winner.

(10) For language practice, vary the sentence that you say in Indonesian when asking for a card from another player, from '*ada*' to any sentence from the conversations: '*Saya mencari plester,*' (I'm looking for bandaids), or '*Saya perlukan kartu plester*' (The card I need is plaster), for example.

2. 50 ESSENTIAL VERBS

For the Indonesian, all of the verbs are given in their root form, which can usually be either a verb or noun. Knowing the root, you can add prefixes and suffixes to form nouns, verbs, adjectives, and adverbs (explained in the unit: Indonesian Grammar Basics). For Javanese, roots alone are not likely to be used as verbs, so in the Javanese list the verb form of the word is given rather than the root form.

English	Indonesian	Javanese
agree, approve	setuju	s /mathuk
ask	tanya, minta*	takon
accept	terima	nampa
bathe (take a bath)	mandi	adus
borrow	pinjam	nyili'h
buy	beli	tuku
can	bisa, dapat*	isa
carry	bawa	gawa
clean	bersih	resik
come	datang	teka
do	laku(kan), kerja(kan)*	lakoni, garap
drink, take medicine	minum*	ngombé
eat	makan	mangan, maem*
get up (wake)	bangun	tangi
give	beri	wenéhi, kéi
go	pergi	lunga
have/already	(s)udah	(u)wés
have to do	harus	kudu
know (something)	tahu	weruh, ngerti
know someone, introduce	kenal	s, wanuh
learn, study	belajar	sinau
like	suka, senang*	seneng

21

love	cinta	tresna
make, build	buat	gawé
meet someone	jumpa, temu*	ketemu
need, be needed	butuh, perlu	s
not (with verbs, adj, adv)	tidak/nggak/gak/tak*	ora
not (with nouns)	bukan	dudu
open	buka	mbukak
own, belong to (possessive)	milik, punya*	duwé
please (do for me), to aid	tolong	tulung
please (go ahead, do it)	silahkan	mangga
put in order, straighten up	rapi	rapih
read	baca	maca
receive	terima	nampa
reply	jawab	mangsuli
see	lihat	ndelok
sell	jual	adol
send	kirim	s
sit	duduk	lungguh
sleep	tidur	turu
take	ambil	jupuk
talk about/discuss	bicara tentang/membicarakan*	rembug
teach	ajar	mulang
turn on	hidupkan	uripké
turn off	matikan	paténi
understand	paham /mengerti	ngerti
use/wear	pakai, gunakan*	angga
watch	nonton, saksi*	delok
want	mau, ingin, péngén*	gelem, arep*
work	kerja	nyambut gawé
write	tulis	s

Language Notes

1. The root *tanya* often takes a *ber* prefix and is used actively as *bertanya* – to ask, and as a noun, *pertanyaan* - question. It is very broad in meaning (like the verb 'ask' in English), versus *minta*, which is used more narrowly only in situations where one is asking a favor of someone or requesting something. *Minta ma'af* - I beg your pardon /ask your forgiveness. *Aku mau minta ayah belikan aku mobil*- I'll ask Dad to give me the car. In the sentence *Dia bertanya kalau aku pernah ke sana* - She asked if I have ever been there, *bertanya* cannot be replaced by *minta*.

2. *Bisa* and *dapat* are interchangeable, when used for the verb 'can.' *Dapat* has the additional meaning of 'get.' In Java, the verb *bisa* is more common, while in some outlying areas where a form of Malay is the mother tongue, *dapat* tends to be more common. In Javanese, the verb is spelled *isa*, but pronounced *iso*.

3. The difference in *lakukan* and *kerjakan* for do: *Lakukan* is more general in use and applicable in more situations (which is why I seem to always use *lakukan* for everything and never use *kerjakan*). *Kerjakan* has a physical sense and refers only to some kind of work or task. *Sudah kamu kerjakan skripsi mu?* Did you do your thesis? *Dia kerjakan tugasnya* - He did his duty. *Apa yang kamu lakukan sekarang?* What are you doing now? *Ada beberapa hal yang harus saya lakukan* - There are several things I have to do.

4. As in many Asian languages, the verb *minum* – to drink, is also the way to say 'take medicine' – *minum obat*.

5. In Javanese, *mangan* is more polite and used for adults, *maem* is ngoko, and reserved usually for kids or used between friends to be funny or cute, as in 'chow down.'

6. *Suka* is the more direct way of saying 'like,' especially with food or something material. *Aku suka coklat* - I like chocolate. *Senang* has more of a sense of to be happy with/about. It seems that with Javanese, at least, *seneng* is very common and less direct than using *suka*, when they are interchangeable. *Aku senang rumah ini* - I like this house/I'm happy with this house. This sentence could just as well be *Aku suka rumah ini*, but the former is more common.

7. For the verb 'meet,' *jumpa* is more restricted in meaning, while *temu* is broader in meaning, and can also mean 'to find.' *Aku belum temu(kan) kuncinya* – I haven't found the key yet. 'Until we meet again,' can be either *Sampai bertemu lagi*, or *Sampai jumpa lagi*, but the latter is not as formal sounding and is more popular, especially in emails, sms texts, and so on.

8. *Tidak* is the most formal way to say 'not' or 'no' for the negative. *Nggak* is common in informal speech. *Gak* is even more informal/contracted, while *tak* is the popular shortened form of *tidak* in writing or text.

9. *Punya* is fairly broad in meaning, and translates as 'have.' *Aku punya motor* - I have a motorcycle, versus *motor ini milik siapa* – Whose motorcycle is this? Or, *Dia pemilik rumahnya* – He's the owner of the house. versus *Dia punya rumah besar* – He has a big house.

10. The root *bicara* means to talk. When used with the *ber* prefix, the preposition *tentang* (about) has to be used with it: *Kita tidak berbicara tentang apa pun* – We didn't talk about anything. When used with the *mem* prefix and *kan* suffix, it becomes 'discuss' and does not require *tentang: Kita tidak membicarakan apa pun* – We didn't discuss anything.

11. The difference in *pakai* and *gunakan*: *Pakai* is broader and more general in meaning, and is also used for the verb 'to wear.' *Gunakan* is usually used for something that is physical and often has a procedure. The word 'utilize' in English translates well as *gunakan*.

12. *Saksi* is the word for witness. But, it is used by Indonesian TV and in general to mean the same as *nonton*, to watch - *Saksikan acara ini sabtu malam jam 2100 WIB* - Watch this program Sat night at 9pm Western Indonesian Time. Otherwise, words with the *saksi* root have the meaning of eyewitness, witness, give evidence, etc.

13. The differences between *mau, ingin, and péngén*: *Mau* has a future sense/intention as 'going to' does in English, while *ingin* has purely a physical wanting of something. *Mau ke mana Mister?* Where are you going Mister? *Aku mau pergi ke Bali* – I'm going to go to Bali/I want to go to Bali. *Aku ingin hp baru* – I want a new mobile phone. *Péngén* is simply the popular slang for the word *ingin*. In Javanese, *arep* is like *mau*, with the same broad/dual meaning, and *gelem* is like *ingin*, with a restricted physical desire.

3. INDONESIAN GRAMMMAR BASICS

Prefixes & Suffixes for Verbs

1. (Prefix) me/men/meng + root = action verb that has a direct or indirect object.

potong = cut. This root can be used as either a noun or verb. To be more precise and accurate, it can and should be changed to memotong when the verb is an active one with an object. Note: *Dia memotong jarinya* - He cut his finger. Here are the rules for attaching the prefix to roots:

Root = l, m, n, ng, ny, r, w, y	add *me: lihat → melihat*
Root = c, d, j, t (c/j or t/d sound)	add *me: cari → mencari*
Root = b, p, f	add *mem* drop p: *pikir→ memikir*
Root = all vowels, g, k, h	add *meng* *the k gets dropped
Root = s	add *men,* s to y: *sukai→ menyukai*

2. Other action verbs sometimes take the prefix 'ber' when they do not have a direct object:

berlari - run, *berbahasa* - speak, *berpérang* - go to war, *berbicara* - talk

3. me + root + kan/i = to make it happen, to do for someone. Always has a direct object. In the Jakarta area, *kan* is changed to *i* by most speakers in informal/colloquial speech, with the same meaning.

mengingatkan – to remind someone of x, for me
memanasi – to heat something up
membelikan – to buy it for someone

4. me + root + i = to keep doing something repeatedly.

mengambili – keep taking, *membacai* – read over and over

5. ter + root = the most

terbaik – the best, *terburuk* – the worst, *termahal* – the most expensive, *terkenal* – famous (most known)

6. ter + root = to happen by accident

terjadi – to happen, *terjatuh* – to drop something, *termakan* – accidentally swallow

7. ke + root + an = to be on receiving end of a bad thing

kehujanan – to be caught in the rain
kesakitan – to be really sick, suffering from an illness
kecurian – to have been robbed

Prefixes & Suffixes with a 'Passive voice' function

This occurs frequently in Indonesian, and to become proficient in the spoken language, it is necessary to learn to use the following naturally.

1. ter + root = be verb + past participle in English

terputus – *Koneksi telpon terputus.* The phone connection was cut off.

2. di + root = passive (be vb. + p.p. in English)

Coklatnya dimakan. The chocolate was eaten. / Someone ate the chocolate.

Mobil ini dijual. This car is for sale.

3. di + root + kan (in cases where the active form has a 'kan' suffix)

membelikan – buy for someone; *dibelikan* – was bought

4. di + root + i (in cases where the active verb has an 'i' suffix)

Motor ku sudah diperbaiki. – My motorcycle has already been fixed. / They already fixed my motorcycle.

Dia disukai semua siswa. – All the students like him. /
(He's liked by all the students.)

Prefixes & Suffixes which form nouns

1. pe/pem/pen + root = a person or thing that does it, like the suffix 'er' in English.

pencuri - thief, *pemotong* - cutter, *pendengar* - listener, *pekerja* - worker

2. root + an = noun. Like English suffixes 'ion, al, ment, y,' this results in a number of meanings, but always some kind of noun derived from the root/verb.

makanan - food, *ratusan* - hundreds, *pikiran* - thought, *pilihan* - choice, *kerjaan* - job

3. ke + root + an = an abstract noun.

kejadian - outcome, *kemajuan* - progress, *keselamatan* - security, *kekuatan* - strength, *kewajiban* - duty

---

Adverbs

se + root + nya	to make an adverb ('ly' or time phrase)
sebenarnya	actually, in fact
sebelumnya	before that
seadanya	as much as there is
secepatnya	as fast as possible

Recommended Self-Study Activities

Jumbled Word Parts:

(1) You can use either strips of paper or cards to make the word parts for this activity. For paper strips, use 6 sheets of paper. Cut the sheets into strips (about 10 strips/page). Now cut the strips into 3 sections. One long section in the middle, two equal short sections at each end, like this:

_____cut_____cut_____

(2) If using cards, use a regular-sized index/playing card for the middle section and half a card each for the end sections. You will need about 150 cards total.

(3) Now, write all of the root words of all the verbs in Unit 2 on the long strips of paper (middle section). Get rid of any long strips (blank) remaining. The only strips not written on are now the short strips.

(4) Write the prefix 'ke' on 12 short strips. Write 'an' on 12. Write 'ber' on 12. And, write 'kan' on 10 strips.

(5) Write 'me' on 6, 'men' on 6, and 'meng' on 6. Write 'pe' 'pen' and 'pem' on 6 short strips each as well. And finally, write 'i' on 6 strips.

(6) You now have a complete set of roots, prefixes, and suffixes to work with.

(7) Separate all the strips into three categories/piles: prefixes, roots, and suffixes.

(8) If working by yourself, use the strips to make words. Time yourself, seeing how many words you can make in a minute. Get faster.

(9) If working with another person in a pair or group, divide up the prefix and suffix strips equally, make additional copies of the roots. See which person or team can make the most words in a minute.

Rules for Jumbled Word Parts (cont.)

(10) With three or more players, one person throws a root word in the middle and the other players must choose a prefix or suffix that makes an appropriate word. Whoever is the quickest gets to keep the word. The winner gets to throw the next root word in the middle and the other players throw in a prefix or suffix and the fastest correct word wins. Keep going until all root words are used up. The winner is the one with the most words at the end.

Sentence Practice:

(1) Use the verbs from Unit 2 in sentences.

(2) Write two sentences using the active form of the verb, then 2 more sentences using a noun form of the root made from adding a prefix, suffix, or both.

(3) Have your teacher/tutor check the sentences and correct them.

(4) Make careful note of the difference in grammar and usage between the verb and noun sentence forms.

Crossword Puzzles:

(1) Use crossword puzzle software to make a crossword puzzle. A good free online maker can be found at www.eclipsecrossword.com

(2) Use the Indonesian words in the vocabulary section of Unit 2 as the answers, and write the clues in English.

(3) Use both root words and also related words formed with prefixes and/or suffixes for the word list (answers) to your puzzle. For example, clue/answer pairs for the root word *cinta* could be:
Love (n.) / *cinta*
To love someone. / *mencinta*
To have sex with/make love to someone. / *bercinta*

(4) Use a good bilingual dictionary/app to help you make the word list for step number 3.

(5) Have a native Indonesian speaker check your word list when you are finished to make sure all the words you have created/used for your puzzle are actually used in real-life.

(6) Solve the puzzle/share it with your friends.

4. JAVANESE PRONUNCIATION

1. The letter A and the long o (ō) sound (as in vote)

- Words tend to end in a long o (ō) sound, as in Suhart*o*. This usually happens when they are spelled with final 'a' as well as 'o'

- A word spelled with two a's separated by consonants will nearly always be pronounced as long o. Example *basa* (language) = bōsō. *Jawa* (Java) = jōwō. So, *basa jawa* = bōsō jōwō, the Javanese language. *Surabaya* is pronounced 'Suroboyo.'

(As stated in 'Markings and Spellings' page 7, the latter appears as Sura<u>ba</u>ya in this text, to help the reader know when 'a' is pronounced as long 'o'.)

2. Pronunciation of C / K / P

- '*c*' is not aspirated as English 'ch'; it is close to a soft '*j*'
- '*k*' is close to a soft '*g*' sound, not aspirated as in English
- '*p*' is also non-aspirated, like a soft '*b*'

3. The letter E

- For speakers semi-proficient in Indonesian, the pronunciation of 'e' in Javanese presents very few difficulties and is usually obvious
- Letter 'e' in Javanese can make 3 sounds: (1) schwa/soft u, (2) soft 'e', or (3) long 'a':
- (1) If e makes a schwa sound in Indonesian, it usually does in Javanese: *rendang, benar/bener*
- (2) Makes a soft 'e' sound (red) in few words – usually same as Indonesian or evident: *wortel, pendek, nek, ket, pengen*
- (3) Many words in Javanese end in 'e.' When one does, it is <u>always</u> pronounced as the sound found in words like *hey, fiancé, frappé*

To keep markings as simple as possible, an accent mark has not been placed over the final e in words, except in the vocabulary lists and in Unit 7 (so you get used to reading it as sound 3). Throughout the text, in words where the pronunciation of 'e' may not be clear, an accent mark (é) has been used when the word first appears in a given conversation, to show that e should be pronounced as either long 'a' (fiancé) or soft 'e' (red). Later in the same conversation, the same word may not be marked.

4. The letter I

As in Indonesian, 'i' is pronounced as long 'e' (**see**). However, words ending in *'ih'* are not pronounced with long ēē, but like soft 'i' (sit) but with stronger emphasis, or often more like a soft 'e' as in 'envelope.'

5. KE

For words ending in *'ke'* if *ke* is a suffix added to the root word, the k is pronounced. But, if the *ke* is part of the word, the k is not pronounced. For example, *deweke* (he/she) is pronounced: *dé · wé · é* while *macake* (read for someone) is pronounced: *mo · cho · ké*

6. T's and D's

There are 4 consonants in Javanese that cover the d-t spectrum; each has a slightly different sound and none exactly match either 'd' or 't' in English. But, no worries! From a practical standpoint, everyone should understand you even if the pronunciation of each d or t is not exact.

When using the English/romanized alphabet, these 4 consonants are spelled: d, dh, t, th
Here's what sounds they roughly correlate to:

d = a regular 'd' in English

dh = a d sound, but with a back of the throat soft 'h' added.

t = close to 't' in English, but not so aspirated

th = non-aspirated soft 't' but with a strong h (air) sound added from back of throat.   *Yes, this adoption of spelling for Javanese can cause some confusion because the 'th' spelling does not make the same sound as 'th' in English.

Practice: Have a Javanese native speaker say a word with each of these 4 sounds and listen and copy him/her, until you can tell the difference between them and are able to closely parrot each t-d sound as correctly as possible.

5. JAVANESE GRAMMAR BASICS

Good news! Javanese grammar is very similar to Indonesian grammar, if not always the same. Practically, it is mostly a matter of substituting Javanese words and particles (prefixes, suffixes, linking phrases) for Indonesian ones. You will note that the content in this section follows the previous 'Indonesian Grammar' section as closely as possible.

Prefixes & Suffixes which form Verbs

1. m/n/ng + root = action verb.

Unlike informal Indonesian, where it is often okay to be lazy and use the root word as either a verb or noun, it is more essential in Javanese to use this prefix to make the root an active verb. Here are the rules for attaching the prefix to roots, based on the initial consonant or vowel:

Root = b   add m: *bales* → *mbales* (to give X back)
Root = p, w   drop and add m: *pijet* → *mijet* (press X)

Root = d, dh, j   add n: *delok* → *ndelok* (watch xthing)
Root = t, th   drop and add n: *tuku* → *nuku* (buy xthing)

Root = vowel   add ng: *adus* → *ngadus* (bathe/wash)
Root = g, r, l   add ng: *garap* → *nggarap* (do xthing)
Root = k   drop and add ng: *kumpul* → *ngumpul* (gather x)

Root = c, s   drop, add ny: *silih* → *nyilih* (borrow xthing)

This is not more complicated than Indonesian, but slightly different. The main point to remember is that a nasalized ng/n/m sound at beginning of a word indicates an action verb.

**2. m/n/ng + root + ké = to make it happen, to do for someone.
Always has a direct object. Same general functions as 'kan' suffix in
Indonesian. (Note 'aké' is the written form in ngaka and it is 'aken'
in krama)**

nukoké	to buy something for someone (*membelikan*)
nggawaké	bring for someone (*membawakan*)
macaké (mocoké)	to read for someone (*membacakan*)

**3. Unfortunately, there are a few basic rules for adding suffixes
(follow these for the other suffixes that follow as well):**

Word ends in any consonant except n	= add suffix
Word ends in n	= drop n, add suffix
Word ends in a, e, o	= add suffix
Word ends in i	= change o to é, add suffix
Word ends in u	= change u to o, add suffix

Don't worry; it won't take long to get the hang of this, once you've begun
trying to use the prefixes and suffixes. Just make sure your
teacher/tutor/friends correct you so you don't keep making the same
mistakes over and over.

Prefixes & Suffixes which form Nouns

root + an

**Same as Indonesian; this results in a variety of nouns of different
kinds.**

suket → *suketan* (grass → grassy area)
slamet → *slametan* (safe → ceremony wishing a safe trip)
pikir → *pikiran* (think → thought)

ke/ka + root + an

To make an abstract noun

slamet → *keslametan* (safe → safety)

pa + root

nemu → *panemu* (find → finding, opinion)
mikir → *pamikir* (think → thinking, thought)
njaluk → *panjaluk* (ask → request)
awe'h → *paweh* (give → gift)

pa + root + an/n

For a place or thing

adus → *padusan* (take a bath → a bathing place)
turu → *paturon* (sleep → bed)
sinau → *pasinaon* (study → course of study)

pi + root

A few words take this form rather than 'pa'

tulung → *pitulung* (help → assistance)
takon → *pitakon* (ask → question)

**Unfortunately, Javanese has no equivalent to the Indonesian pe/pem + root, to form the 'doer' of a verb.

k/ke + root + = to 'suffer from'

kudanan -   be caught in the rain (Indonesian: *kehujanan*)
kecolongan -   to be robbed (Indonesian: *kecurian*)

Adverbs

sa + root + é to make an adverb ('ly' or time word)

sabeneré	actually, in fact
sadurungé	before that
saanané	as much as there is
sacepeté	as fast as possible

Pronouns of Space & Direction

iki	ini	this
kuwi	itu	that
kaé	itu	that

Like some other Asian languages, Javanese has three concepts of space, *iki* for 'near me,' *kuwi* for 'in your vicinity,' and *kaé* for objects beyond both of us, either physically or metaphorically, or for something both speakers already know about.

kéné	sini	here, this one here
kono	sana	there, that one

mréné (mriki = krama)	ke sini	to here
mrono (mriku = krama)	ke sana	to there

Reflexive Pronouns

awakku (dhéwé)	aku sendiri	myself
awakmu (dhéwé)	kamu sendiri	yourself
dhéweké (dhéwé)	dia sendiri	himself, herself, themselves

In each case, the *dhewe* does not need to be said, and typically isn't.

General Rules for Changing Indonesian to Javanese

1. *nya* in Indonesian = *é* in Javanese

   - sebenar*nya* (actually) = sebenern*é*

   - Saya pergi ke rumah*nya*. (I went to her house.) Javanese = Aku lungo neng omah*é*. Notice the exact match of vocabulary words in the sentence.

   - Rumahnya besar. (His house is big.) Javanese = Omah*é* gedhé.

2. di = di

   - dibeli
   - dijual

3. meng/men/me = m/n/ng, making the verb active

   - ngabari = memberitahu

4. kan or i = ké or i.

   - hidup = urip, hidupkan = uripké
   - dengar = krungu, dengarkan → ngrungoké
   - mati = paten, matikan → pateni

5. a in final consonant → e (sometimes)

   - malam = malem
   - benar = bener

6. USEFUL LINKING WORDS

These lists of linking words and particles do not follow the format and spelling conventions used in other units. They have been organized alphabetically in Indonesian in order to be useful to those trying to learn Javanese, and the Javanese words are spelled with 'o' for long o.

Indonesian	Javanese	English
agar	supaya	in order to
aja/saja	waé	just
bagai	laksana	like (rarely used, poetic)
bagi	kanggo	for
begini	ngéné	like this, in this way
begitu	ngono	like that, in that way
belum	durung	not yet
bersama	bareng	together (with)
berturut-turut	urut-urutan	in a row, consecutively
berulang-ulang	bola bali	repeatedly
contohnya	contohé	for example
cuma	mung	only
dalam	néng, njero	inside
dan	lan	and
dengan	karo	with
di	ning/néng	in, at
dulu	mbiyén	first (before doing X else)
hampir	améh, méh	almost
hanya	mung	only
jika	nék	if
justru	kasunyatan	on top of that, in fact
kalo/kalau	nék	if
kecuali	kejaba	except (for)
kemudian	njur, banjur	later (5 months later...)
khususnya	khususé	especially
kurang dari	kurang saka	less than
kurang lebih	kurang luwih	more or less
lagi	manéh	again, more
lalu	njur	then
langsung	langsung	directly
lebih (banyak)	luwih (akéh)	more than
masih	isih	still
maksudnya	maksudé	meaning, that is to say,
malah	malah	in fact, on the contrary

maksimal	s	at most, at maximum
menurut	miturut	according to
meskipun	senajan	despite, although
minimal	s	at least, at minimum
namun/demikian	nanging	however
nyaris	méh	nearly
pas	s	exact(ly)
pernah	tau	have (have done, experienced)
pun	ugo	even, too (gives emphasis)
rasanya	rasané	it seems like
rupanya	jebulé	apparently, evidently
sama	padha	the same
sama seperti	padha karo	the same as, just like
sampai	tekan	until
sebaliknya	sewaliké (silent k)	on the contrary
sebagai	dadi	as (*As* a teacher, I …)
sebelum	sakdurungé	before
sebenarnya	sakjané	actually
sehingga	saéngga	until, so X that
se jauh ini	tekan saiki	so far (so far, so good..)
selain	sakliyané	besides
selain itu	sakliyané kuwi	besides that
selanjutnya	sakuwisé (silent k)	continuing
semakin	tambah	as ... (as fast as)
seperti	kaya	like
sesudah	setelah, sakuwisé	after
sesuai dengan	miturut	according to (what you use)
sudah	uwis (uwés)	already
supaya	supaya	so that
soal	bab	about, concerning (not spoken)
tanpa	s (pron. long 'o')	without
tapi/tetapi	tur	but
tentang	bab	about
tergantung	s	depending on
terus	s	keep/continue (doing)
tetap	tetep	still, already
tersebut	kuwi	that already mentioned
	(Written only, not spoken. In English: 'the/it/them.')	
udah	wis (wés)	already (short for *sudah*)
walaupun	senajan	even though

List of Common Particles / Expressions / Interjections

Indonesian	English
aduh	Oh no! Ouch! Crap!
ampun	Good God! Oh Lord!
astaga	Oh my God! My Goodness!
banget	so, really (*Hari ini dingin banget.*)
bo	! , like (at end of sentence, used by girls and gays – girly sounding: 'He's like so cute!'
deh	alright, c'mon (urging) (*Oke deh* = Alright then) So/such emphasis (*Hari ini dingin banget deh!*)
dong	for sure, of course, man (certainty) *Ya, dong* – I'm sure!
hah?	Huh?
hei	hey
hore	hurray!
kek	you could've
kok	why, how come (*Kok lama banget kamu?* – What's taking you so long?)
la/lha	well, well then, well now, of course
lah	c'mon (urging) or believe me (requesting belief)
lo/lho	1. What? No way! (doubt, disbelief, surprise) 2. Oh hey, remember …
nah	You know.., So… (a fact or conclusion)
nih	this, here, (*ini*)

Oya		Oh yeah, ? (a new topic, or doubt…?)
pas		exact(ly)
pun		even, emphasises a word/part of sentence (Di dalam rumah pun dia pakai topi – He (even) wears a hat in the house.
sih		Hmm.. ?? (wondering to self) *Apa sih* – Hmm, what is it again?
sip		Perfect! Cool! Alright! (thumbs up)
to(h)		1. right? isn't it? - same as *kan* ending, but informal 2. After all, … (at beginning of phrase)
tuh		that, there (*itu*) he/she, him/her
waduh		Oh no! Ouch! Crap!
Wah		Wow, Oh!
ya		yeah, you know, right, okay

Common Slang/Colloquialisms

kayak	seperti	like
gué	aku	I
lu/lo/loe	mu/kamu	you
ngapain	kenapa	what for, why, how come
ngarep	mengharap	hope
pula	juga	too
sob	sobat	friend, pal
suka males	tidak suka	don't want to

7. VILLAGE LIFE

English	Indonesian	Javanese
bicycle	sepéda	pit
broom	sapu	s
call to prayer	adzan	s
carnival/festival	pasar malam	pasar malem
chicken	ayam	pithik
clinic (in village)	puskesmas*	s
collection of money by village	iuran*	urunan
contributions (to charity)	sumbangan	s
community work project	kerja bakti* /Gotong Royong	s
cow, ox (usually white)	sapi	s
pen, coral (for animals)	kandang	krangkéng
dry	kering	garing
ditch	parit	kalén
fallen leaves	daun kering	godhong garing
farmer	petani	tani
festival/carnival with dancing and spirit possessions	—	Reog/Jathilan*
field (not rice)	ladang	tegalan
field (for public use, football)	tanah lapang	lapangan
fishing	mancing	s
food peddler	gerobak / kaki lima	gerobak
garden	kebun	kebon
gate, fence, hedge	pagar	pager
guard duty	ronda (kamling)*	s
guard post neighborhood	pos kamling	cakruk
harvest (n.)	panén	panen

head of neighborhood (1st level)	Pak RT	s
head of neighborhoods (2nd level)	Pak RW	s
head of village	Kadés (Kepala Desa)	s
household	rumah tangga	s
Javanese almanac/horoscope	kalendar jawa	petungan
land	tanah	lemah
machete	golok	s
measurement of land	méter persegi (m²)	s
meeting-regular social gathering	arisan*	s
meeting of heads of family- to solve a problem	musyawarah	rembuga
mosque	masjid	mesjid
mutual support/cooperation	Gotong Royong	s
nightly round of guard	ronda pos kamling*	s
beating sticks together by ronda	kentungan*	s
open plot of land	tanah kosong	lemah kosong
pick (fruit)	petik	s
plant (n, v)	tanam/menanam	nandur (v)
plough (v, n)	(mem)bajak	s, (ng)luku
porch	téras	s
rake (v, n)	(meng)garu	(ng)garu
religious meeting (Muslim)	pengajian	s
rice drying (on road or in yard)	gabah	s
rice field	sawah	s
rice –growing in field	padi	s
rice-uncooked	beras	s
rooster	(ayam) jago	(pithik) jago
rotating lottery	lotere (lotré)*	s
sack	karung	s
sack of rice	karung beras	s

44

school	sekolah	s
sickle	arit	s
solicitor wanting contributions	pencari sumbangan	wong golék sumb.
spread out (on ground, table)	gelar	jéréng
storage of harvest by village	lumbung	s
street light	lampu jalan	lampu dalan
sweep (with broom)	menyapu	nyapu
traditional healer	dukun*	s
water buffalo	kerbau	kebo
yard	halaman	latar

Language & Culture Notes

1. *Ronda* is the term used by most people to refer to the nightly neighborhood watch duty, or rounds, in which several men camp themselves out overnight in the raised wooden neighborhood guard hut/shack, referred to as the *pos kamling,* and periodically (on the hour) make a round on foot of the neighborhood to ensure all is well. *Kamling* is the official name given to this system of neighborhood watch. *Kamu ada ronda malam ini?* (Do you have guard duty tonight?); *Apa suara itu? Itu kentungan ronda aja.* (What's that sound? It's just the guard on his nightly round beating his sticks). Every man in the neighborhood is expected to take his turn at the duty, with the schedule being overseen by the *Pak RT*. While on duty, men generally play cards or other games, drink coffee or tea, and chat. An increasing number of TVs are also seen in *pos kamling* around the country.

2. *Puskesmas* is short for Pusat Kesehatan Masyarakat –Public Health Center.

3. *Iuran* is collected by the authority of the *Pak RT* and used for the welfare of the neighborhood when there is a need, such as when someone falls ill but does not have money to pay for care, a death, a natural disaster, or a road that needs repaving, etc.

4. *Kerja bakti* includes such things as cleanup of an area, paving of a street, planting trees, painting, etc. *Gotong Royong* is the underlying principle of mutual, neighborly support and cooperation, while *kerja bakti* is the physical work project/allocation of work itself, but some people use the terms interchangeably when talking about village work. All able-bodied men and youth are expected to participate, while women often cook food and help with less physical aspects of the project. As a foreigner living in a rural area, it is unlikely anyone will be brave enough to inform you of when such a project is scheduled to take place, but typically, it occurs on a Sunday morning, and the neighborhood will be pleasantly surprised if you turn out to lend a hand.

5. At *Reog* or *Jathilan*, one of the main attractions is dancers who typically work themselves into a kind of trance/frenzy and eventually become 'possessed' by a spirit. Across the country, such local attractions go by a number of local names. *Reog* is a term familiar to Javanese, and *Jathilan* specific to Central Java, where *Reog* is the name used by many people for the dancing/possessions part of the larger *Jathilan* festival.

6. As the guard makes his rounds of the village/neighborhood, or '*ronda*,' he beats sticks together (*kentungan*). Traditionally, a code exists, based on the manner they are beaten. A regular beat indicates all is well. If there is a village emergency, for example, the sticks are beat together rapidly and loudly. Today, not everyone is aware of the codes for their neighborhood, but in many villages such a code is still in use.

7. *Dukun*, or traditional healers, or 'medicine men' are very much still consulted by many traditional Indonesians, often in tandem with a clinic or doctor trained in Western medicine.

8. *Arisan* are held regularly, usually involving only women and youth, while *musyawarah* are held when a problem arises, and attended by the men, in their traditional position as head of household.

9. Various *lotere* are extremely popular in Indonesia, and in neighborhoods, drawings for the winner are usually held at the *arisan*. Neighbors gamble/contribute an amount based on their wealth and ability to pay, and it bestows social prestige to put more money into the pot. Individual neighborhoods make their own rules for the lottery, such as how often and when the drawings take place, along with the distribution of the funds to winners.

Indonesian Conversations

1. Meeting the Family

Daughter: Bu! Bapak! Bisa kemari sebentar? Ini ada temanku.

Mom: Tunggu sebentar.

Dad: Teman dari mana? (Shakes hands.) Nama mu siapa?

Friend: Saya teman sekolah. Saya berasal dari Surabaya. Nama saya Wisnu.

Mom: Silakan duduk (di teras, di luar). Mau minum apa?

Friend: Nggak usah Bu. Air putih saja cukup.

(Everyone sits down except Mom, who goes gets water & snacks, and brings them out.)

Friend: Terima kasih Bu.

Father: Silakan diambil makanannya. Saya permisi dulu sebentar ya. (He leaves the two alone.)

2. Women Gossiping in Street

Mbak Putri: Kemarin Pak RT udah datang minta iuran bulanan untuk lampu jalan?

Bu Candi: Belum, mungkin nanti sore.

Bu Desi: Aduh! Aku sedang tidak punya uang.

Bu Candi: Aku juga gak punya uang. Uangku habis buat beli lotere. Gimana aku membayarnya?

Mbak Putri:	Mungkin kamu bisa bayarnya setelah menjual hasil panen gabahmu.
Bu Candi:	Benar ide mu, Mbak.
Bu Desi:	Kamu tahu tidak kapan kerja bakti untuk lampu itu?
Mbak Putri:	Mungkin beberapa minggu lagi ya.
Bu Candi:	Oh ya, udah Bu. Kalo begitu, sekarang aku pulang untuk memasak di rumah. Suamiku hampir pulang dari kantor.

3. Arisan for a New Neighbor

Bu RT:	Selamat malam Ibu-ibu warga desa. Di sebelah saya ada warga baru yang pindah dari Yogya. Namanya bu Desi. Silakan Bu Desi untuk bicara diri sendiri saja.
Desi:	Terima kasih Bu. Nama saya Desi dari Yogya. Saya baru pindah ke rumah nomer A-6 minggu lalu bersama keluarga saya.
Bu RT:	Untuk Ibu Desi kami ucapkan selamat datang. Semoga betah tinggal di lingkungan warga sini. Bu Desi kami punya beberapa kegiatan salah satunya pengajian di masjid dan masak bersama tiap minggu. Silakan kalau Bu Desi ingin bergabung.
Desi:	Terima kasih atas sambutannya.
Bu RT:	Malam ini kita tidak ada banyak hal yang perlu diskusikan. Bu Yeti, gimana bakti sosial minggu lalu?
Bu Yeti:	Kami berhasil mengumpulkan uang sebanyak 2 juta untuk korban gempa bumi.
Bu RT:	Wah, bagus itu. Ibu-ibu saya ingatkan bahwa minggu depan ada acara memasak bersama untuk kerja bakti.

4. Carnival Comes to Town

Pak Gusti: Katanya di desa ini akan ada acara jathilan. Kapan ya?

Pak Agus: Sepertinya minggu depan.

Pak Gusti: Acaranya di mana?

Pak Agus: Di lapangan dekat rumah Pak RT. Semuanya sudah
               disiapkan – jathilan, dukun, dan perlengkapan lainnya
sudah   siap. Tinggal sedikit yang belum ada.

Pak Gusti: Apa itu? Mungkin aku bisa bantu.

Pak Agus: Saya butuh ayam, kelapa, dan buah-buahan lain untuk
               acara itu.

Pak Gusti: Kalo untuk ayam, ambil saja di kandang samping
               rumahku. Kelapanya kamu bisa petik di belakang
               rumahku, minta saja golok pada isteriku.

Pak Agus: Terima kasih Pak sudah dibantu. Acara ini pasti seru.
               Jangan lupa nonton ya Pak. Saya tunggu.

5. On Guard Duty with the Guys

*Men in the village are at the Pos Kamling, playing cards together and
talking about a new neighbor who has just moved into the
neighborhood.*

Pak Rudi: Pak, sudah dengar kabar tentang keluarga yang baru
               pindah di Jalan Merak itu?

Pak Alex: Oh, Pak Teguh itu, ya? Ada kabar apa, ya Pak?

Pak Rudi: Kabarnya Pak Teguh itu orangnya kurang ramah dengan
               warga. Ketika pemuda minta iuran, eh... Pak Teguh malah
               mengusir pergi.

Pak Alex:	Ah, yang benar, Pak?
Pak Rudi:	Iya, saya juga tahu dari bapak-bapak dan pemuda yang lain. Sepertinya sudah banyak yang tahu tentang itu.
Pak Alex:	Wah, saya kok tidak pernah mendengar ya?
Pak Rudi:	Kabarnya Pak Teguh itu dulu punya perusahaan di Jakarta, lalu bangkrut karena krisis ekonomi, dan akhirnya mereka pindah ke Yogya.
Pak Alex:	Oh begitu, ya?
Pak Rudi:	Kabarnya keluarga Pak Teguh punya hutang banyak. Karena itu banyak orang datang untuk menagih hutang. Makanya Pak Teguh kurang ramah dengan tamu yang datang.
Pak Alex:	Wah, saya sebenarnya kasihan dengan Pak Teguh, tetapi dia juga tidak bisa seperti ini terus. Ini akan menganggu kampung kita.
Pak Rudi:	Jadi sebaiknya bagaimana ya, Pak?
Pak Alex:	Kita harus mengadakan rapat dengan Pak RT untuk membahas ini. Lalu kita harus bicara baik-baik dengan Pak Teguh.
Pak Rudi:	Wah, saya setuju itu.

Reading Sample: An Invitation to a Neighborhood Meeting

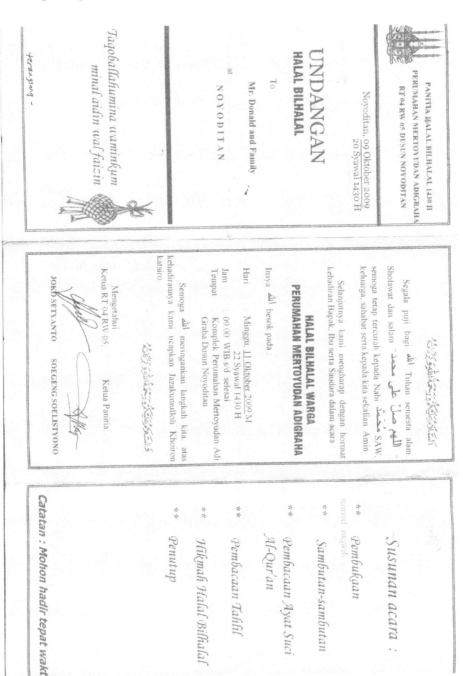

Javanese Conversations

1. Meeting the Family

Daughter:	Bu, Bapak! Saged tindak mriki sekedhap? Menika wonten rencang kula.
Mom:	Enténi sedhilit.
Dad:	Kanca saka ngendi? Jenengmu sapa?
Friend:	Kula réncang sekolah. Kula asalipun saking Surabaya. Nami kula Wisnu.
Mom:	Ayo, lungguh. Arep ngombé apa?
Friend:	Mboten sisah repot-repot Bu. Toya pethak kémawon sampun cekap.
Friend:	Matur nuwun, Bu.
Father:	Ayo dijukuk panganané. Aku pamit sikik sedhilit ya.

2. Women Gossiping

Mbak Putri:	Wingi Pak RT wis teka njaluk iuran wulanan kanggo lampu dalan?
Bu Candi:	Durung, mungkin mengko soré.
Bu Desi:	Aduh! Aku lagi ora duwé duit.
Bu Candi:	Aku uga ora duwé duit. Duitku entek kanggo tuku loteré. Piyé cara aku bayaré?
Mbak Putri:	Mungkin kowé isa bayaré sakuwisé adol panénan gabahmu.

Bu Candi:	Bener idemu Mbak.
Bu Desi:	Kowé ngerti ora kapan kerja bakti kanggo lampu kuwi?
Mbak Putri:	Mungkin pirang minggu manéh ya.
Bu Candi:	Oh ya, wis Bu. Nek ngono saiki aku bali kanggo masak neng omah. Bojoku meh bali saka kantor.

3. Arisan

Bu RT:	Sugeng ndalu Ibu-ibu wargi desa. Ing sebelah kula wonten wargi énggal pindahan saking Yogya. Asmanipun Bu Desi. Mangga Bu Desi saged matur piyambak kemawon.
Desi:	Matur nuwun Bu. Nami kula Desi saking Yogya. Kula enggal pindah ing griya nomer A6 minggu kepanggeh sesarengan kaluwargi kula.
Bu RT:	Kagem Ibu Desi kawula sesarengan matur sugeng rawuh. Mugi-mugi, betah anggénipun tinggal ing lingkungan wergi. Bu Desi, kawula sesarengan gadhah kegiatan-kegiatan, salah sawijining punika pengajian ing masjid lan masak sesarengan saben minggu. Monggo mbokmenawa Ibu badhé ndérék.
Desi:	Matur nuwun kagem sambetanipun.
Bu RT:	Ndalu menika kawula sesarengan mboten gadhah kathah perihal kagem dipun bahas. Bu Yeti, pripun bakti sosial mingu kepanggéh?
Bu Yeti:	Kawula sesarengan saged ngempalaken arto kalih juta kagem korban gempa bumi.

Bu RT: Oh inggih, Ibu-ibu, kule elingaken menawi minggu lajeng wonten acara memasak sesarengan kagem kerja bakti.

(Arisan finishes and all women chat while walking back home.)

4. Carnival – *This conversation has not been translated into Javanese so that you can try it yourself, from the Indonesian. Have your friend or teacher help you and check your work.*

5. At the Guard Post

Men in the village are at the Pos Kamling, playing cards together and talking about a new neighbor who has just moved into the neighborhood.

Pak Rudi: Pak, wis krungu kabar keluarga sing bar waé pindah neng Dalan Merak kuwi?

Pak Alex: Oh, Pak Teguh kuwi, ya? Ana kabar apa, ya Pak?

Pak Rudi: Kabaré Pak Teguh kuwi wongé kurang ramah karo warga. Pas pemuda njaluk urunan, eh... Pak Teguh malah ngusir lunga.

Pak Alex: Ah, sing bener, Pak?

Pak Rudi: Iyo, aku uga ngertiné saka bapak-bapak lan pemuda liyane. Kayané wis akéh sing ngerti bab kuwi.

Pak Alex: Wah, aku kok ra tau krungu ya?

Pak Rudi: Kabaré Pak Teguh kuwi mbiyén duwé perusahaan neng Jakarta, trus bangkrut merga krisis ekonomi, lan akhiré padha pindah neng Yogya.

Pak Alex: Oh, ngono, ya?

54

Pak Rudi:	Kabaré keluarga Pak Teguh duwé utang akéh. Sebab kuwi ana akéh wong teka kanggo nagih utang. Mangkane Pak Teguh kurang ramah karo tamu sing teka.
Pak Alex:	Wah, aku sakjané mesakaké karo Pak Teguh, nanging déwé(k)e ya raisa kaya ngéné terus. Iki bakal ngganggu kampungé awa(k)édhéwé.
Pak Rudi:	Dadi apiké piyé ya, Pak?
Pak Alex:	Awa(k)édéwé kudu nganakaké rapat karo Pak RT kanggo mbahas iki. Trus awa(k)édéwé kudu omong apik-apik karo Pak Teguh.
Pak Rudi:	Wah, aku setuju kuwi.

Unit 7: English Translations of Conversations

1. Meeting the Family

Daughter:	Mom! Dad! Can you come here for a minute? This is my friend.
Mom:	Wait a minute.
Dad:	Your friend from where? What is your name?
Friend:	I'm a friend from school. I'm originally from Surabaya. My name is Wisnu.
Mom:	Please, sit down. What would you like to drink?
Friend:	Don't bother Mam. Just water is fine.
Friend:	Thank you, Mam.
Father:	Please help yourself. If you'll excuse me for a moment...

2. Women Gossiping

Miss Putri:	Did the RT (already) come yesterday and ask for the monthly collection, for the street lamp?
Mrs. Candi:	Not yet, maybe later this evening.
Mrs. Desi:	Oh no! I don't have any money right now.
Mrs. Candi:	I don't have any money either. I spent all my money on the lottery. How will I pay for it?
Ms. Putri:	Maybe you can pay after you sell your rice harvest.
Mrs. Candi:	That's a good idea, Putri.
Mrs. Desi:	You don't (happen to) know when the work project is for the lamp?
Ms. Putri:	Maybe in a few more weeks.
Mrs. Candi:	Okay then, in that case, I'll go back home now and cook. My husband is almost back home from the office.

3. Women's Meeting for a new Neighbor

Head Mom: Good evening neighborhood Moms. At my side I have a new neighbor who moved here from Jogja. Her name is Daisy. Please say a few words about yourself Daisy.

Daisy: Thank you Mrs _____. My name is Daisy, from Jogja. I just moved into house A-6 last week with my family.

Head: We'd like to say welcome. We're all happy to have you join our circle. We have several regular get-togethers/events, one of which is the religious meeting at the mosque and cooking together each week. Please feel free if you would like to join us.

Daisy: Thank you for the warm welcome.

Head: Tonight, we don't have much that needs to be discussed. Mrs Yeti, how was the work bee/neighborhood social project last week?

Mrs. Yeti: We successfully raised up to 2 million for victims of the earthquake.

Head: Wow, that's great. I want to remind all of you that next week we are scheduled to cook together for the neighborhood work project.

(The welcome party finishes and all the moms chat and return home.)

4. Carnival Comes to Town

Mr. Gusti: The word is a jathilan (carnival) is coming to town. I wonder when...

Mr. Agus   It looks like next week.

Mr. Gusti: Where will it be?

Agus: In the open field near the RT's house. Everything is already ready - the dancers, the dukun (fortune teller/medicine man), and everything else is ready too. Only a few things left that aren't.

Gusti: What's that? Maybe I can help.

Agus: I need a chicken, a coconut, and some other things for it.

Gusti:	For the chicken, just take one from the pen next to my house. You can pick the coconut from behind my house - just ask my wife for a machete.
Agus:	Thank you for your help. This (carnival) is going to be fun. Don't forget to watch, okay? I'm looking forward to it.

5. On Guard Duty

Rudi:	Have you heard the news about that family that just moved in – on Merak Street?
Alex:	Oh, Mr. Teguh yeah? What's the news?
Rudi:	The news is Mr. Teguh is someone who doesn't get along with the neighbors. When a young man asked for the neighborhood contribution, Mr. Teguh got mad and chased him out.
Alex:	Oh, is that right?
Rudi:	Yeah, I also heard it from some dads and another young man. It seems almost everyone knows about it.
Alex:	Oh man! It's just me that never hears about these things.
Rudi:	They say Mr. Teguh used to have a business in Jakarta. Then, they went bankrupt because of the economic crisis, and finally they moved to Jogja.
Alex:	Oh really?
Rudi:	They say Mr. Teguh's family had a lot of debts. Because of that, a lot of people came to collect their debts. It's no wonder Mr. Teguh isn't too friendly with people who come by.
Alex:	You know, I actually feel sorry for Mr. Teguh, but he still can't keep being/acting like this. It's going to disturb our neighborhood.
Rudi:	So what would be a good thing to do Alex?
Alex:	We have to have a meeting with the RT to discuss this. Then, we should have a good talk with Mr. Teguh.
Rudi:	I agree with that.

Blank Page for Notes / Vocabulary

8. HOME SWEET HOME

Please review the Electric & Household vocabulary in unit 1: Words You Already Know before continuing this unit.

English	Indonesian	Javanese
Where	*Di mana*	*Neng Ngende*
address	alamat	s
alley/lane	gang	s
city	kota	kuta
country(side)	kampung	s
house	rumah	omah
housing compound	perumahan	s
street	jalan	dalan
suburbs	désa, kampung*	s
village, 'hamlet'	désa, dusun	s

Outside the House	*Di Luar Rumah*	*Eng Jobo Omah*
clothesline	tali jemuran	tali pémÉan
doormat	késet	s
'for rent' sign	'dikontrakkan'*	dikontrakké
hose	selang	s
porch	téras	s
wall (around yard)	témbok	s
yard (front yard)	halaman	latar

In the House	*Di Dalam Rumah*	*Eng Jero Omah*
bathroom	kamar mandi*	s
bed	tempat tidur	dipan
bedroom	kamar tidur	kamar
broom	sapu	s
cabinet	bufét	bupét

60

ceiling	plafon	s
chair	kursi	s
closet	lemari	s
door	pintu	lawang
electricity	listrik	s
electric socket	stop kontak	s
flashlight	sénter	s / béter
floor mat (vinyl/plastic)	karpet	s
floor mat (straw)	tikar	s
furniture	perabotan/mebel	perkakas
leak	bocor	s
light bulb	lampu/bolam	s
maid/servant	pembantu	réwang
mattress	kasur	s
roof/ceiling	atap	payon
tub in bathroom	bak mandi	s
wall	dinding	témbok
well	sumur	s
window	jendéla	jéndéla

In the Kitchen	*Di Dapur*	*Eng Bawon*
bowl	mangkuk	mangkok
candle	lilin	s
cooking oil*	minyak goréng	lengo goréng
cover for food	tutup ségo	tudung saji
cup	mug/cangkir	cangkir
fork	garpu	porok
gas tank	tank élpiji	s
glasses	gelas	s

kitchen	dapur	pawon
knife	pisau	lading
matches	korék api	korék
plate	piring	s
pot	panci	s
refrigerator	lemari es	kulkas
rice cooker	rice cooker, penanak nasi	s
sink	wastafel	s
spoon	sendok	s
stove (with burners)	kompor	s
sugar	gula	gula
tap/faucet	kran	s
toaster oven	toster, pemanggang roti	panggangan roti
water dispenser	dispenser (aqua)	s

Language & Cultural Notes

1. For bathroom, *kamar mandi* and *kamar kecil* are both used, but refer to different functions. In a house, there is usually just a single room, so either word suffices. Outside the home, however, '*kamar mandi*' refers to the room with a water basin and tap for washing hands; '*kamar kecil*' or *WC* the room with the toilet. Since Indonesian bathrooms are usually in the back of the house, it makes sense that saying '*Saya mau ke belakang*' indirectly accomplishes the same thing as asking 'Where's the bathroom?' (It's kind of like 'I need to go powder my nose,' or some such saying in English.)

2. In a majority of Indonesian homes, there is no toilet paper in the bathroom. Usually, there is a spray nozzle attached to the toilet. In public places often a bucket, water scoop, and your hand are it. If you're like most expats, you'll end up preferring the water nozzle over TP, but will be in heaven if you get both. If you're stuck on having TP, buy a plastic box of wet wipes, found in the hygiene/baby section of any Indonesian store, and carry it in your bag.

3. A clean bathroom tends to be a wet bathroom in Indonesia; from a typical Westerner's perspective, the floor is always wet.

4. The term *jelantah* is used in Javanese for the cheapest, dirtiest cooking oil, like that found at street stands, which use it over and over.

5. People who live on the outskirts of large cities in Java, in what would be considered the suburbs in the USA, regard themselves as living in the *desa* or *kampung* despite being so close to the city and surrounded by so many people. This would certainly not be considered 'the countryside' in the USA, much less 'a village' (still the most common translations for these terms). Nevertheless, these suburban neighborhoods are still organized very much along village lines (see Appendix: Organization of Society). You will also find chickens, roosters, goats, sheep, etc. just like you would on a farm or in the countryside.

6. Like anywhere in the world, finding a place to rent in Indonesia can be a challenge. Unlike North America, most cities outside Jakarta do not typically have many small apartments designed for individuals or couples. The ones that exist and offer monthly rent are typically quite expensive by Indonesian standards. On the other hand, renting a house for the entire year is quite cheap, ranging from $700 to $2000 (outside Jakarta) per year – but unfortunately, it does have to be paid up-front. The downside to this is having a lot more space than you usually need and not having any bargaining power when it comes to getting the owners to live up to their responsibilities, such as fixing things that go wrong with the house over the course of the year. Another negative aspect to house renting in Indonesia is that they are usually not constructed well at all, very often resulting in leaks in the roof, crumbling concrete, and having to share your home with mosquitoes, rats, spiders, ants, large lizards, jungle snakes, etc.

7. It is extremely common for any Indonesian family who is not on the poor end of the social ladder to have a maid, or *pembantu*. Duties range from cooking and cleaning, to being nannies to the children. Many well-to-do Indonesians have a gardener/handyman (*tukang kebon*) as well. There are several reasons for this: (1) the desire to help out someone who is poorer and in need of a job, (2) it is a status symbol to have a maid, (3) necessity due to lifestyle. (In many well-to-do families, both parents work out of town.) In addition, menial jobs are not highly regarded, and compared to the West, it is very cheap to hire a *pembantu* so that almost anyone can afford to hire one for several hours/week. There is also a huge difference in mindset between most Indonesians with money and blue-collar, middle-class Westerners. Indonesians are generally surprised when I tell them I get satisfaction from gardening, repairing my own motorcycle, performing household repairs and upkeep, and doing other manual labor.

8. *PBB* (in the housing contract) stands for *Pajak Bumi dan Bangunan*, or 'property tax.' It is often included in contracts with water and electric, and is extremely minimal (by Western standards).

Indonesian Conversations

1. Where is Your House?

Mbak Siti: Apakah pésta Mbak Wiwin bésok?

Mbak Wiwin: Ya, benar Mbak. Mbak sudah dapat undangannya?

Mbak Siti: Ya sudah. Cuma saya belum tahu di mana rumahmu. bisakah beritahu di mana alamatmu?

Mbak Wiwin: Kampung rambutan, RT 5, RW 10, Dusun Makmur, Kecamatan Majalengka.

Mbak Siti: Sesudah sampai kampung itu, bagaimana caranya sampai ke rumah mu?

Mbak Wiwin: Ada masjid di jalan utama, rumahku di sebelahnya.

2. Looking for a House to Rent

Mas Agus is driving thru a neighborhood looking for 'For Rent' (dikontrakkan) signs or houses to rent. He doesn't see any, but asks a neighbor or the security guard if there are any in the area.

Mas Agus: Permisi, Pak. Di perumahan ini apa ada rumah yg dikontrakkan?

Pak Gembong: Ya, ada. Rumah di sana, dengan halaman depan dan jendela serta pintu berwarna hijau. (Points to the house he means.)

Mas Agus: Yang itu, dengan teras besar?

Pak G: Tidak, yang di sebelahnya. Mari, saya tunjukkan rumahnya.
               (They walk to the house together.)

Pak G:	Pemiliknya tinggal di Jakarta Mas, tapi besok bisa saya bawakan kuncinya.
Mas Agus:	Ada berapa kamar?
Pak G:	Dua kamar aja. Di belakang ada tempat jemuran juga.
Mas Agus:	Sudah termasuk perabotan?
Pak G:	Lengkap Mas.
Mas Agus:	Berapa séwanya per tahun?
Pak G:	Kurang tahu, besok Mas tanya langsung saja pada pemiliknya. Ini nomornya. (He gives Agus the mobile number of owner using his own mobile phone.)
Mas Agus:	Terima kasih Pak. Besok jam berapa sebaiknya saya datang lagi?
Pak G:	Jam berapa saja, sebelum jam enam. Kalau malam, saya Sudah pulang.
Mas Agus:	Besok saya datang pagi sekitar jam sepuluh ya Pak.
Pak G:	Ya, saya tunggu kedatangannya.
Mas Agus:	Terima kasih. (Agus shakes hands, then gets on his motorcycle, gives Pak Gembong a head nod and leaves.)

3. Cooking a Meal Together

Bu Andras: Ambilkan telur dari dalam kulkas.

Mbak Yusti: Ya Bu. Berapa?

Bu: Dua. (Mbak brings eggs to the stove.)

Bu: Sekalian ambilkan piring.

(Mbak gets plates from shelf.)

Mbak: Mau masak apa Bu?

Bu: Nasi goreng.

Mbak: Semalam kan juga nasi goreng?

Bu: Itu yang bapakmu suka. Ambilkan minyak goreng.

Mbak: Apa lagi Bu?

Bu: Di mana séndoknya?

Mbak: Di sini Bu.

(Bu lights stove, cooks food.)

Bu: Elpijinya sudah mau habis. Besok harus beli lagi.

(Dinner is served!)

4. Electricity Goes Out

Two guys are watching a football match on TV when the electricity goes out.

Mas Indra: Aduh! pas lagi seru-serunya. Listrik mati! Tempat tetangga mati juga?

(Mas Dwi goes and checks outside to see if neighborhood is dark.)

Mas Dwi: Ya, semuanya mati.

Mas Indra: Sénternya ada di meja.

(Mas Dwi grabs flashlight, turns it on.)

Mas Dwi: Di mana lilin?

Mas Indra: Di rak, di dapur. Koréknya di mana ya?

Mas Dwi: Di sini, di dekat lilinnya. (Lights a candle, grabs a plate to put candle on, & carries it over to floor, where both are sitting.)

Mas Indra: Lama nggak ya matinya?

Mas Dwi: Semoga tidak lama.

(Beberapa menit lagi listrik hidup.)

Mas Dwi: Wa, untung mati listriknya tidak lama ... bisa nonton pertandingan lagi..

Mas Indra: Jangan lupa matikan lilinnya.

Reading Sample: Author's Personal Story

Tahun ini (2010), saya baru pindah ke Jakarta, dari Jawa Tengah. Sudah hampir tiga tahun di sana dan sudah bosan. Walaupun saya pernah tinggal di rumah dan di perumahan yang dekat kota serta lumayan besar (Yogyakarta dan Magelang), tinggal di sana memang seperti tinggal di desa. Contohnya, sebelum saya bisa pindah ke setiap rumah tersebut, saya harus bertemu Pak RT.

Di perumahan pertama ada formulir yang harus diisi dengan pertanyaan tentang agama, umur, dan lain-lainya. Di perumahan, saya harus mendengarkan Pak RT menjelaskan tata tertib perumahan, seperti misalnya tamu wanita harus melapor dan tidak boleh menginap jika dating sendirian dan juga, tidak baik kalau saya minum banyak bir di luar (teras rumah). Tentu saja di setiap tempat, saya harus memberi Pak RT photocopy Kitas dan paspor, dengan surat dari sekolah bahasa yang membuktikan saya bekerja di sana.

Di Yogya, ketika pacar saya datang ke rumah, pintu rumah harus di buka supaya semua tetangga tidak akan pikir dia pelacur dan hanya datang untuk bercinta aja. Di dalam rumah pertama, suatu hari ketika saya mandi, ular hutan hitam dan labah-labah besar masuk kedalam kamar mandi dan dua-duanya bersembunyi di pintu. Hanya memakai handuk, saya gunakan sapu untuk membuang ular itu ke luar.

Setiap rumah ada bocor karena rumah-rumah di sana umumnya tidak dibangun dengan bagus, dan semuanya ada semut, nyamuk, dan tikus. Sesudah hujan khususnya, ada banyak serangga masuk ke dalam rumah. Itu biasa dan sebagian dari kehidupan kalau kita akan tinggal di Indonesia.

Reading Sample: A House Contract (1-Yr Rental)

SURAT KONTRAK

Yang bertanda tangan dibawah ini :
Nama : Edward N█████████
Alamat : Jalan Kaliurang km ██ No ███
Selanjutnya disebut PIHAK PERTAMA

Nama : Donald E███ Hobbs (warga negara Amerika)
No Passpor : ████4976
Selanjutnya disebut PIHAK KEDUA

PIHAK PERTAMA menyewakan sebuah rumah dengan alamat Jalan Kaliurang km 6,5 Gang Timor Timur, Jalan Kayen Raya, Siberut 3 No ███ kepada PIHAK KEDUA dengan biaya kompensasi sebesar Rp.10.000.000,- (sepuluh juta rupiah) yang telah diterima seluruhnya oleh PIHAK PERTAMA.

PIHAK KEDUA telah menempati rumah tersebut sejak hari Senin, 5 januari 2009. Namun masa sewa selama satu tahun akan dimulai pada hari yang sama dengan keluarnya visa kerja PIHAK KEDUA.

PIHAK KEDUA wajib membayar biaya PBB, air, dan listrik selama menempati rumah tersebut dan mengembalikan rumah tersebut pada masanya dengan kondisi yang sama baiknya pada saat diterima.

Demikian surat kontrak ini dibuat berdasarkan kesepakatan PIHAK PERTAMA dan PIHAK KEDUA.

PIHAK PERTAMA   PIHAK KEDUA

Edward N████   Donald E███ Hobbs
(atas nama Dina N█████████)

Reading Sample: Kost Receipt

Kwitansi Kost, Jakarta Timur

No.

Telah terima dari
Mr. Don

Uang sejumlah
Lima juta rupiah

Untuk pembayaran
Sewa kost kamar No 4 (AC) Selama 2 bulan

Mulai tanggal 25 Oktober Sd 25 Desember 2010

Jakarta 25 Oktober 2010

Rp. 5.000.000

Javanese Conversations

1. Where is your House?

Mbak Siti: Apa bener pesta Mbak Wiwin sésuk?

Mbak Wiwin: Iya bener, Mbak. Mbak wis éntuk undangane?

Mbak Siti: Iya wis. Mung aku durung ngerti néng endi omahmu.
                 Isa kandhani neng endi alamatmu?

Mbak Wiwin: Kampung Rambutan, RT 5, RW 10, Dusun Makmur,
                 Kecamatan Majalengka.

Mbak Siti: Sakuwise tekan kampung kuwi, piye carane tekan neng
                 omahmu?

Mbak Wiwin: Ana mesjid neng dalan gedhe. Omahku neng sebelahe.

2. Looking for a House to Rent

*Mas Agus is driving thru a neighborhood looking for 'di kontrakkan'
signs or houses to rent. He doesn't see any signs but asks a neighbor or
the security guard.*

Mas Agus: Nuwun sewu, Pak. Ing perumahan menika menapa
                 wonten griya ingkang dipun kontrakaken?

Pak Gembong: Inggih, wonten. Griya ingkang mrika, ingkang gadhah latar
                 ngajeng lan jendela mawi pintu werni ijem.

Mas Agus: Ingkang menika, mawi émpér ageng?

Pak G: Mboten, ingkang ing sebelahipun. Mangga, kula
                 dherekaken dhateng griyanipun.

(They walk to the house together.)

71

Pak G:	Ingkang kagungan tinggal ing Jakarta Mas, nanging mbenjang sonten, saged kula bethake kuncinipun.
Mas Agus:	Wonten pinten kamar?
Pak G:	Kalih kamar kémawon. Ing wingking ugo wonten panggén mémén.
Mas Agus:	Sampun kaliyan perabotan?
Pak G:	Lengkap, Mas.
Mas Agus:	Pinten séwanipun per tahun?
Pak G:	Kirang mangertos, mbénjang énjing Mas tanglet dhateng ingkang kagungan kemawon. Menika nomeripun.

(Gives Agus the mobile phone number of owner using his own mobile phone.)

Mas Agus:	Matur nuwun, Pak. Mbénjang jam pinten langkung sae kula dugi mriki malih?
Pak G:	Jam pinten kémawon, sekdéréngipun jam enem. Menawi ndalu kula sampun wangsul.
Mas Agus:	Mbenjang énjing kula dugi sekitar jam sedoso nggih, Pak.
Pak G:	Inggih, kula tenggo rawuhipun.
Mas Agus:	Matur nuwun.

(Agus gets on his motorcycle, gives Pak Gembong a head nod, and rides off.)

3. Cooking a Meal Together

Bu Andras: Jukokake endhog seka njero kulkas.

Mbak Yusti: Inggih Bu, pinten?

Bu Andras: Loro.   (Mbak brings eggs to the stove.)

Bu Andras: Sekaliyan jukokake piring ya.
               (Mbak gets plates from shelf.)

Mbak Yusti: Badhe masak menapa, Bu?

Bu Andras: Sega goreng.

Mbak Yusti: Wau ndalu uga sekul goreng, leres Bu?

Bu Andras: Kuwi sing ramamu remen. Jukokake lenga goreng.

Mbak Yusti: Menapa malih, Bu?

Bu Andras: Néng endi sendoke?

Mbak Yusti: Ing mriki, Bu. (Lights kompor, cooks food.)

Bu Andras: Gase wis méh enthék. Sésuk kudu tuku manéh.

(Dinner is served!)

4. Electricity Goes Out

Two guys are watching a football match on TV when the electricity goes out.

Mas Indra: Aduh, pas lagi seru-serune. Listrik mati.
Panggone tangga sebelah uga mati ya?

(Mas Dwi goes and checks outside to see if neighborhood is dark.)

Mas Dwi: Ya, kabéh mati.

Mas Indra: Séntere ana néng méja.
(Mas Dwi grabs flashlight, turns it on.)

Mas Dwi: Néng endi lilin?

Mas Indra: Neng rak, neng dapur. Korek ana neng endi ya?

Mas Dwi: Neng kéné, neng cedhak lilin. (Lights candle, gets a plate to put it on, & carries it over to floor where both are sitting.)

Mas Indra: Suwe ora ya matine?

Mas Dwi: Muga-muga ora suwe.

(Beberapa menit lagi listrik hidup.)

Mas Dwi: Wah..., untung mati listrik ora suwe.... isa nonton pertandingan manéh.

Mas Indra: Ojo lali pateni liline.

Unit 8: English Translations of Conversations

1. Where is Your House?

Ms. Siti: Is your party tomorrow?

Ms. Wiwin: Yes, that's right. Have you already received the invitation?

Ms Siti: Yes, I did. Only I don't know where your house is yet. Can you let me know where your address is?

Ms. Wiwin: Kampung rambutan, RT 5, RW 10, Dusun Makmur, Kecamatan Magalengka. (See Appendix: Organization of Society to see how these equate. Like most Western addresses, it starts with neighborhood and gets larger, to one of the districts of the city.)

Ms. Siti: After I get to your neighborhood, what is the way to your house?

Ms. Wiwin: There is a mosque on the main road; my house is next to it.

2. Looking for a House to Rent

Agus: Excuse me. Is there any house for rent in this compound?

Mr. Gembong: Yes, there is. The house over there, with the yard in front and the window along with the green gate.

Agus: That one, with the big porch?

Mr. G: No, the one next to it. C'mon, I'll show you the house.

Mr. G: The owner lives in Jakarta young man, but tomorrow I can bring the key.

Agus: How many rooms are there?

Mr. G: Just two rooms. In back, there's a place to hang laundry too.

Agus: Is it already furnished?

Mr. G: Completely furnished.

Agus: How much is the rent per year?

Mr. G: I don't really know. Tomorrow, you can ask the owner directly. Here is his number.

Agus:	Thank you sir. Tomorrow, what time would be good for me to come again?
Mr. G:	Anytime before six. If it's nighttime, I'll have already gone home.
Agus:	Tomorrow I'll come in the morning, around 10, okay?
Mr. G:	Yeah okay, I'll be waiting (for your arrival).
Agus:	Thank you.

3. Cooking a Meal Together

Mrs. Andras:	Get some eggs from inside the fridge.
Yusti:	Okay Mom. How many?
Mom:	Two. (The daughter brings the eggs to the stove.)
Mom:	Next, get some plates.

(Daughter gets plates from shelf.)

Daughter:	What are we going to cook Mom?
Mom:	Fried Rice.
Daughter:	Fried rice again – tonight?
Mom:	It's what your father likes. Get the cooking oil.
Daughter:	What else?
Mom:	Where's a spoon?
Daughter:	Here.
Bu:	The gas is almost out. Tomorrow we have to buy some more.

4. Electricity Goes Out

Indra:	Oh no! It was just getting good and the electricity goes out. Are the neighbors out too?
Dwi:	Yeah, they're all out.
Indra:	There's a flashlight on the table.

Dwi:	Where are the candles?
Indra:	On the shelf in the kitchen. Now, where are the matches?
Dwi:	Here, near the candles. (Lights a candle.)
Indra:	I wonder if the outage will last long?
Dwi:	I hope it's not long.

(A few minutes later the electricity comes on.)

Dwi:	Man, we're lucky it wasn't out long ... we can watch the game again.
Indra:	Don't forget to put out the candles.

Reading Sample: Author's Personal Story

This year (2010), I just moved to Jakarta, from Central Java. I had been in Central Java for almost three years and was already bored. Even though I had lived in a house and in a housing compound that were close to cities which were fairly large (Yogyakarta and Magelang), living there was really like living in a village. For example, before I could move into either of the houses I lived in, I had to meet the RT.

In the first house there was a form which had to be filled out, with questions about religion, age, and so on. In the housing community, I had to listen to the RT explain the rules of the community, like a girl guest had to report and couldn't come and stay if she was by herself, and it wouldn't be good if I drank a lot of beer outside (on the porch). Of course in each place, I had to give the RT a photocopy of my work permit and passport, with a letter from the language school that proved I was working there.

In Yogya, when my girlfriend came to the house, the front door had to be open so that all the neighbors wouldn't think she was a prostitute and just came over to have sex. In the first house I lived in, one day while I was taking a shower, a black jungle snake and a large spider came into the bathroom and both hid in the door. Wearing only a towel, I used a broom to chase the snake outside.

Each house had leaks because the houses there generally aren't built well, and all of them had ants, mosquitoes, and rats. After rain especially, a lot of termites/white ants came into the house. This is normal and part of life if you are going to live in Indonesia.

Letter of Contract/Contract Agreement

The signatories (below):
Name: Edward N.
Address: Kaliurang Road, Km — , #
Henceforth referred to as the First Party

Name: Donald E Hobbs (citizen of the USA)
Passport No: —4976
Henceforth referred to as the Second Party

The First Party rents a house with address Kaliurang Road, Km 6.5, East Timor Lane, Kayen Raya Street, Siberut 3, # — to the Second Party with compensation in the amount of 10,000,000 rupiah (ten million rupiah), which has already been received in full by the First Party.

The Second Party has occupied the house in question since Monday, 5 January 2009. However, the one-year rental period will begin the same day as the Second Party's leaving (the country) for a work visa.

The Second Party is required to pay the cost of property tax, water, and electricity while he resides in the house, and to return the house after the period in the same condition as at the time he received it.

Thus, this letter of contract was made based on the agreement reached between the First Party and the Second Party.

First Party   Second Party

9. FOOD AND DRINK

Please review the food and drink section in Unit 1: Words You Already Know before continuing.

Basic Foods & Ingredients

English	Indonesian	Javanese
basil leaves	daun kemangi	godhong kemangi
bay leaves	daun salam	godhong salam
bean (green)	buncis	s
bean sprouts	taugé	tokolan
beef	daging sapi	s
beef, ground	sapi giling	s
bread	roti	s
butter	mentéga	mertégo
cabbage	kubis, kol	kubis
carrot	wortél	s
cassava	singkong	telo
catfish	lélé	s
cheese	keju	s
chicken	ayam	pithik
chili peppers	cabé, lombok	s
chili sauce	(saus) sambal	sambel
coconut	kelapa	kambil
coconut cream custard	srikaya	s
coconut milk	santan	santen
cooking oil	minyak goreng	lengo goreng
corn	jagung	s
cucumber	ketimun/timun	s
curry	karé (Indian), gulai (Sumatran)	s
duck	bébék, itik	s
egg	telur	éndhog
eggplant	térong/terung	s
egg noodles	mie telur	bakmi éndhog
fish	ikan	iwak
flour	tepung	glepung
food	makanan	panganan
fried rice	nasi goréng	sego goréng
galanga l	laos, kencur (stronger)	s
garlic	bawang/bawang putih	s
ginger	jahé	s
goat	kambing	iwak wedhus

79

honey	madu	s
innards, intestines	jerohan, usus, isi perut	jeroan
lamb	domba	s
lemon grass	seréh	s
lime leaves	daun jeruk (purut)	godhong jeruk
meat	daging	s / iwak
milk	susu	s
MSG	vetsin, micin, sasa*	s / moto
mung bean	kacang hijau	kacang ijo
mushroom	jamur, cendawan	s
nut, pea, bean, peanut	kacang	s
oatmeal, porridge	bubur	s
onion	bawang bombay	s
onion -small (Ishallot)	bawang mérah,	brambang
palm sugar (like molasses)	gula mérah	gula jawa
peanut sauce, spicy	bumbu/saus/sambal kacang	s
pepper	lada	merico
portion, serving	porsi	s
potato	kentang	s
ramen noodles	mi, mie	s
r. noodles w/ veg in wok	bakmi	s
ramen, fried	mi goréng	bakmi goréng
ramen, with broth	mi rebus	bakmi godhok
rice (cooked)	nasi	sega
salt	garam	uyah
shrimp /prawn	udang*	urang
side dishes	lauk-pauk	lawuh
sago	sagu (starch from palm)	kanji
soup	sop, soto	s
soybean cake, fermented	témpé	s
soy sauce	kecap asin	s
soy sauce (sweet/teriyaki)	kecap	s
spinach (water)	kangkung	s
squash, gourd	labu	walu
sticky rice	nasi ketan	sego ketan
sugar	gula	gula
tapioca	tapioka, sagu	s
taro	talas	tales, kimpul
tofu	tahu	s

Fruit

Indonesian	Javanese	English
anggur	s	grapes
alpokat	s	avocado
asam	asem	tamarind
belimbing	s	starfruit
buah naga	s	dragon fruit
delima	s	pomegranate
jambu	s	guava
jeruk	s	orange
jeruk Bali/besar	s	grapefruit
jeruk nipis	s	lime
kelapa, kopyor	klapa, kambil	coconut
kesemek	s	persimmon
kolan kaling	s	sugar palm fruit
kiwi	s	kiwi
kurma	kurma	date
leci	s	lychee
mangga	pelem	mango
manggi	s	mangosteen
nanas	s	pineapple
nangka	nangka	jackfruit
pepaya	katés	papaya
pisang	gedhang	banana
pisang batu	s	banana - white, hard
salak*	s	snake fruit
semangka	s	watermelon
sirsak/sirsat	s	sirsak, soursop
sukun, ketimbul	s	breadfruit

Indonesian Specific Food

acar   pickled relishes, cucumber, carrots, etc.

bakpi(a)   flaky dough ball filled with bean paste & sugar

bawal   fresh water fish, rather bony but cheap

buras   rice cake in banana leaf, cooked in coconut milk

bakwan jagung	deep fried battered corn fritter
bakso	small spongy meatballs, often in soup with noodles
balado/belado	any dish cooked in red chili pepper sauce
déndéng belado	jerky (beef) fried with red peppers (Sumateran)
bergedé / perkedel	potato ball/croquette/patty
daun singkong	cassava leaf, spinach-like, always at padang places
dodol	a 'fudge' made of sticky rice, palm sugar, coconut milk, and choice of fruit
gado-gado	mixed steamed vegetables topped with peanut sauce
gudeg	unripe jackfruit in coconut milk (Yogya specialty)
Guramé	fresh water carp, like a bass or trout
karedok	raw vegetable salad with galangal and peanut sauce
kelepon	green sticky rice balls with syrup & grated coconut
kerupuk	chips of flour flavored with shrimp, fish, or onion with texture like pork rinds, eaten with most meals
ketoprak	bean sprouts, tofu, rice noodles with sweet soy sauce, sweet & sour peanut sauce
ketan urap	sticky rice with grated coconut
ketupat	boiled, pressed rice cake in woven coconut leaf basket, sliced, eaten at Lebaran
laksa	rice noodles, chicken, hard boiled egg, and bean sprouts with ginger in chicken broth with coconut milk: specialty of Bogor, West Java
lapis Surabaya	3 layer cake, 2 vanilla, 1 chocolate, jam filling
lodéh	coconut milk with leaves & nuts from melinjo tree

lontong	rice boiled in banana leaf, sliced, at sate stands
loték	vegetables, galangal, peanut sauce
lumpia	fried egg/spring roll, in several varieties
martabak	egg crepe fried with meat, vegetables, cheese
mi bakso	egg noodle soup with bakso
nasi campur	rice, meat, vegetables, eggs, sauce, krupuk
nasi jagung	rice mixed with corn flour (East Java)
nasi kapau	rice with variety of meat, vegetables, spices, chili peppers (West Sumatran)
nasi kuning	yellow rice, eaten on special occassions
nasi lemang	sticky rice with coconut milk in green bamboo
nasi pecel	sampler plate of rice, vegetables, tofu, rice noodles and peanut sauce
nasi santen/uduk	rice cooked in coconut milk, in banana leaf
Nila	fresh water fish, cheaper than *Gurame*
oléh-oléh	food as souvenir - any region specific treats bought while traveling and brought back for coworkers and friends
opor ayam	simmered in tart coconut milk with spices
padang	food/food stalls/restaurants from sumatera, buffet style, spicy and open late at night
pangsit	fried wonton
pécel	kind of vegetable salad with peanut sauce
pémpék / empek-empek	fish dumplings with sweet soy sauce, chopped cucumber, and chilis (Palembang)
rawon	spicy meat stew, black (East Java)
rujak	sliced pieces of various fruits, with spicy peanut sauce, often eaten with ice cream, sold by peddlers
rempeyek	fritter, wafer, cracker
rempeyek kacang	salty peanut brittle

rendang	meat simmered in a spicy brown coconut sauce at Padang restaurants/stands (Sumatra)
saté sate buntel sate manis	satay/shishkabob/skewered meat with peanut sauce minced lamb balls & onion kabob (Solo) sate marinated in palm sugar & soy sauce
semanggi	potatoes, sprouts, clover leaves, top with spicy sweet potato & fish paste, in banana leaf (Surabaya)
semar	sticky rice with shredded chicken, in banana leaf
siomay	*pari* (a bitter veg.), potato, egg, cabbage, fish dumplings, topped w/ peanut sauce
soto soto Bandung soto mi	meat/vegetable soup (richly seasoned) beef soup, fried soybeans, radish, lemon grass beef soup with noodles, tomato, cabbage
tapé	fermented, alcoholic cassava fudge eaten during *puasa* & *Lebaran*
urap	steamed vegetables with spices & grated coconut

Describing Food

bitter	pahit
bland	hambar
delicious, great	énak
fresh	segar
fried	goréng
grilled, barbecued	bakar
not good	tidak énak
salty	asin
spicy	pedas
spicy & sour	asam pedas (to describe Padang food)
sour	asam / kecut
stir-fried	tumis
strong (thick)	kental
sweet	manis
sweet & sour	asam manis
thick (strong)	kental
too X	terlalu X
not X enough	kurang X

Eating Out

cup of coffee	secangkir kopi
check, bill	bon
food stall/stand	kedai
food tent, small restaurant	warung
halal, kosher	halal
menu	daftar makan, ménu
order	pesan
take out/take away	dibungkus

Drinks *(one of the Indonesia's great accomplishments)*

arak	brandy-like liquor distilled from *tuak*
bajigur	coffee, coconut milk, spices (west Java)
bandrék	hot coconut milk, ginger, pepper, sugar
brem	sweet Balinese rice wine
és campur	ice, fruit, syrup
es coklat	chocolate milk
es dawet	coconut milk, pieces of tapioca, sugar

es jeruk	lemon/orange juice w/water + sugar
es kacang hijau	mung bean porridge drink
es kelapa	sugar water with cubes of coconut
es kelapa muda	fresh coconut juice in coconut with ice
es kopyor	the highest quality of coconut, which has soft flesh, blended with the juice
es lemon	lemonade
es stroberi	strawberry milk
es téh	ice tea, sweetened
es téh lémon	ice tea lemon, sweetened
es teh tawar/pahit	ice tea, unsweetened
es télér	iced fruit cocktail with condensed milk
jamu	traditional herbal drink, many kinds for various ailments
jus apolkat coklat	avocado juice with chocolate syrup
kopi tubruk	coffee, ground
kopi luwak*	coffee from the undigested coffee beans that civets eat and excrete
kopi hitam/jawa*	black coffee, usually unfiltered
kopi instan	instant coffee
kopi manis	coffee with sugar
kopi three in one	instant coffee with sugar and creamer
rondé	hot drink of beans, fruit, sticky rice balls, ginger syrup. Great!
STMJ	Susu, Telur, Madu, Jahe - milk, eggs, honey, ginger. A virility drink
soda gembira	soda water, red syrup, condensed milk
teh celup	tea in bags
teh asli	tea leaves, made from leaves
teh melati	jasmine tea
teh panas	hot tea
teh jahe	ginger tea
tuak wayah	yeasty toddy from fermenting palm tree flowers

Language & Cultural Notes

1. In conversation 1, notice the use of '*pakai*' for with. This is the preferred word in similar food situations, not 'dengan.' In other cases, '*sama*' is used.

2. As in English, numbers can sometimes be shortened, like saying 'twenty five' instead of 'twenty-five hundred ,' so in Indonesian the '*ribu*' is not always voiced in all cases or transactions where 'thousand' is already understood.

3. *Kopi luwak* is unique to Indonesia and the Philippines, more aromatic, better tasting, and more expensive than regular beans, made from undigested beans eaten and excreted (shat out) by the civet.

4. Hot coffee outside the upper scale coffee shops is usually unfiltered; you just wait for all the grounds to settle then scrape the surface with a spoon a couple times before drinking. *Kopi Jawa* = Cowboy coffee. Starbucks are extremely expensive, and seem to charge the same prices they would in the States (the coffee is actually imported via the Starbucks supply chain, even if it is Sumateran coffee). The best bet for a good, reasonable cup of Indonesian grown coffee seems to be local coffee houses in various cities, although they are few and far between.

5. Indonesia is the only place I've lived where you have to be careful eating rice that you get from any food stand. I know several people who have chipped teeth biting into small pebbles in the rice, which is dried on the road and not carefully cleaned by either farmers or vendors before selling or cooking.

6. Fast food chains and convenience stores in Indonesia are not geared to Westerners' preferences and leave much to be desired. Like the rest of SE Asia, Mexican fast food does not exist. Unlike neighboring countries, Indonesian McDonald's does not have some items like the quarter pounder, milk shakes or decent coffee. If you order anything besides chicken or the basic hamburger '*beef burger*' or cheeseburger, you'll likely have to wait for it to be cooked and brought out to you. Seven Elevens are new to Indonesia; currently there are only a few in the Jakarta area. The Circle Ks and Indomarets are comparatively more expensive and lacking, but can be counted on to carry a full range of cold beer available in Indonesia, including San Miguel, Carlsberg, Heineken, and Fosters. KFC does not carry the best sides – no mashed potatoes, gravy, beans, or coleslaw. On a positive note for North Americans, A&W restaurants are popular in malls and carry the same classic root beer float you enjoyed as a kid.

7. Tax on liquor is substantial and was raised again in 2010. This means hard liquor prices in Indonesia are rather expensive, and on par with Singapore or Malaysia, versus cheaper prices in other SE Asian countries. On the other hand, large bottles of *Bintang bir* are cheap and available everywhere, and it's a light-bodied lager, that goes down smoothly. A negative result of high taxes on hard liquor is that there are a fair number of deaths each year from Indonesians (and a few foreigners) drinking cheap/locally distilled liquor at local *warung*, which turns out to be toxic. Beware of drinking anything locally distilled, such as you might get at an unknown *warung*, as you may be risking your life. One of the absolute cheapest, but safe (when it was original) available hard liquors for many years was *Mansion House - 'Mensin'*, available in two varieties: *biasa/hitam* ('whiskey'), and *Mensin putih* (a clear 'Vodka'). Since the work on this text began, Mansion House has become largely unavailable, but that may change again in the near future. A recent addition to spirits available in Indonesia is the brand *'Vibe,'* which is made in Indonesia, cheap, and of drinkable quality (vodka, gin, and some mixed liquors). In Jakarta, there are a number of duty free liquor stores, which generally sell liquor at reasonable prices to any foreigners, except when they are inspected or harassed by authorities, during which time they either close or sell only to those with a diplomatic passport. An affordable favorite among local youth is to share a bottle or two of the common, very sweet, red wine (*anngur*), which is perfectly safe. Local *arak* drinks are also popular and at bars catering to foreigners or the wilder Indonesian crowd, you can get it mixed with orange, or honey, or a combination of juices, which is sometimes rather nice.

8. When eating at a local warung, use the following vocabulary if you want your egg fried (*telur goreng*) the way you want: sunny-side up = *mata sapi*, over-easy = *setengah matang*. Otherwise, it will be fried so the yoke is hard (and probably extremely greasy – most places tend to use way too much oil). Scrambled (but no milk, spicy) = *telur dadar*.

9. Almost all *warung* food uses a large amount of MSG. If you want to ask someplace not to use it - which is an uncommon request unless you happen to be somewhere trendy frequented by backpackers – saya *'tidak pakai vetsin/micin or 'tanpa vetsin.'* Even better, tell them you are allergic to MSG – *Saya alergi vetsin/micin*. Then, they will be extra careful and won't forget. Often it's just habitual to throw it in and by the time they are cooking, they've forgotten and sometimes, rather than cooking it all over again without the MSG, they just give it to you anyway and hope you won't be able to tell the difference.

10. Many expats find the Javanese tendency to add sugar to everything unsuitable to their taste. The breakfast cereals such as *Choco* and *Honey Bites* and *Energen* instant oatmeal (vanilla, green bean, and chocolate) are so sweet, they make you gag. No worries - Quaker oatmeal is sold in grocery stores. Similarly, almost all the *saus sambal* (chili sauce) is a little on the sweet side, but one brand, *Jari Ibu*, is not. You can find Del Monte ketchup and Kraft Real Mayonnaise as well, rather than buying local sweet versions of the same thing. For unsweetened ice tea, ask for *es teh tawar*, and be sure to specify you don't want sugar in your coffee: *kopi pahit/tidak pakai gula*.

11. In most cases shrimp are cooked and served with the skin on and heads attached, so they're quite difficult to eat as you have to peel each one before you can eat them. This is especially messy when they are cooked in a sweet and sour sauce.

12. When eating in any eateries not located in intenational hotels, the waiting staff will not remove any plates or glasses until you leave. This is not laziness - it is considered rude to remove plates as it can be construed as a sign they are asking a customer to leave. (Such as sweeping around your table while you are still eating might be construed the same way in the West.) Therefore, if you want them to take the plates/glasses you need to ask them to do so if you are running out of room or flies and ants have begun to take undue notice of your table.

13. Most eateries do not have smoking areas and people who are eating with you or beside you will light up cigarettes as soon as they are finished eating regardless of whether others are still eating. It is considered unusual to complain or ask someone not to smoke unless there are no-smoking signs present (which are still ignored much of the time).

14. In most cases, dinner parties such as Westerners are accustomed to where everyone has conversation throughout the meals are not the normal custom in many regions. Most people only talk before and after the meals but not during the meals. It's often quite silent when everyone is eating. People eating with mouths open, burping and slurping are commonly heard noises and not considered rude in many places (especially in villages and at tables surrounded by Indonesians of Chinese descent). It is considered rude, however, to make the noise of silverware clinking against plates, or spoons clinking against cups or glasses when stirring.

Indonesian Conversations

1. Di Warung Sate – At a Satay Stand

Tom:	Minta saté ayam satu, dibungkus.
Bu Warung:	Pakai lontong?
Tom:	Ngak Bu, pakai nasi. (Waits for order.)
Bu:	Bapak sudah lama di sini?
Tom:	Apa? Ma'af, tolong ulangi lagi ya.
Bu:	Sudah lama di sini?
Tom:	Oh, belum. Saya belajar bahasa Indonesia di sini, baru satu bulan aja.
Bu:	Wah, sudah pintar bahasa Indonesia.
Tom:	(Laughs/smiles) Belum, belum begitu bagus. Saténya berapa?
Bu:	Dua belas ribu.
Tom:	(Hands over money.)
Bu:	Terima kasih.
Tom:	Sama-sama.

2. Di Kedai Kopi – At the Coffee Shop

Heri and Wawan are local English teachers and are meeting at an upscale coffee shop in the city.

(Heri has already arrived and ordered coffee. His friend, Wawan, just came.)

Wawan:	Malam. Udah lama menunggu di sini?
Heri:	Nggak. Sepuluh menit aja.
Wawan:	(Sits at the table with Heri.) Udah pesan kan?
Heri:	Cuma kopi, makanannya belum.
Wawan:	Gimana kopinya?
Heri:	Énak banget, tapi sedikit mahal.
Wawan:	(Looks at menu.) Ya, benar. Lebih mahal dari Kedai Kopi. Aku sebenarnya mau minum apa ya ...

(The waiter comes to take the order.)

Heri:	Mau berbagi kentang goreng?
Wawan:	Sip.
Pelayan:	Mau pesan apa?
Heri:	Kentang goreng satu Mas.
Wawan:	Saya minta kopi Toraja ini – pahit.
Pelayan:	Apa lagi?
Heri:	Mm - ya, Cappuccino satu lagi.

Pelayan:	Boleh saya mengulang lagi pesanannya - satu kentang goreng, satu Toraja (kopi), satu Cappuccino.
Heri:	Ya. Terima kasih.
Wawan:	Aku capék. Sibuk sekali di tempat kerja.
Heri:	Bagus kan ada lebih banyak kelas.
Wawan:	Aku nggak suka lebih banyak kelas kalo jumlah guru yang ada masih sama.

(The waiter comes bringing the coffees and french fries.)

3. Di Pasar Swalayan – At the Supermarket

Ani:	Apakah kita sudah membeli semua barang yang dibutuhkan?
Rini:	Sebentar, aku akan cék lagi daftar belanja kita. Kécap, sudah. Bawang juga sudah. Oh ya, tinggal daging sapi giling.
Ani:	Berapa kilo daging kita harus beli?
Rini:	Kira-kira ya 2 kilo. Kupikir.

(Ani takes Rini to the meat section.)

Rini:	Pak, ada daging sapi giling selain ini? Kalau ada, minta dagingnya yang masih segar ya..
Penjual:	Jangan khawatir, Mbak, daging giling spesial di sini paling segar.
Rini:	Kalau begitu, saya minta 2 kilo, ya Pak.
Penjual:	Baik, Mbak. Daging ayamnya nggak beli sekalian?
Rini:	Nggak, Pak, terima kasih. Lain kali saja.

(Ani and Rini go to the cashier.)

Kasir: Sudah semua, Mbak? Ini susunya sedang diskon lho. Nggak beli sekalian?

Ani: Nggak, terima kasih, Mbak.

Rini: Oh ya, aku ingat, Ani, sepertinya kita nggak butuh bawang. Kupikir kita masih punya bawang di laci dapur.

Ani: Kamu yakin?

Rini: Ya, aku yakin.

Ani: Mbak, bawangnya tidak jadi dibeli.

Kasir: Baik, Mbak. Tidak apa-apa.

4. Memasak – Cooking

Ani: Kita akan masak apa bésok?

Rista: Aku pikir kita bisa masak sayur lodéh. Kita masih punya bahan-bahannya.

Ani: Baik, karena aku agak malas berbelanja ke pasar hari ini.

Rista: Ya aku juga, tetapi lebih baik aku cék bahan-bahan yang ada dulu.

Ani: Aduh, kupikir santan ini sudah basi. Baunya aneh.

Rista: Iya, kamu benar. Lalu bagaimana, kita jadi masak sayur lodeh besok?

Ani: Aku capek dan tidak mau pergi ke pasar. Bagaimana kalau kita masak seadanya besok?

Rista: Aku juga agak malas berbelanja. Bagaimana kalau besok kita masak tumis kacang panjang saja?

Ani: Baiklah.

DAFTAR MENU

Menu Spesial

Spaghetti Bolognaise	13.000
Mie Ayam Teriyaki	15.000
Nasi + Ayam Teriyaki	15.000
Chicken Steak Cheesy *disajikan dengan salad + french fries atau nasi	23.000
Chicken Cordon Bleu *disajikan dengan salad + french fries atau nasi	23.500
Nasi + Ayam Katsu Teriyaki Saos	15.500
Steak Hot Plate *daging sapi lokal dgn sayuran + kentang goreng	24.000
Sate Ayam + lontong/nasi	15.000
Sapi Rendang + nasi	18.000
Opor Ayam	15.000

Kwetiau

Kwetiau Ayam	10.000
Kwetiau Ayam Bakso	15.000
Kwetiau Ayam Pangsit Goreng	14.500
Kwetiau Ayam Pangsit Rebus	16.200
Kwetiau Ayam Siram	18.000
Kwetiau Masak Ayam	17.700
Kwetiau Sapi Goreng	19.000
Kwetiau Seafood Goreng	20.500

DAFTAR MENU   Harga sudah termasuk PBI 10%

Bihun

Bihun Ayam Bakso	13.500
Bihun Ayam Pangsit Rebus Bakso	15.300
Bihun Goreng Ayam	15.700
Bihun Goreng Seafood	19.200
Bihun Goreng Sapi	18.500
Bihun Siram Sapi	18.500

Bakso

Bakso Urat Mie/Bihun	8.000
Bakso Halus Mie/Bihun	8.000
Bakso Campur Mie/Bihun	8.000

Mie

Mie Ayam	8.000
Mie Goreng Ayam	12.000
Mie Ayam Pangsit Rebus	11.000
Mie Kuah Ayam	12.500
Mie Goreng Spesial	14.000
Mie Goreng Seafood	15.500
Mie Siram Sapi	13.500
Mie Aceh Ayam/Telur	15.000
Lo Mie	16.000
I Fu Mie	16.000

DAFTAR MENU   Harga belum termasuk PBI 10%

Nasi Goreng

Nasi Goreng	10.000
Nasi Goreng Spesial	12.000
Nasi Goreng Seafood	14.000
Nasi Goreng Kambing	14.000
Nasi Goreng Sapi	15.000
Nasi Goreng Udang	14.000
Nasi Goreng Kepiting	14.000
Nasi Goreng Petai	13.000
Nasi Goreng Ikan Asin	14.200
Nasi Goreng Sosis	13.000
Nasi Goreng Teri Medan	14.200

Paket Ayam
*semuanya termasuk nasi, acar, krupuk, sambal

Ayam Goreng Mentega	19.000
Ayam Goreng Tepung	19.000
Ayam Goreng Rica-rica	19.000
Ayam Asam Manis	19.000
Ayam Bakar	18.000
Ayam Bakar Bumbu Bali	20.000

Menu Lain

Nasi Cap Cay	14.000
Nasi Ayam Cah Jamur	14.000
Nasi Ayam Cah Kembang Kol	14.000
Nasi Fu Yung Hai	14.000

DAFTAR MENU
Harga belum termasuk PBI 10%

Soto Ayam	10.500
Kentang Goreng	7.500
Chef's salad (telur, ayam, keju)	14.000
Lodeh	10.500
Tempe Goreng (2 potong)	3.000
Nasi Uduk	4.000
Nasi Putih	3.500

Ikan/Makanan Laut
*Termasuk nasi

Gurame Bakar	22.000
Pecel Lele	12.500
Bawal/Nila	15.000
Cumi Goreng Tepung	23.500
Cumi Goreng Mentega	23.500
Cumi Goreng Rica-Rica	24.000
Ikan Laut Asam Manis	25.000

Minuman

Teh Tarik	7.000
Es Teh Tawar	1.500
Es Teh Manis	2.500
Teh Botol Sosro	2.500
Teh Panas	2.000
Teh Panas Manis	2.500
Jus Alpukat	8.000
Jus Melon	8.000
Jus Sirzak	8.000
Jus Mangga	8.000

Jus Tomat	8.000
Es Juruk	8.000
Es Lemon	8.000
Air Mineral Botol	3.000
Coke/Sprite/Fanta	4.500
Kopi Hitam	3.500
Es Kopi	4.500
Es Capucino	9.000
Es Coklat	8.000
Es Dawet	10.000
Es Soda Susu	9.000
Es Soda Gembira	11.000
Jahe	10.000
STMJ	14.000
Milkshek (Coklat, Vanila, Stroberi)	12.000
Es Kelapa Muda	15.000

Notes on the Menu

1. You won't find a single restaurant's menu quite this varied in Indonesia – it is strictly a made-up composite useful for this chapter, although a few chain restaurants found in malls serve most of what is on the menu.

2. Prices here are typical of those found on the outskirts of Jakarta, in 2010. Food prices vary greatly and in other cities, like Yogya or Padang, are still cheaper, but have gone up significantly in the last several years and are still increasing.

3. If you find a *warung* or restaurant you like, stick with it. There are many mediocre to very bad restaurants and *warung* in Indonesia that stay in business year after year only because they are cheap and convenient.

Javanese Conversations

1. At a Satay Stand *(Neng Warung Sate)*

Tom: Nyuwun sate ayam setunggal, dipunwungkus.

Bu: Ngagem lontong?

Tom: Mboten Bu, ngaggem sekul.

Bu: Bapak, sampun dangu wonten mriki?

Tom: Men_apa_. Pangapunten, nyuwun dipun ambali malih?

Bu: Sampun dangu wonten mriki, Pak?

Tom: Oh déréng, kul_a_ sinau b_asa_ J_awa_ wonten mriki, saweg setunggal wulan kémawon.

Bu: Sampun pinter b_asa_ J_awa_.

Tom: Déréng, dereng sae, saténipun pintén Bu?

Bu: Kalihwelas éwu. (Takes money.) Matur nuwun.

Tom: Sami-sami

2. At the Coffee Shop *(Neng Kedai Kopi)*

Wawan: Wis suwe kowe néng kéné?

Heri :   Ora. Lagi sepuluh menit wae.

Wawan: (Sits at the table with Heri.) Wis pesen to?

Heri: Mung kopi, panganane durung.

Wawan: Piye kopine?

Heri: Enak tenan. Tapi rada larang sithik.

Wawan: (Looks at menu). Ya bener. Luwih larang saka Kedai Kopi.
Aku sakjane péngén ngombe apa to?
(The waiter comes to take their order.)

Heri: Gelem paroan kentang goreng?

Wawan: Sip.

Pelayan: Badhe pesen menapa?

Heri: Kentang goreng setunggal, Mas.

Wawan: Kula kopi Toraja menika - pahit.

Pelayan: Menapa malih?

Heri: Mm – inggih, cappucino setunggal malih.

Pelayan: Saged kula ulang malih pesenanipun –setunggal kentang
goreng, setunggal Toraja, setunggal cappucino.

Heri: Inggih leres, matur nuwun.

Wawan: Aku kesel. Sibuk banget neng kantor.

Heri: Apik to, kan ana luwih akéh kelas.

Wawan: Aku ora seneng luwih akeh kelas nék jumlah guru
sing ana isih tetep . . .

(The waiter arrives bringing coffee and French fries.)

3. At the Supermarket (Neng Pasar Swalayan)

Ani: Awa(k)édhéwé wis tuku kabéh sing dibutuhke?

Rini: Sedhilit, aku arep ngecék daftar belanjan awakedhewe. Kécap, uwis. Bawang uga uwis. Oh ya, tinggal daging sapi giling.

Ani: Pirang kilo awakedhewe kudu tuku?

Rini: Kira-kira ya 2 kilo. Takpikir.

Ani: Pak, wonten daging sapi giling, mboten? Menawi wonten, nyuwun daging ingkang - taksih seger nggih.

Penjual: Ampun khawatir, Mbak. Sedaya daging wonten mriki paling seger.

Rini: Menawi mengaten, kula nyuwun 2 kilo, nggih Pak?

Penjual: Inggih, Mbak. Daging ayamipun mboten ditumbasi sekalian?

Rini: Mboten, Pak, matur nuwun. Sanés wedhal kémawon.

Kasir: Sampun sedhaya, Mbak? Menika susunipun taksih diskon. Mboten tumbas sekaliyan?

Ani: Mboten, matur nuwun, Mbak.

Rini: Oh ya, aku kelingan, Ani, kétoke awakedhewe ora butuh bawang. Tak pikir awakedhewe isih nyimpen bawang neng laci dapur.

Ani: Kowe yakin?

Rini: Iya, aku yakin.

Ani:	(To the cashier) Mbak, bawangipun mboten sios ditumbas.
Kasir:	Inggih, Mbak. Mboten punapa-punapa.

4. Cooking

Ani:	Awa(k)édhéwé arep masak apa sésuk?
Rista:	Tak pikir, awakedhewe isa masak sayur lodéh. Awakedhewe isih dhuwe bahan-bahane.
Ani:	Kepeneran, kerana aku radha males belanja neng pasar dina iki.
Rista:	Ya, aku uga iya, tapi luwih becik aku ngecék bahan-bahan sing ana sikik.
Ani:	Aduh, tak pikir santen iki wis mambu. Ambune anéh.
Rista:	Iya, kowe bener. Trus, piye, awakedhewe sida masak sayur lodéh sesuk?
Ani:	Aku kesel lan ora péngén lunga menyang pasar. Piye nék sesuk awakedhewe masak sakanane wae?
Rista:	Aku uga males belanja. Piye nék sesuk awakehewe masak tumis kancang panjang wae?
Ani:	Ya.

Unit 9: English Translations of Conversations

1. At a Satay Stand

Tom:	One chicken satay please, to go.
Stand Owner:	With lontong?
Tom:	No Mam, with rice.
Owner:	Have you been here long?
Tom:	What? Sorry, could you please repeat that?
Owner:	Have you been here long?
Tom:	Oh, not yet. I'm studying Indonesian here; it's been just one month.
Owner:	Wow, you're already good at Indonesian.
Tom:	Not yet. Not that good yet. How much is the satay?
Owner:	Twelve-thousand.
Tom:	(Hands over money.)
Owner:	Thank you.
Tom:	You're Welcome.

2. At the Coffee Shop

Heri has already arrived and ordered coffee. His friend, Wawan, just came.

Wawan:	Evening. Been waiting here long?
Heri:	No. Just 10 minutes.
Wawan:	(Sits down.) You already ordered, right?
Heri:	Only coffee – nothing to eat yet.
Wawan:	How's the coffee?
Heri:	Real good, but a little expensive.

Wawan:	(Looks at menu.) Yeah, you're right. It's more expensive than Coffee Kedai (name of a coffee house in Yogya.) What do I actually want to drink....

(The waiter comes and wants to take the order.)

Heri:	Do you want to share some French fries?
Wawan:	Yep.
Waiter:	What would you like to order?
Heri:	One fries please.
Wawan:	I'll have this Toraja coffee – black.
Waiter:	Anything else?
Heri:	Hmm, yeah, one more Cappuccino.
Waiter:	May I repeat your order – one french fries, one Toraja (coffee), one Cappuccino.
Heri:	Yes. Thank you.
Wawan:	I'm tired. It's so busy at work.
Heri:	It's good isn't it – that there are more classes?
Wawan:	I don't like more classes if the total number of teachers that we have is still the same!

(The waiter comes, bringing coffee and french fries.)

3. At the Supermarket

Ani:	Did we already buy everything that we need?
Rini:	Just a moment, I'll check our shopping list again. Ketchup, got it. Garlic – got it too. Oh yeah, ground beef is left.
Ani:	How many kilograms of meat should we buy?
Rini:	About 2 kg. I think.
Rini:	Sir, do you have any ground beef besides this? If you do, I'd like some (meat) that is more fresh...

Seller:	Don't worry Miss. The special ground beef here is the freshest.
Rini:	In that case, I'd like 2 kg please.
Seller:	My pleasure. You don't want to buy any chicken today?
Rini:	No, thank you. Some other time. (Rini and Ani kemudian go to the cashier.)
Cashier:	Is that everything Miss? This milk is now on sale. You wouldn't like any today?
Ani:	No, thank you.
Rini:	Oh yeah, I remember Ani, it seems we don't need any garlic. I think we've still got some in the kitchen cupboard.
Ani:	Are you sure?
Rini:	Yes, I'm sure.
Ani:	Miss, we're not going to need the garlic.
Cashier:	Very well Mam, No problem.

4. Cooking

Ani:	What are we going to cook tomorrow?
Rista:	I think we can cook *lodeh* and vegetables. We still have the ingredients.
Ani:	Good, because I'm don't really feel like going shopping in the market today.
Rista:	Yeah, me neither, but I'd better check what ingredients we have first.
Ani:	Darn! I think this coconut milk is already soured/gone bad. It smells strange.
Rista:	Yeah, you're right. Then how are we going to cook *lodeh* and vegetables tomorrow?
Ani:	I'm tired and don't want to go to the market. What if we cook something we've got for tomorrow?

Rista: I really don't feel like shopping either. What if tomorrow we just cook stir-fried long beans?

Ani: Sounds good.

10. FUN AND GAMES

Please review the activities, games, sports section in Unit 1: Words You Already Know before continuing.

English	Indonesian	Javanese
Abra kadabra!	Simsalabim!	s
ant/elephant/man	suit	pingsut
astrology	pernujuman	s
baseball	kasti, baseball	kasti
beach	pantai	s, kisik
blackjack	blackjack	s
camping	berkemah	kemah
cards	kartu	kertu
carnival, show	jatilan	jatilan
catch (with a ball)	lempar tangkap	nangkep
chat online	chatting, ngobrol online	ngobrol
cheat	main curang/contek*	nyonto
chess	catur	sekak
chinese checkers	halma	s
dance	menari	njogéd
dancer	penari	beksa
deck/pack of cards	kartu rémi	s
exhibit(ion)	exhibisi, paméran	s
field (football)	lapangan	s
firecracker	mercon	s
fireworks	kembang api	s
fishing	mancing	s
fortune teller	peramal	dukun
gamble	judi	totohan
game	permainan	dolanan
Go Fish (card game)	cangkul	macul
go shopping	belanja	blanja
hang out/look around	nongkrong, jalan-jalan	mlaku-mlaku
hard liquor	minuman keras	lapén
hide and seek	petak umpet/umpet-umpetan	delikan
hopscotch	bitek gunung	sunda mandah

jump rope	lompat tali	lumpatan, yéyé
kite (v.-fly)	(v.-main) layang-layang	layangan
liquor from palm sugar	arak	tuak
magic	ajaib	sulapan
magician	pesulap*	tukang sulap
make/place a bet	bertaruh	totohan
marbles	keléréng	néker
meet friends	bertemu teman	ketemu kanca
mobile phone	hp	s
monkey bars	restok berjalan	gandulan
movie	cinema, film	félem
movie theater	bioskop*	s
outdoor improvised theater	layar tancap	layar tancep
park (n)	taman	s
play guitar	bermain gitar	dolanan gitar
(greased) pole climb	panjat pinang	ménék pinang
pool/billiard hall	tempat bilyar	s
put on a show, exhibit	mengadakan pameran	mamerké
relay race	lari éstafét/beranting baton	mlayu éstafét
rock, paper, scissors	suit / hom pim pa*	pingsut / s
sack race	balap karung	s
shuffle cards	mengocok	ngasut
sing	bernyanyi	nyanyi
singer	penyanyi	s
snakes & ladders	ular tangga	s
sweet wine	anggur	s
swim	berenang	nglangi
swimming pool	kolam renang	s
tag	gobak sodor*	s
tic tac toe	tebak-tebakan dengan angka	bedhék-bedhékan
text /sms	sms	s
track (n) (around a field)	lintasan lari, lapangan trék	s
tug of war	tarik tambang	s
video	dvd, vcd	s
volleyball	voli	s
village lottery	lotré	s
zoo*	kebun binatang	s

Language & Culture Notes

1. Notice that Indonesians enjoy many of the same traditional games as North Americans and Aussies. Picnic/outdoor games are the same as found in the USA. Similarly, these are also played only occasionally at similar times - around Indonesian Independence Day or at some kind of fair or special event.

2. In conversation 2, the clerk asks if the customer has a smaller bill/note; this is common and stores often don't carry enough change for larger bills, or the clerk doesn't want to take the effort to break a larger bill, even just 20.000 rupiah.

3. It is common practice in department and other stores to be given a receipt/purchase order by a particular section of the store and to have to take it to a central cashier to pay before being given the merchandise.

4. *Main curang* is to cheat, for most games (by not following the rules, moving too many spaces, etc.). *Contek* means to look at another person's cards (or another student's test at school).

5. *Gobok sodor* is a kind of tag, which requires at least 4 people to play - 3 guards and 1 runner. If there are more kids, they line up as runners and wait their turn (runners go one by one). Each guard has a zone that he has to stay in. He can move within the zone but cannot cross the lines that make it up. The runner has to make his way thru each zone in turn, to the next line and if he makes it across all 3 zones to the 4th, he wins. Unlike tag, the guards have to catch a runner, rather than just touch/tag him to get him out and change places, from being a guard to the next runner.

6. *Suit* is 'ant, elephant, man' and played the same as rock, paper, scissors (ant beats elephant, elephant beats man, man beats ant). *Hom Pim Pa* is like 'odd man out' and used to determine who is on the same team or in/out at the start of a game when there are a number of players and rock paper scissors would be too complicated. Everyone holds out their hands and chants 'hom pim pa.' At the end of this, everyone's palms are either face up or face down. Everyone with palms down are on the same team or in/out; everyone with palms up likewise. Several rounds can be used to eliminate players and choose a winner.

7. There are a couple famous magicians who regularly appear on Indonesian TV - Deddy Corbuzier (an Indonesian magician who used to perform with a painted face like the members of the band Kiss) and Criss Angel, with his popular show 'Mindfreak.'

8. Horoscopes and fortune telling are popular in Indonesia, as they are the world over. For a few they are just for fun, but for most they provide answers to the same range of problems customers in the West are seeking: love, money, happiness, etc. Nighttime TV ads encourage viewers to call or sms fortune tellers with their problems (only X rupiah per call!) to find the answers they need in life. Mama Loren, a psychic always on TV, died in 2010 – others will undoubtedly take her place.

9. Although the word for a movie theater is *bioskop*, you may hear your younger friends say they are going to 'cinema 21' or just '21.' Cinema 21 is the name of the most successful chain of theaters, found in most shopping malls.

10. Pool halls in the not-so-distant past were always either small local joints, or seedy, dimly lit places that offered alcohol and had women attendants. There were a number of scandals involving sex being sold with girls who worked in the latter. In both cases, the clientele were all chain-smoking younger men. This has changed over the last ten years, and '*bilyar*' is now popular with a more upscale crowd, and becoming popular with many young women. Upscale pool halls now cater to this changed market. They cost more than the neighborhood pool halls do, but offer newer, better tables, a larger variety of food/drinks, and trendy music. They often have attractive young female attendants wearing visually appealing (read: sexy) uniforms as well.

11. Indonesia's zoos are often sad, disappointing, or upsetting (depending on how much you love wild animals) for Westerners, because they are like our zoos in the past – underfunded and with little concern about the animals' comfort or natural habitat. Cages are generally small, concrete, and often filled with trash thown in by the visitors. Nevertheless, they provide a green space in cities where public parks are in short supply, and an excellent chance to see some unique species of animals, as well as being a good place to take a date.

Indonesian Conversations

1. In Gramedia

Pak toko: Bisa membantu cari apa?

Dodi: Ya, saya mau lihat catur.

Pak: Boléh. Silakan.

Dodi: Saya mau yang tidak terlalu mahal tapi bagus.

Pak: Ini murah, yang ini lebih mahal.

Dodi: (Picks up cheaper item and examines it.)
             Kualitas ini tidak terlalu bagus apa?

Pak: Iya. Yang ini lebih baik.

Dodi: Boleh lihat sebentar?

Pak: Ya, boleh. (Gives item to Dodi.)

Dodi: Ya ini bagus. Berapa harganya?

Pak: Empat puluh dua ribu.

Dodi: Kalau yang itu?

Pak: Yang itu dua puluh lima ribu.

Dodi: Oké. Yang bagus ini aja. (Hands item back to Pak.)

Pak: (Writes out receipt at counter, hands to Dodi.)
             Ini ke kasir dulu.

Dodi: (Goes to cashier & pays, brings stamped receipt back.)

Pak: (Brings item in bag out, gives it to Dodi.) Terima kasih.

2. What should we play?

Two kids are bored and trying to decide what to do.

Budi: Aku bosan. Kita main aja yuk...

Arif: Main apa?

Budi: Main petak umpet saja bagaimana?

Arif: Ah, malas kalau cuma kita berdua. Nanti cuma kita yang gantian sembunyi dan mencari. Nggak seru.

Budi: Kalau begitu, bagaimana kalau kita ajak teman-teman yang lain?

Arif: Ya, kamu panggil Husni, Wawan, dan Yanto. Aku pergi ke rumah Lintang, Bagus, dan Chandra. Mereka mungkin mau main petak umpet juga.

Budi: Kalau begitu kita pergi sekarang yuk, biar nanti kita bisa main lama sebelum maghrib.

3. Boys Go Fishing

Wawan :   Aku dengar dari Yanto ada banyak ikan lele di sawah Pak Paijo.

Lintang: Ah masa?

Wawan: Benar, sumpah! Kemarin Yanto mancing di sana dan dapat banyak.

Lintang: Pak Paijo nggak apa-apa kita mancing di sawahnya?

Wawan: Kata Yanto sih nggak apa-apa selama kita nggak injak padi di sawahnya.

Lintang: Oh begitu. Kita memancing di sana yuk!

Wawan: Sekarang?

Lintang: Iya, kamu bisa kan?

Wawan: Bisa, aku akan pinjam tali pancing Yanto ya.

Lintang: Asyik... kita langsung ketemu di sawah Pak Paijo aja ya?

Wawan: Sip.

4. Magic Show at Shopping Mall

Rudi: Lihat itu! Ada apa di sana? Mengapa banyak orang berkumpul di kios itu?

Endang: Ya, benar. Lihat ke sana yuk!

Rudi: Oh, ternyata ada tukang sulap di sini.

Endang: Iya, dia bermain sulap dengan kartu.

Rudi: Mengapa kartunya bisa menjadi As semua, ya?

Endang: Iya itu membuatku heran.

Rudi: Lihat, sekarang dia melakukan sulap dengan burung merpati. Dia memasukkan kelinci itu ke dalam topi....

Endang: Wah, burung itu hilang. Hilang ke mana burung itu?

Rudi: Wah, dia memang pintar sekali.

5. Traditional Events for Independence Day

Arif: Mister, mau lihat kegiatan tujuh belasan?

Mister: Ya, Aku sudah lihat. Tadi malam ada apa - orang yang berlari bawa tongkat, lalu beri itu kepada orang di depan. Apa namanya di bahasa Indonesia?

Arif: Oh, lari estafet.

Mr: Lari apa?

Arif: Estafet mister. Beranting baton.

Mr: Lari estafet?

Arif: Ya betul.

Mr: Sore ini ada apa lagi?

Arif: Ada voli, ada tarik tambang, balap karung, permainan anak-anak...

Mr: Sebentar - kurang ngerti. Itu apa?

Arif: Voli Mister, Voli. Tau kan?

Mr: Ya, tau voli. Tapi yang lainnya...tarik apa?

Arif: Tarik tambang. Ada tali panjang dan tebal, dua tim begini (mimes pulling a rope with body).

Mister: Oh, mengerti. di bahasa Inggris namanya itu 'tug of war'

Arif: Apa?

Mr: Namanya 'tug of war.' Tug artinya tarik. Tug of war. War, perang ya. 'Tug of war.'

Arif: Tug of war ... di Amerika ada ya Mister?

Mr:	Ya, ada. Itu sama. Selain itu, yang terakhir – bilang apa? Apa karung?
Arif:	Balap karung.
Mr:	Karung seperti karung dari pasar swalayan?
Arif:	Nggak mister. Karung beras. Karung besar.
Mr:	Balap artinya apa?
Arif:	Lari, lomba.
Mr:	Oke. Di Amerika ada juga. Namanya 'sack race.' Jam berapa mulai?
Arif:	Jam empat, setengah lima.
Mr:	Baik. Aku datang untung lihat. Galah itu untuk apa? (Points at two poles in field.)
Arif:	Itu panjat pinang.
Mr:	Panjat apa?
Arif:	Pinang.
Mr:	Orang panjat galah ya.
Arif:	Ya. Di Amerika ada panjat pinang?
Mr:	Ada. Sama, tapi biasanya pakai oli buat licin jadi lebih susa ya.
Arif:	Sama. kadang kadang, ya. Mungkin nanti tambah oli.
Mr:	Oh, gitu. Oke, aku mau pulang sekarang. Sampai nanti sore ya.
Arif:	Jam empat mister. Empat.
Mr:	Ya, udah. Aku datang nanti sore ini.

Javanese Conversations

1. In Gramedia

Pak: Saged dibantu pados menapa?

Dodi: Inggih, kula badhe mirsani sekak.

Pak: Angsal. Mangga.

Dodi: Kula péngén ingkang mboten pati awis nanging sae.

Pak: Menika murah, seng menika langkung awis.

Dodi: (Picks up cheaper item, looks at it.)
       Kualitas menika mboten pati sae penapa?

Pak: Inggih. Menika langkung sae.

Dodi: Saged ningali sekedap?

Pak: Ingih saged. (Gives item to Dodi.)

Dodi: Nggih menika sae, reginipun pinten?

Pak: Sekawan dasa kalih éwu.

Dodi: Menawi ingkang menika?

Pak: Ingkang menika selangkung éwu.

Dodi: Inggih sampun. Ingkang sae menika kémawon.
       (Hands item back to clerk.)

Pak: (Writes out receipt at counter, hands to Dodi.)
       Menika, wonten kasir rumiyin.

Dodi: (Goes to cashier and pays, brings stamped receipt back.)

Pak: (Brings item out to Dodi in bag.) Matur nuwun.

2. What should we play?

Budi: Aku bosen. Awa(k)édhéwé dolanan wae yuk.

Arif: Dolanan ap̲a̲?

Budi: Main dhelikan wae piye?

Arif: Ah, males nek mung awakdhewe wong loro. Mengko mung
        awakedhewe sing gantian dhelik lan nggoléki. Ora seru.

Budi: Nék ngono, piye nek awakedhewe ngajak k̲anc̲a̲-k̲anc̲a̲ liy̲a̲?

Arif: Y̲a̲, kowe ngundang Husni, Wawan, lan Yanti. Aku lung̲a̲ neng
        omahe Lintang, Bagus, lan Chandra. Mungkin uga p̲adh̲a̲
        péngén main dhelikan.

Budi: Nek ngono, ayo awakedhewe lung̲a̲ saiki, men mengko is̲a̲ main
        r̲adh̲a̲ suwe sakdurunge maghrib.

3. Boys Go Fishing

Wawan: Aku krungu soko Yanti, an̲a̲ akeh iwak lélé néng sawahe
         Pak Paijo.

Lintang: Ah, masa?

Wawan: Bener, sumpah. Wingi Yanto mancing rana lan éntuk akeh.

Lintang: Pak Paijo ora ap̲a̲-ap̲a̲ awa(k)édhéwé mancing neng sawahe?

117

Wawan: Omonge Yanto sih ora papa asal awakedhewe ora ngidak pari neng sawahe.

Lintang: Oh ngono. Awakedhewe mancing neng kono yuk!

Wawan: Saiki?

Lintang: Iyo, kowe isa to?

Wawan: Isa, aku nyilih tali pancing Yanto sikik, ya.

Lintang: Asyik, awakedhewe langsung ketemu neng sawahe Pak Paijo wae ya?

Wawan: Sip.

4. Magic Show at Shopping Mall

Rudi : Delok kuwi! Ana apa néng kono? Kenapa akeh wong padha ngumpul neng kios kuwi?

Endang : Ya, bener. Ndelok rono yuk!

Rudi : Oh, tibake ana tukang sulap neng kéné.

Endang : Iya, dhéwé main sulap nganggo kertu.

Rudi : Kenapa kertune isa dadi As kabeh ya?

Endang : Iya, kuwi nggawe aku gumun.

Rudi: Delok, saiki dheweke sulap nganggo manuk dara. Dheweke ngelebokke manuk kuwi neng njero topi....

Endang : Wah, manuk kuwi ilang. Ilang néng endi manuk kuwi?

Rudi : Wah, dheweke pancen pinter tenan.

5. Traditional Events for Independence Day

Arif: Mister, badhe ningali kegiatan tujuh belasan?

Mr: Ya, aku wis ndelok. Mau bengi ana apa – wong sing mlayu nggawa tongkat, ngenéhi tongkat néng orang neng ngarepe.
Apa jenenge neng bahasa Indonesia?

Arif: Oh menika mlayu éstafét.

Mr: Mlayu apa?

Arif: Éstafét, Mister. Beranting baton.

Mr: Estafet?

Arif: Inggih leres.

Mr: Sore iki ana apa maneh?

Arif: Wonten voli, tarik tambang, balap karung, ugi permainan kagem laré-laré.

Mr: Sik – kurang ngerti. Kuwi apa?

Arif: Voli mister, mangertos mboten?

Mr: Ya, ngerti voli. Tapi sing liyane...tarik apa?

Arif: Tarik tambang. Wonten tali panjang lan ageng, wonten kalih tim kados mekaten. (Mimes pulling a rope with body.)

Mr: Oh ngerti. Neng bahasa Inggris jenenge 'tug of war'

Arif: Menapa?

Mr: Jenenge 'tug of war.' Tug artine narik. Tug of war. War, pérang ya. 'Tug of war.'

Arif: Tug of war..... ing Amerika ugi wonten Mister?

Mr: Ya, ana. Kuwi padha. Sakliyane kuwi, sing kéri mau...omong apa? Apa karung?

Arif: Balap karung.

Mr: Karung kaya karung saka pasar swalayan?

Arif: Sanes Mister. Karung beras. Karung beras.

Mr: Balap artine apa?

Arif: Mlajar, lomba.

Mr: Oh. Neng Amerika uga ana. Jenenge 'sack race.' Jam pira mulaine?

Arif: Jam sekawan, setengah gangsal.

Mr: Oke. Aku teka nggo ndelok. Cagak kuwi kanggo apa? (Nuding cagak loro neng lapangan.)

Arif: Menika panjat pinang.

Mr: Panjat apa?

Arif: Pinang.

Mr: Wong ménék cagak ya?

Arif: Inggih. Ing Amerika wonten panjat pinang?

Mr: Ana padha, tapi biasane nganggo oli supaya lunyu. Dadine luwih rekoso ya?

Arif: Sami. Kadang kala inggih. Mungkin mangke ditambahi oli.

Mr: Oh, ngono. Oke, aku méh bali saiki. Ketemu mengko sore ya.

Arif: Mangke jam sekawan, Mister, sekawan.

Mr: Yo, wis. Aku teka mengko sore iki.

Unit 10: English Translation of Conversations

1. In Gramedia (Bookstore)

Store clerk: Can I help you find something?

Dodi: Yes, I'm looking for a chess game.

Clerk: I can help you. Please (follow me).

Dodi: I want one that's not too expensive but still good.

Clerk: This one is cheap; this one is more expensive.

Dodi: (Looks at the cheaper one.)
The quality of this one isn't too good, is it?

Clerk: No. This one's better.

Dodi: May I see it for a moment?

Clerk: You may. / Here you are.

Dodi: Yes, this one is good. How much is the price?

Clerk: Forty-two thousand.

Dodi: And that one?

Clerk: That one is twenty-five thousand.

Dodi: Okay. (I'll) just (take) the good one.

Clerk: Take this to the cashier first.

Dodi: (Goes to the cashier and pays, brings back the stamped receipt.)

Clerk: (Brings the item out and gives it to Dodi.) Thank you.

2. What Should We Play?

Budi: I'm bored. Let's play (something)...

Arif: Play what?

Budi: How about just playing hide-and-seek?

Arif:	Oh, I don't want to if it's only us two. Later it'll only be us who switch the hiding and seeking. It's not any fun.
Budi:	Okay then, how about we get our other friends?
Arif:	Yeah, you call Husni, Wawan, and Yanto. I'll go to Lintang, Bagus, and Chandra's house. Maybe they want to play hide-and-seek too.
Budi:	Okay then, let's go now so then we can play a long time before evening prayer time.

3. Boys Go Fishing

Wawan:	I heard from Yanto there's lots of catfish in Mr. Paijo's rice paddies.
Lintang:	Oh? When?
Wawan:	It's true, I swear! Yesterday Yanto went fishing there and caught lots.
Lintang:	Mr. Paijo doesn't mind us fishing in his fields?
Wawan:	Yanto says he doesn't mind when we step on his rice paddies.
Lintang:	Oh, okay then let's go fishing there!
Wawan:	Now?
Lintang:	Yes, you can right?
Wawan:	I can – I'll borrow Yanto's fishing pole.
Lintang:	Cool. Let's just meet right after at Mr. Paijo's field okay?
Wawan:	Cool/Okay.

4. Magic Show at a Shopping Mall

Rudi:	Look at that! What's going on there? Why are a lot of people gathered at that stand?
Endang:	Yeah you're right. Let's take a look!
Rudi:	Oh, apparently there's a magician here.

Endang:	Yep. He's doing magic tricks with cards.
Rudi:	How can all the cards turn into Aces?
Endang:	Yep. It's amazing.
Rudi:	Look, now he's doing magic with a dove. He's putting that rabbit into a hat...
Endang:	What? The bird disappeared. Where did it disappear to?
Rudi:	Wow, he's really very good.

5. Traditional Events for Independence Day

Arif:	Mister, are you going to see the August 17th / Independence Day events?
Mr.:	Yes. I've already seen some. Last night there was – a person who runs carrying a stick, then gives it to the person in front. What's the name for it in Indonesian?
Arif:	Oh, *lari estafet* (relay race).
Mr.:	*Lari* what?
Arif:	Estafet Mister. Swinging/passing a baton.
Mr.:	Lari estafat?
Arif:	Yeah, that's right.
Mr.:	This afternoon what else is there?
Arif:	There's volleyball, the tug-of-war, sack race, kid's games...
Mr.:	Hold on – I don't understand. What's that?
Arif:	Volleyball, Mister, volleyball. You know, don't you?
Mr.:	Yes, I know volleyball. But the other one – *tarik* what?
Arif:	Tarik tambang. There's a long, thick rope and two teams go like this (mimes pulling action).
Mr.:	Oh, I understand. In English it's name is the tug-of-war.

Arif:	What?
Mr.:	It's called 'tug of war.' Tug means pull. 'Tug of war.' War – is *perang*. 'Tug of war.'
Arif:	Tug of war … They have it in America right Mister?
Mr.:	They have it. It's the same. Besides that, the last one – what did you say? Something *karung*?
Arif:	*Balap karung.*
Mr.:	'Sack' like the sack from the grocery store?
Arif:	No Mister. A rice sack. A big sack.
Mr.:	What's the meaning of '*balap*?'
Arif:	Run, race.
Mr.:	Okay. We have it in America too. It's name is 'sack race.' What time does it start?
Arif:	4 or 4:30.
Mr.:	Great. I'll come see it. What are those poles for? (Points at two poles in the field.)
Arif:	Those are *panjat pinang* (the pole climb).
Mr.:	*Panjat* what?
Arif:	*Pinang.*
Mr.:	People climb the pole right?
Arif:	Yeah. In America do they have the pole climb?
Mr.:	We have it. It's the same but usually they use grease to make it more difficult.
Arif:	The same here. Sometimes yeah. Maybe later they'll add oil.
Mr.:	Oh, I see. Okay, I'm going to go home now. See you later this evening yeah.
Arif:	Four o'clock Mister, at four.
Mr.:	Yeah, I know. I'll come later this evening.

11. TRAVEL AND TRANSPORT

Please review the Travel & Transport section of Unit One: Words You Already Know, before continuing.

English	Indonesian	Javanese
airline	maskapai penerbangan	s
airplane/aircraft	kapal terbang/pesawat	montor mabur
airport	bandara (bandar udara)	lapangan terbang
bicycle	sepéda	pit
bridge	jembatan	kretek
bus stop	halte bus	halte bis
chain	rantai	s
driver	supir	s
drivers license	SIM	s
fix a flat	tambal ban	s
flat (tire)	kempés	gembos
flight	penerbangan	s
gear (1st, 2nd)	gigi/persnéling	s
horse carriage	andong	dokar
minivan (city bus/routes)	angkot (angkutan kota)	s
minivan (long distance)	travel*	s
motorcycle taxi	ojék	s
old, trash, worn-out (a car)	sampah, payah	payah
overpass/flyover	jalan layang	s
patch a tire, tube	tambal	s
pedicab	bécak	s
port/harbor	pelabuhan	s
rowboat, skiff	perahu	prau
roundabout/circle	bundaran	bunderan
ship/ferry	kapal	s
souvenirs (always food)	oléh-oléh	s
spare tire	ban cadangan	ban sérep
speed bump	polisi tidur	s
taxi meter	argo*	s
tickets	karcis, tikét	s
ticket window	lokét	s
tire	ban	s
toll road	jalan tol	dalan tol
train	keréta api	sepur

traffic	lalu lintas	s
traffic jam/bad traffic	macet	s
traffic police stop/checkpt	razia, operasi	cegatan polisi
tube of tire	ban dalam	ban jero
vehicle 'blue book'	(buku) BPKB*	s
vehicle registration	STNK*	s
wheel	roda	ro<u>da</u>

Language & Culture Notes

1. BPKB stands for *Bukti Pemilikan Kendaraan Bermotor*, the proof of ownership. It is a blue book that contains the ownership record and incidents involving the motorcycle. It is generally kept at home.

2. STNK stands for *Surat Tanda Nomer Kendaraan*, or vehicle registration. SIM stands for *Surat Izin Mengemudi*, or driver's license. As elsewhere, Indonesian police typically ask for license and registration. Parking lots/garages often ask to see STNK when you leave, to ensure nobody is stealing motorcycles (a common crime in Indonesia). If you aren't carrying the STNK, you will either get a ticket or have to pay a bribe on-the-spot. At the worst, the police will impound the motorbike and you will have to bring evidence of ownership to the station and pay an even larger fine to get your bike back.

3. Domestic Indonesian airlines are cheap and basically reliable. On the other hand, flights are commonly delayed, and there have been numerous accidents. Investigations of the industry have ensued after such incidents, and charges that many carriers opt to pay off inspectors rather than comply with upkeep and regular safety inspections are believable. For short flights outside Indonesia, Air Asia flies into numerous Indonesian cities and has a much better record and reputation. Of the Indonesian carriers, only Garuda Airlines meets the international standards necessary to operate outside the country.

4. Small shops or spots beside the road advertising '*stel roda*' or *tambal ban*' are frequent, and you will rarely have to travel far in order to have a flat tire fixed. It will cost you less than a dollar in U.S. currency anywhere, to have a motorcycle tire patched. If you have to replace a tube, it will cost a little more: 30 – 40.000 rupiah, or a few dollars.

5. *Angkot* are old *Colt* minivans with an open side door that run regular routes in and around the cities. Payment depends on the distance you go, from 500 rupiah for just down the road up to several thousand rupiah. *Travel* are minivans that operate like long-distance buses, city–city. You buy a ticket and can take luggage. On Java, they are a good alternative to buses or trains.

6. Trains on Java are a great way to travel and see the countryside. There are 3 classes: 'ekonomi, business, and executive.' The *ekonomi* trains can get very uncomfortable and crammed with passengers, like cattle cars (I would only recommend them for between small towns not serviced by the larger trains). Business Class has dedicated, semi-comfortable seating with open windows as the means of staying cool, although at busy times, lots of people without seats can stand or sit in the aisle and sometimes try to take your arm rest to sit on. Executive Class has reclining comfortable seats with AC, which can often get downright freezing on night trains – be sure to bring a jacket. Business and Executive Class trains often use different stations within the same city, so check for times and schedule, as well as which station the train leaves from/arrives at.

7. City-to-city buses are almost always cheaper than train, but you will be subject to the drivers' death defying driving tactics. Buses do not hesitate to pass, even when it is not clear, and have no qualms about using their size to run smaller vehicles (motorcycles) off the road as necessary. The up-side is that you tend to get there quickly, especially considering traffic conditions. A kind of unspoken agreement exists between the driver and the passengers. He can go ahead and drive like a madman, as long as everyone arrives safely and he doesn't have an accident. If he happens to kill someone, the crowd (including passengers) will likely beat him to death. If he escapes the angry crowd, he will not be able to work as a driver again, and will be on the run.

8. Driving in cities in Indonesia is often stressful and maddening. In Yogya, the combination of *angkot, sepeda, becak, andong, mobil, and sepeda motor*, all on the same streets, makes for an interesting mix of stop-and-go traffic and suddenly appearing hazards to avoid. But, owning and driving a motorcycle can sometimes be enjoyable when traffic is not too bad, and is convenient and preferable to taking buses or taxis all the time. In Jakarta, traffic is congested or *macet* much of the time, and it can take hours to get anywhere, just creeping along in low gear. Indonesians are rarely considerate to other drivers in the same sense that Westerners are, so intersections are a mess, with everyone trying to gain the advantage and get ahead, at the other vehicles' expense. Many expats in Jakarta hire a driver so they do not have to deal with the traffic, and I myself gave up trying to drive my motorcycle in Jakarta fairly quickly, in favor of relatively more expensive taxis (less stressful, AC, not breathing in fumes).

9. Driving cross country, from city to city, on the island of Java can also be stressful and annoying. As of yet, there is no major highway system linking cities, so travel is often on two-lane roads in need of repair, with buses and trucks stacked up, lines of traffic both directions, the smell of exhaust in the air, and aggressive drivers intent on passing you, regardless of conditions. If you are on a motorcycle, you will eventually be run off the road (hopefully onto a decent shoulder) by a bus or truck heading at you in your lane. Rather than visible signs or cones of some kind, the preferred warning for a dangerous hole or obstruction in the road tends to be a few tree branches stuck into the road or hanging off the obstruction, which at night and at high speeds cannot always be seen until you are upon them. Reliable road signs are also lacking on Java, so that when you come to an intersection of some kind in the next city, it is unclear which way you should go. People in smaller towns, when asked for directions for a larger city farther away, often have no idea how to get there. However, to save face, they will tend to give you directions anyway, even if they have no idea and cannot read a map. This leads to lots of backtracking.

10. Traffic is at its absolute worst during the Idul Fitri or Lebaran holiday, following Ramadan. Similar to American Thanksgiving, nearly everyone travels to their family's home for several days. Millions (yes millions) leave Jakarta by car and motorcycle to travel across Java or to Sumatera. The gridlock in places cannot be imagined. Trains and planes are sold out and the transport companies charge customers more money as the holiday nears. Needless to say, there are also a large number of road accidents and deaths.

11. In contrast to Java, driving around the island of Bali and some other outer islands in the east is enjoyable. In Bali, the roads are well kept and well-marked, owing to the Balinese practice of promoting tourism and of using tourist dollars on infrastructure which will generate and allow for more tourism in the long-term. This is a concept most of Indonesia has yet to embrace.

12. The *busway* is Jakarta's attempt at clean, reliable, affordable public transportation for workers and tourists, without the expense of an overhead or underground train, like KL, Bangkok, or Singapore. It has been partially successful, but is still plagued by problems. The dedicated bus lanes are routinely used by other cars and the bus lanes have not been maintained in places so that buses frequently have to use the regular traffic lanes. Routes on the periphery of the city are not frequent enough to compete with other forms of transportation, like an inner city or city-city bus, and in many places, it is easier and faster to take another kind of bus or combination of *angkot* and bus. Despite this, in certain parts of the city, especially the city center, the bus way is a cheap, convenient, clean and fairly quick way to get from A to B.

13. About 10 years ago, the city of Jakarta decided it would build a monorail, which of course, was never completed. Jakarta has recently announced that it plans to build a subway, due to be completed in a few years. Given the city's massive problems with flooding, inability to maintain current infrastructure, corruption, and lack of technical knowledge for such a project, I cannot imagine that the city will be successful in this endeavor any more than it was with a monorail, although it would be greatly welcome.

14. Taxis - in Jakarta and other larger cities, Blue Bird (and its more expensive affiliate 'Silver Bird' in Jakarta) is the best known professional taxi company and one of the few that meets some kind of standard. They are recognizable by their clean metallic blue body with wings on top. They are slightly more expensive than some other taxis, but generally worth it, although there is no guarantee. I have personally had trouble with a few Blue Bird drivers. However, Blue Bird taxis go back to a garage at night and receive periodic maintenance, and the taxis all have a driver placard with the driver's name. The drivers receive a percentage of total daily fares, according to the meter. Other reputable taxi companies include Putra (non-metallic dull blue), Express (white with a yellow 'E'), and my personal favorite, Gamya (green - www.gamya.com). These are operated in contrast to most taxi companies where 2 drivers (friends) often share operation of a taxi and pay a daily rent - say 200.000 rupiah - to the taxi company, but keep all profits above that amount, take the taxi home, may have to pay maintenance out of their own pocket, but own the taxi after several years. It is not hard to see how this system encourages large fares and cheating customers. Out of all Indonesian cities, Jakarta is the only city where I have had regular bad encounters with dishonest taxi drivers. Dishonest taxi drivers are rare in most other parts of the country.

15. Using the meter (*argo*) is always the way to go when taking a taxi somewhere you are not familiar with, although you can nearly always beat a meter rate by haggling a flat rate if the distance is far and you know how much it generally costs by meter. Be sure to carry plenty of small bills, as taxi drivers generally don't have/claim not to have proper change. In Jakarta, an easy way to do this is to pay with a large bill at the toll gates, when you get on the *jalan tol*.

Indonesian Conversations

1. Taking a Becak (Naik Becak)

Pak: Bécak Mister! Becak!

Mister: Oke. Kalau saya mau ke Jalan Prawirotaman berapa harganya?

Pak: Berapa Mister mau?

Mr: Sepuluh ribu gimana?

Pak: Itu jauh dari sini Mister.

Mr: Kalau lima belas ribu boleh?

Pak: Boleh. Silahkan. (Mr. climbs in and they begin the trip.)
        Dari mana Mister?

Mr: Asalnya dari Amerika, tapi sekarang tinggal di sini.

Pak: Siswa?

Mr: Bukan siswa. Saya ajar bahasa Inggris di sekolah bahasa Inggris.
        (The rest of the ride proceeds without conversation.)

Mr: Kiri Pak. Di sini aja cukup. (Gets out.) Lima belas ribu ya?
        (Hands money to Pak.) Terima kasih Pak.

Pak: Sama-sama.

2. Traffic Checkpoint (Razia)

There is a police checkpoint set up, all motorcycle traffic is being diverted through the checkpoint.

Polisi: STNK dan SIM. Siapa pemilik motor ini?

Wida: Saya Pak.

Polisi: Kenapa alamat STNK dan SIM tidak sama? Ada KTP?

Wida: (Gives the police her national ID card.) Karena saya sekarang kuliah ke UGM dan tidak tinggal di rumah keluarga yang di desa.

Polisi: Tinggal sendiri di Yogya? Belum menikah? (Reaches and turns on headlight and checks turn signals.) Reting kanan tidak berfungsi.

Wida: Tinggal sendiri Pak. Minta permisi Pak, Saya ada kelas sekarang.

Polisi: Sudah lama reting tidak berfungsi tapi anda tidak memperbaikinya – Ya kan? Jadi begini – tolong membawa motor ke sebelah sana. (Points to the side of the checkpoint, where the trouble cases are dealt with.)

(Police check all documents again).

Wida: Ma'af Pak tapi saya belum bisa bayar. Sekarang tidak punya cukup uang dan sekarang hari untuk bayar sekolah. Saya akan pinjam uang dan memperbaiki segera Pak.

Polisi: Kalau dibiarkan berbahaya. Tidak bisa. Motor anda bisa diambil di kantor POLRES. Ada biaya yang harus dibayar.

Wida: Tapi bagaimana saya bisa pergi ke sana? Saya tidak boleh membayar biaya sekarang di sini saja?

Polisi: Tidak bisa. Harus ke dalam kantor polisi.

3. Flat Tire on the Motorcycle

Mr. Don: Pak, tolong ban belakang saya kemps.

(Pak turns on compressor, fills the tire.)

Pak Ban: Mister tidak bisa, ban dalamnya ada lubang.

Mr. Don: Baiklah, tolong diperbaiki ya Pak.

(Pak gets out his tire kit, runs the tire thru water, looks for the hole.)

Pak Ban: Dari mana Mister?

Mr. Don: Aslinya? Amerika.

Pak Ban: Sudah pintar bahasa Indonesia

Mr. Don: Belum, tapi bisa sedikit-sedikit.

Pak Ban: Bannya sudah banyak tambalanya, Mister.

Mr. Don   Ya, benar. Ban dalam memang udah lama.

Pak Ban: Lebih baik kalo diganti aja.

Mr. Don   Ban dalam yang baru berapa?

Pak Ban: Yang murah dua puluh tapi nggak bagus,
                yang kualitas bagus dua puluh lima.

Mr. Don: (checks wallet). Ma'af Pak, sekarang kantongku kempes.
                Sekarang tambal itu satu kali lagi ke sini aja. Besok saya
                datang lagi ganti ban dalam ya.

Pak: Baik. (Patches tire, which takes 5 min.) Sudah Mister.

Mr. Don: Berapa?

Pak: Lima ribu.

Mr. Don:	Terima kasih Pak. Sampai besok, saya datang lagi untuk ganti ban dalam.
Pak:	Hati-hati Mister.

4. Bring us Back Oleh-Oleh!

Mas Anto just returned from vacation in Jogja.

Aris:	Gimana liburannya?
Anto:	Wah, seru. Suasana di sana berbeda dengan di sini, jadi malas kembali pulang dan kerja.
Tuti:	Pergi ke mana saja di sana?
Anto:	Semua tempat menarik kudatangi. Mulai dari Kraton sampai Candi Borobudur, juga pantai.
Aris:	Mana nih, oleh-olehnya? Masa hanya cerita saja.
Anto:	(Mengeluarkan bungkusan dari dalam tasnya.) Tenang, aku bawakan beberapa makanan khas dari sana. Ada bakpia dan geplak.
Aris:	Wah, lumayan untuk camilan di kantor. Makasih ya.
Anto:	Aku tidak sempat membeli yang lain, karena tidak ada waktu lagi. Terlalu sibuk jalan-jalan.
Tuti:	Nggak apa-apa, ini sudah cukup.

5. Bus trip to Bali

Andri and Rinto are on their way to Bali.

Andri: Baru pertama kali lho, aku pergi ke Bali naik bus.
           Biasanya aku lebih suka naik kapal terbang, lebih cepat.

Rinto: Iya, naik bus memang lebih lama tapi ongkosnya kan
           lebih murah.

Andri: Ya, memang lebih murah tapi pinggangku sakit karena
           terlalu lama duduk di bus.
           Untung tadi aku nggak mabuk laut di kapal.

Rinto: Nanti kalau sudah sampai, kamu bisa istirahat di hotel.

Andri: Kita langsung jalan-jalan ke pantai saja. Mungkin capékku
           hilang kalau sudah lihat pantai, ha ha.

Rinto: Ya, boleh. Tapi sebelum itu, kita makan dulu. Aku dengar
           ada banyak restoran énak di Kuta. Aku ingin coba.

Andri: Pasti ada banyak bulé di sana dong. Mungkin kamu bisa
           ketemu céwék bule yang cantik di sana, ha ha.

Rinto: Kita harus ke club di Kuta kalau mau mencari cewek-
           cewek. Ada banyak turis dari seluruh Indonesia dan dunia
           ini. Mungkin kita beruntung.

Andri: Ya dong. Aku senang kalo bisa ke luar dari bus aja. Gak
           peduli mencari cewek.

Rinto: Di Kuta ada banyak hotel yang murah. Naik taksi aja
           langsung dari stasiun yuk! Aku gak ingin naik bus lagi.

Andri: Aku juga pikir gitu.

Reading Sample 1: Train Ticket

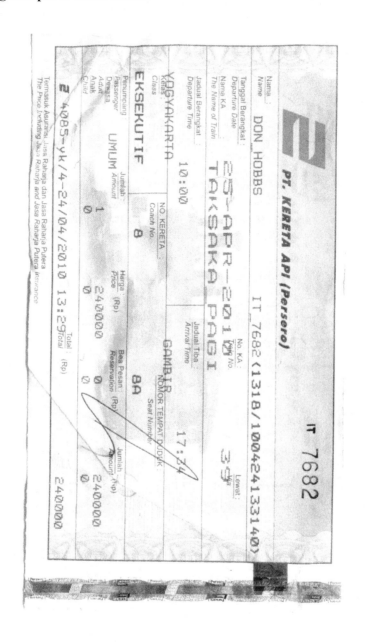

Reading Sample 2: Shipping Company Form

PERNYATAAN KIRIM PACKET MOTOR
(HP. 0274.71829XX)

PACKET MOTOR DITUJUNKAN
KEPADA YTH.

DIKIRIM DARI:

Don HOBBS / KOST Karywan
Jl. Pinang Ranti II RTXX RWXX
#4 Jkta TMR

PUTHUT
Jl. Supadi No. 9
YOGYA
0818278XXX

BAHWA SEMUA PENGIRIMAN <u>PACKET MOTOR</u> APABILA TERJADI KERUSAKAN ATAUPUN TERJADI

RETAK <u>2</u> PECAH PATAH MOTOR YG DIKRIM ADLAH MENJADI <u>TANGGUNG JAWAB PENGIRIM/RESIKO</u>

<u>SENDIRI</u> .

KEADAAN MOTOR YG DIKIRIM TERDIRI SEBAGAI BERIKUT :

1. JENIS MOTOR	*HONDA GLP*	11. ACCU & TUTUP ACCU	*Ada*
2. WARNA CAT MOTOR	*Hijau*	12. PUSTEP & KARET SLAH	*Ada*
3. NO. PLAT POLISI	*AB53XX TK*	13. KLAKSON KETENGKAS	*Ada*
4. BAN DAN PELEKMOTOR	*Ada*	14. JOB MOTOR	*Ada*
5. MESIN MOTOR	*Ada*	15. SLEBOR MOTOR	*Ada*
6. KACA SPION MOTOR	*Ada - 2 buah*	16. STANDAR ENGKDOUBEL	*Ada*
7. LAMPU DPN & BLK	*Ada*	17. BAN SEREP	—
8. LAMPU RETING	*Ada*	18. KUNCI TOLKIT	—
9. SPEDO METER MOTOR	*Ada*	19. KUNCI KONTAK	*Ada*
10. SAYAP/TEBENG MOTOR	—	20. SURAT2 MOTOR	*STNK*

NB. *P32362*

Helm 1 buah

DEMIKIANLAH KETERANGAN PACKET MOTOR YG KAMI KIRIMKAN DG PERINCIAN TERSEBUT

DIATAS MOHON TRIMA KASIH.

TGL KIRIM : *9/2 - 10*

HORMAT KAMI,

Ardianto

(PENGIRIM)
PUTHUT ARDIANTO

137

Javanese Conversations

1. Taking a Becak

Pak: Bécak Mister! Becak!

Mr: Ya. Nék aku arep neng dalan Prawiro Taman pira regané?

Pak: Kersane panjenengan?

Mr: Sepuluh éwu…. Piye?

Pak: Menika tebih saking mriki….

Mr: Nek limalas ewu, isa?

Pak: Angsal. Monggo. Saking pundi Mister?

Mr: Asale saka Amerika, tur saiki tinggal néng kéné.

Pak: Murid?

Mr: Dudu murid, aku mulang boso Inggris neng sekolah boso Inggris.
(Rest of ride proceeds without conversation.)

Mr: Kiwa Pak. Neng kene wae cukup. Limolas ewu ya? Nuwun, Pak.

Pak: Sami sami.

2. Traffic Checkpoint (Jekatan Polisi)

There is a checkpoint; all motorcycle traffic is being diverted through it.

Polisi: STNK lan SIM. S<u>apa</u> sing nduwe motor iki?

Wida: Kul<u>a</u> Pak.

Polisi: Kok alamat SIM lan STNK ora p<u>ada</u>? An<u>a</u> KTP?

Wida: (Gives the police her national ID card.) Sakniki kul<u>a</u> kuliah ing UGM, lan mboten tinngal ing griy<u>a</u> kul<u>a</u> ing desa.

Polisi: Manggon dewe neng Jogja? Durung nikah? (Reaches and turns on headlight and checks turn signals.) Lampu reting ora urip.

Wida: Piyambakan.. [sendirian] ngapunten Pak, kul<u>a</u> wonten kelas sakmenik<u>a</u>.

Polisi: Wis suwe reting ora urip tur kowe ora ndandani. Iya to? Dadi ngéné. Tulung nggowo motor neng sebelah k<u>ana</u>.

(Leads her to side of checkpoint and checks all documents again.)

Wida: Ngapunten Pak, nanging kul<u>a</u> dereng angsal bayar. Sakmenik<u>a</u> mboten gadhah art<u>a</u> lan sakmenik<u>a</u> dinten bayaran sekolah. Kul<u>a</u> badhe nyambut art<u>a</u> rumiyin lajing kul<u>a</u> dandosi Pak.

Polisi: Nek kowe dijarke bahaya. Ora is<u>a</u>. Motormu is<u>a</u> dijupuk neng kantor Polres. An<u>a</u> biaya sing kudu dibayar.

Wida: Nanging pripun kul<u>a</u> badhe kesah mrika? Kul<u>a</u> mboten saged mbayar sakmenika ing mriki kemawon?

Polisi: Ora is<u>a</u>. Kudu neng kantor polisi.

3. Flat Tire on the Motorcycle

Mr. Don: Pak tulung ban mburiku bocor.
(Pak turns on compressor, fills the tire.)

Pak Ban: Mboten saged Mister, ban lebetipun wonten ingkang bolong.

Mr. Don: Ya wis, tulung didandani ya, Pak.
(Pak gets out his tire kit, runs the tire thru water, looks for the hole.)

Pak Ban: Saking pundi Mister?

Mr. Don: Asline? Amerika.

Pak Ban: Wah, pun sae basa Jawa-nipun nggih.

Mr. Don: Durung, tur isa sithik-sithik.

Pak Ban: Ban sampun kathah tambalanipun, Mister.

Mr. Don   Iya bener. Ban njeroku pancén wis lawas.

Pak Ban: Saénipun digantos kémawon.

Mr. Don   Ban sing anyar pira?

Pak Ban: Ingkang mirah ning mboten patos sae reginipun kalih dasa, ingkang kualitas sae reginipun selangkung.

Mr. Don: Nuwun séwu Pak, saiki aku lagi ora duwe duit. Saiki tambal pisan manéh ya. Sésuk, aku teka maneh mréné ngganti ban njero ya.

Pak: Inggih. (Changes tire in 5 min.) Sampun Mister.

Mr. Don: Pira, Pak?

Pak:	Gangsal éwu.
Mr. Don:	Nuwun Pak. Sesuk aku teka mréné kanggo ngganti ban njero.
Pak:	Ngatos atos Mister.

4. Bring us Oleh-Oleh back !

Anto just returned from vacation in Yogyakarta.

Aris:	Piye liburane?
Anto:	Wah seru. Suasanane néng kana béda banget karo neng kéné. Marakke males bali lan nyambut gawe.
Tuti:	Lunga nengdi wae neng kana?
Anto:	Kabeh panggonan sing apik tak tekani. Mulai saka Kraton nganti Candi Borobudur, uga kisik.
Aris:	Endi oleh-olehé? Masa mung crita thok?
Anto:	Aja kuatir, tak gawake panganan khas saka kana. Ana bakpia karo geplak.
Aris:	Wah, lumayan kanggo camilan neng kantor, nuwun ya.
Anto:	Aku ora sempat tuku liyane, merga wis ora ana waktu menéh, kakehan mlaku-mlaku.
Tuti:	Ora apa-apa, iki wis cukup.

5. Bus trip to Bali

Andri dan Rinto sedang dalam perjalanan ke Bali.

Andri: Lagi pisan iki aku lunga néng Bali numpak bis. Biasane
           aku luwih seneng numpak motor mabur, lewih cepet.

Rinto: Iya, numpak bis pancén luwih suwe ning regane luwih
           murah.

Andri: Pancen luwih murah, tur boyokku pegel kesuwén lingguh
           neng bis. Untung mau aku ra mabuk neng kapal.

Rinto: Mengko nék wis ketuk kowe isa istirahat neng hotel.

Andri: Awa(k)édéwé langsung mlaku-mlaku neng pantai wae..
           mungkin keselku ilang nek wis ndelok pantai.

Rinto: Oleh, tur sakdurunge kuwi awakedewe mangan sik.
           Aku krungu akéh restoran énak neng Kuta. Aku péngén
           nyoba.

Andri: Ana akéh bulé mesti neng kana ya. Mungkin kowe isa
           ketemu karo bule wédok sing ayu lan apikan neng kana, ha ha.

Rinto: Awakedewe kudu lunga neng klub neng Kuta nek arep
           golek céwék. Neng kana ana akeh turis saka Indonesia lan
           manca. Mungkin awakedewe beja.

Andri: Iya lah. Aku seneng nek isa metu saka bis,
           Ora peduli nggolék cewek.

Rinto: Neng Kuta ana hotel sing murah banget. Numpak taksi
           saka terminal langsung wae yuk! Aku wegah numpak
           bis maneh!

Andri: Aku ya mikir ngono.

Unit 11: English Translation of Conversations

1. Taking a Pedicab

Driver:	Pedicab Mister! Pedicab!
Mr. Don:	Okay. If I want to go to Prawirotaman Street, how much is it?
Driver:	How much do you want (to pay)?
Mr.:	How about 10,000?
Driver:	It's far away from here Mister.
Mr.:	Will you do it for 15,000?
Driver:	I will. Please (get in). Where are you from?
Mr.:	Originally from America, but now I live here.
Driver:	Student?
Mr.:	I'm not a student. I teach English at an English language school.
Mr.:	Pull over here sir. Here's good enough. 15,000 right? Thank you sir.
Driver:	You're welcome.

2. Traffic Checkpoint

Police:	License and registration. Who's the owner of this motorcycle?
Wida:	I am.
Police:	Why isn't the address on the registration and license the same? Do you have your ID card?
Wida:	(Gives the police her national ID card.) Because I now am going to college at UGM and I don't live in my family's house in the country.
Police:	You live alone in Jogja? You're not married? (He reaches and turns on the headlight and checks turn signals.) The right blinker/turn signal doesn't work.

Wida:	I live alone sir. I'm sorry sir, but I have class now.
Police:	You're right blinker hasn't worked for a long time, but you haven't fixed it. Isn't that right? So here's what's going to happen. Please bring your motorcycle to the side over there.
Wida:	I'm sorry sir, but I haven't been able to pay for it yet. I don't have enough money right now and today's the day to pay tuition. I'll borrow some money and get it fixed right away, sir.
Police:	If I let you do that, it's dangerous. I can't. Your bike can be picked up at the City Police station. There is a fine that will have to be payed.
Wida:	But how can I get there? I can't just pay the fine now, right here?
Police:	You can't. You have to go to the police station.

3. Flat Tire on the Motorcycle

Mr. Don:	Sir, please my rear tire is flat.
Tire Man:	(Turns on the compressor, fills the tire.) Sorry, it can't – the inner tube has a leak.
Mr. Don:	Okay then, go ahead and fix/patch it please.
Tire Man:	(Gets out his kit, looks for the hole.)
Tire Man:	Where are you from sir?
Mr. Don:	Originally? America.
Tire Man:	You're already good at Indonesian/Javanese.
Mr. Don:	Not yet, but I can speak a little bit.
Tire Man:	The tire has already been patched many times.
Mr. Don:	That's right. The tube is really old.
Tire Man:	It's better just to change it.
Mr. Don:	How much is a new tube?

Tire Man:	A cheap one is 20,000, but it's not good. A good-quality one is 25,000.
Mr. Don:	(Checks his wallet.) Sorry, but I'm flat broke right now. For now, just patch it one more time. Tomorrow I'll come back and change the tube, okay.
Tire Man:	Okay. (5 min. later) It's done.
Mr. Don:	How much?
Tire Man:	5,000.
Mr. Don:	Thank you sir. See you tomorrow – I'll come back to change the tube.
Tire Man:	Take care.

4. Bring Us Back some Souvenirs!

(Anto just returned from vacation in Jogja.)

Aris:	How was your vacation?
Anto:	Wow, it was fun. The atmosphere there was different from here, so I didn't want to come back to work.
Tuti:	Where (exactly) did you go there?
Anto:	We visited all the interesting places. Starting from Kraton (Sultan's Palace) to Borobudur Temple, and also the beach.
Aris:	And where are our souvenirs? Or was it just talk (at the time)?
Anto:	(Takes out packages from inside his bag.) Take it easy. I brought back a few local foods from there. There's *bakpi* and *geplak*.
Aris:	Wow, not bad for snacks for the office. Thanks yeah.
Anto:	I didn't have the chance to buy anything else, because there wasn't any more time. I was too busy looking around.
Tuti:	That's okay, this is just fine/good enough.

5. Bus Trip to Bali

Andri and Rinto are on a trip to Bali

Andri: Wow, this is the first time I've gone to Bali on the bus. Usually I like flying better - it's faster.

Rinto: Yeah, riding the bus takes longer but the cost is cheaper.

Andri: Yeah, it's much cheaper but my butt hurts because of sitting too long on the bus. It's lucky I didn't get car sick a while ago.

Rinto: Later after we're there, we can relax at the hotel.

Andri: Let's just go straight to the beach and look around. Maybe my tiredness will disappear after I've seen the beach, ha ha.

Rinto: Yeah, maybe. But before that, let's eat first. I hear there are a lot of good restaurants in Kuta. I want to try one.

Andri: I'm sure there are a lot of foreigners there, bro. Maybe you can meet a foreign chick there – ha, ha.

Rinto: We have to go to a club on Kuta if we want to find chicks. There are a lot of tourists from all over Indonesia and the world. Maybe we'll get lucky.

Andri: Yeah man. I'll be happy if we can just get off the bus. I don't care about finding chicks.

Rinto: On Kuta there are many cheap hotels. Let's just take a taxi directly from the station. I don't want to ride another bus.

Andri: I'm thinking the same thing.

12. OFFICE, NET, PHONES

Please review Unit 1: Words You Already Know for English office vocabulary before continuing.

English	Indonesian
advertisement	iklan
application (computer)	aplikasi
arrange (a schedule)	atur
asterisk/star (*)	bintang
back-to-back copy	kopi bolak-balik
back/reverse side	balik (belakang)
bind a book	menjilid*
boot up	buting
card paper (colored)	bc warna* (bé sé)
chatting online	chatting (same word)
copier	mesin fotokopi
cover (on book, folder)	sampul
credit (for phone)	pulsa*
envelope	amplop
front and back	bolak-balik
help center	pusat bantuan
in order, fine	bérés
internet shop	warnet
internet access spot	hot spot
keep in touch with	tetap berhubungan dengan
manage	(meng)urus
management	pengurus/manajemen
monitor	monitor
mouse	mouse
neat, orderly, tidy	rapi
number sign (#)	pagar
office	kantor
online	online
options	opsi
overtime	kerja lembur
10 copies	10 kali
page	halaman
paper	kertas
part-time	paruh waktu

password	sandi, password
photocopy	fotokopi*
pieces/counter for paper	lembar
profile	profil
reboot	buting ulang/lagi
schedule	jadwal
space (phone pad/keyboard)	spasi
two-sided copy	bolak-balik
stamp (official)	materai*
sheet (of paper)	lembar
wireless	wi-fi (pron: wee fee)

Indonesian	**English**
akun	account
beranda	home page
dinding	wall
gambar	images, pics
gaptek	technical gap*
ke luar	exit, logoff
kotak	box, mailbox
pencarian	search
penelusuran	search
pengaturan	control, regulation
permintaan	request(s)
pesan	message(s)
pusat bantuan	help center
sandi	password
sekarang berteman	'is now a friend'
serba-serbi	about (all about us)
sunting	edit, proofread
usulan	suggestion
wartél	warung telephone - public telephone center
warnét	warung internet - internet cafe

Language & Cultural Notes

1. Photocopy shops in Indonesia are notorious for messing up large print jobs. Once completed, they do not generally want to give refunds for such problems as poor print quality or misalignment. It's best to always have them do a single copy of the job first and check it before proceeding with the remainder.

2. BC stands for Buffalo Color. It was evidently the first major company selling the paper in Indonesia.

3. Like most the region (and still unlike the USA), cell phones in Indonesia are cheap, convenient, and easy to use, fix, and buy. Sim cards can be bought and swapped out phone to phone with no problem, and there is a huge market in used cell phones, so it's worth getting a cell number while you are in country, even if it's only for a couple weeks. One quirk about numbers is that it will cost more to buy a sim/phone no. with repeating numbers or a pattern that makes the number easier to remember. 085234762391 will be cheaper to buy than 085252225512, for example, and a number like 081700700700 would be the most expensive.

4. Pre-paid phone credit, or '*pulsa*' for handphones can be bought at street side stands or any phone shop, and at some stores. It is available in increments of 5, 10, 20, or 50.000 rupiah. A single sms/text message only costs about 250 rupiah (2-3 cents), so this is how most people communicate.

5. The country phone code for Indonesia is 62. Mobile phone numbers begin with 08. From outside the country, the 0 is left out. So the mobile number 081392333285, for example, is dialed as 6281392333285 from the USA. Within Indonesia, the number is dialed 081392333285. From another mobile phone it can also be dialed as +6281392333285. There are also area/city codes, which also begin with 0. Jakarta is 021, Yogya is 0274. The 0 is omitted when calling from overseas. Area/city codes do not have to be dialed when calling a local number from another phone (mobile or landline) within that same area code.

6. Official stamps (*materai*) and ink stamps are extremely popular in Indonesia - it seems everything needs to be stamped before it is considered legitimate, whether it is a receipt from a cashier in any store, to an office document, to a contract of some kind. Mere signatures usually do not count for much, at least not on important or official documents. Official stamps are bought at the post office or some book stores for 6.000 or 7.000 rupiah (as of 2010) . Your signature goes over the stamp, at the bottom of the document. Most stores and businesses have their own ink pads and rubber stamps, which they love to slap down on receipts, often more than a single time.

Indonesian Conversations

1. At the Photocopy Shop

Tamu:	Siang.
Mbak Kopi:	Siang. Bisa saya bantu?
Tamu:	Ya. (Puts the copies on counter.) Mau halaman ini disusun supaya jadi bikin buku. Bisa begitu?
Mbak:	Bisa. Dijilid ya?
Tamu:	Iya. Halamannya udah beres ya. Ini halaman pertama sampai ini yang terakhir.
Mbak:	Mau jadi berapa buku?
Tamu:	Mungkin sepuluh cukup. Ya, sepuluh pas.
Mbak:	Sampulnya?
Tamu:	Apa?
Mbak:	Sampul di depan dan belakang?
Tamu:	Ya, baik. Ada kertas yang mana yang tebal?

Mbak:	Ini BC Warna. (Points to wall.)
Tamu:	Ya, bagus. Yg hijau muda itu.
Mbak:	Dijilid gimana?
Tamu:	Biasanya yang pakai selotip hitam, ya kan?
Mbak:	Ada. Tapi, kalo mau, spiral juga bisa.
Tamu:	Oh, spiral plastik hitam itu ya? (Points to inside shop.) Boleh saya lihat sebentar?
Mbak:	(Brings the spiraling out.) Ada yg kecil sampe yg besar. Untuk buku ini, yg ini udah bagus. Mau?
Tamu:	Berapa harganya?
Mbak:	10.000 per buku.
Tamu:	Kalo pakai selotip biasa?
Mbak:	7.000
Tamu:	Kalo gitu, spiral aja. Lama tidak?
Mbak:	(Turns to ask man working in store.) Kalau ini, berapa lama Pak? (Man takes a look at pages, they confer.)
Tamu:	Kalo saya mau ambil jam 12:00 bisa?
Mbak:	Boleh.

(Customer comes back in a couple hours at 12:00, but they are not quite finished with the job, so he has to wait about 10 min.)

Mbak:	Sudah Pak.

Tamu:	(Inspects the copies. Most pages are fine, but a few did not copy well and are hard to read.) Fotokopi halaman ini tidak terlalu bagus Mbak. Susah dibaca. Gimana ini sih... Bisa dikasih diskon sedikit?
Mbak:	Maaf Pak, tapi tidak bisa Pak.
Tamu:	Tapi, bagaimana siswaku bisa membacanya... Tapi, tidak apalah. Ya, begini cukup. Berapa?
Mbak:	(Puts the orders in a bag and adds a free pack of copy paper.) Seratus delapan puluh ribu. Terima kasih Pak. Ini kertas kosong gratis ya untuk Bapak.
Tamu:	(Laughs.) Ya, baik. Terima kasih.
Mbak:	Terima kasih kembali. Datang lagi, ya Pak.

2. Request for the OB (Office Boy)

Guru: Halo. Mas bisa fotokopi ini segera, sebelum kelasku yang berikut?

OB: Ya, bisa.

Guru: Baik. Yang ini bolak-balik. Yang lain ini tidak, fotokopi hanya yang di depan.

OB: Baik. Berapa kali?

Guru: Yang ini, 5 kali. Yang lain, 10 kali.

OB: Kertas yang mana?

Guru: Apa ya...A4 warna putih aja. Tapi yang ini, harus BC warna. Ada hijau?

OB: (Opens cabinet.) Hijau kosong Mas. Ada biru, merah, kuning...

Guru: Biru aja bagus.

OB: Kelasnya jam berapa?

Guru: Sepuluh menit lagi ya.

OB: Tidak masalah. (Yells at other OB.) Hendri! Yo, ini harus dikopi
       sekarang. (To teacher): Ya, saya akan
       membawanya ke ruang kelas kalau sudah selesai.

Guru: Makasih Mas.

Reading Sample: Facebook Page

Pencarian

Beranda Profil Cari Teman **Akun**

Sunting Teman
Pengaturan Akun
Pusat Bantuan
Keluar

Donald Hobbs
Sunting Profil Saya

Kabar Berita

Berita Populer · Paling Baru

FAVORIT

Kabar Berita

Pesan 13

Acara

Teman 54

GRUP

Buat Grup...

APLIKASI

Will you KISS me? 3

Koleksi Foto

Permintaan Permainan 33

Permintaan Aplikasi 38

Catatan

Pertanyaan

Teman di Obrolan

Bagikan: **Status** Foto Tautan Video Pertanyaan

Apa yang Anda pikirkan?

Cewek Indo
Very nice n sunny today :___
pengen berpetualangan ke Bali
2 jam yang lalu melalui seluler ·Suka · Komentari

menyukai ini.

Lihat ke-8 komentar

have a good time on the beach love
2 jam yang lalu · Suka

2 jam yang lalu · Suka · 1 orang

Tulis komentar...

Agus I menyukai tautan Monique '

Foto Dinding
We love this custom bike ..canibal power engine.
The art of motor cycle
Oleh : Metalconscious Motorcycle & Tattoo Art

21 jam yang lalu

Salsa I mengomentari statusnya.

Salsa Cintai dan sakiti hati ku kalau itu dpt membawamu
kembali ke pelukanku lagi .. aku rela memberi sgala'a .. _ROSSA_

22 jam yang lalu melalui seluler ·Suka · Komentari

WiNdy menyukai ini.

Herra cocok..
langsung ke tkp..
Kemarin jam 12:41 · Suka

Salsa he ?? opo kwi ?? ono pembunuhan po pye?
22 jam yang lalu · Suka

Tulis komentar...

Acara yang akan datang
Apa acaranya?

Harap masukkan nama acara

Temukan lebih banyak teman
Donald, Teman yang Lain Menunggu

2 teman ini menemukan teman mereka
menggunakan pencari teman. Apakah Anda
sudah menemukan semua teman Anda?
Cobalah.

Cari Teman

privacy lock
Facebook tidak akan
menyimpan kata sandi Anda

Sponsor Buat Iklan

Kunjungi
0.facebook.com untuk
menikmati gratis akses
Facebook Mobile. Untuk
pelanggan AXIS ,
Telkomsel, Three,
Indosat, dan XL.

Colekan

Novi ! · Colek Kembali
Moya · Colek Kembali
Mike . · Colek Kembali

Obrolan (2)

154

Javanese Conversations

1. At the Photocopy Shop

Tamu:	Sugeng siang.
Mbak Kopi:	Sugeng siang, wonten ingkang saged kula binantu?
Tamu:	Inggih. (Puts copies on counter.) Nyuwun halaman niki disusun supados dados buku. Saged?
Mbak:	Saged. Dipun jilid nggih?
Tamu:	Nggih. Halamanipun sampun bérés nggih? Menika halaman setunggal ngantos ingkang pungkasan.
Mbak:	Badhe dados pinten buku?
Tamu:	Kinten-kinten sedasa. Nggih sedasa pas.
Mbak:	Samakipun?
Tamu:	Menapa?
Mbak:	Samak ngajeng kalih wingking?
Tamu:	Nggih. Wonten kertas ingkang kandel?
Mbak:	Menika BC warna.
Tamu:	Nggih, sae. Ingkang ijo énem menika.
Mbak:	Dipun jilid kados pripun?
Tamu:	Biasanipun ngagem selotip ireng, nggih boten?

Mbak:	Wonten, menawi purun badhe ngagem jilid spiral ugi wonten.
Tamu:	Oh spiral plastik ingkang cemeng menika nggih? Saged kula ningali sekedhap?
Mbak:	Wonten ingkang alit dumugi ageng. Kagem buku menika sampun sae, kersa?
Tamu:	Pinten reginipun?
Mbak:	Sedasa éwu per buku.
Tamu:	Menawi ngagem selotip biasa?
Mbak:	Pitung éwu.
Tamu:	Menawi mekaten spiral kémawon – dangu mboten?
Mbak:	Nék iki pirang suwe Pak? (talking to boss)
Tamu:	Menawi kula badhe mendhet jam 12 saged?
Mbak:	Saged.

(Customer comes back in a couple hours at 12:00, but they are not quite finished with the job, so he has to wait about 10 min.)

Mbak:	Sampun Pak.
Tamu:	Foto kopi halaman niki mboten sae Mbak, angél dipun waos. Pripun Mbak? Saged dipun paringi diskon sekedhik Mbak?
Mbak:	Nyuwun ngapunten, menawi menika mboten saged.
Tamu:	Nangin, lha pripun murid kula saged maos? Nanging nggih sampun lha. Menika sampun cekap – Pinten?

Mbak: Satus wolungdasa éwu. Maturnuwun Pak, menika kertas kosong gratis kagem Bapak. (Adds a pack of copy paper.)

Tamu: (Laughs.) Nggih. Matur nuwun.

Mbak: Sami-sami, tindak mriki malih nggih, Pak.

2. Request for the OB (Office Boy)

Guru: Halo. Mas, isa fotokopike iki saiki? Sakedurunge kelasku bar iki?

OB: Inggih, saged.

Guru: Ya. Sing iki bolak balik, sing liyane ora, fotokopine mung sing ngarep.

OB: Nggih, ping pinten?

Guru: Sing iki ping limo. Sing liyane ping sepuluh.

OB: (Ngagem) kertas ingkang kados menapa?

Guru: Apa ya? A4 putih wae. Neng sing iki, kudu BC warna. Ana ijo?

OB: Ijo kosong Mas. Wonten biru, abrit, kaliyan kuning.

Guru: Biru wae apik.

OB: Kelasipun jam pinten?

Guru: Sepuluh menit manéh ya.

OB: Mboten masalah. (Yells at other OB.) Hendri! Yo, iki kudu dikopi saiki. (To teacher): Nggih, mangkéh kula dugike dhateng kelas menawi sampun rampung.

Guru: Nuwun Mas.

Unit 12: English Translation of Conversations

1. At the Photocopy Shop

Customer: Afternoon.

Copy Girl: Good afternoon. Can I help you?

Customer: Yes. I'd like these pages arranged to make/into a book. Can you do that?

Girl: We can. Bound, right?

Customer: Yes. The pages are already in order. This page first until this one that's the last page.

Girl: How many books do you want made?

Customer: Maybe ten is enough. Yeah, exactly ten.

Girl: The cover?

Customer: What?

Girl: A cover on the front and back?

Customer: Yes, good. Which paper do you have that's thick?

Girl: This colored card paper.

Customer: Okay, good. That light green one.

Girl: How do you want it bound?

Customer: Usually you use black tape, don't you?

Girl: We have it. But, if you want, we can use spiral binding too.

Customer: Oh, that black plastic spiral yeah? May I see it a moment?

Girl: (Brings out the spiral binding.) We have a small one up to a large one. For this book, this one is fine. Do you want it?

Customer: How much is it?

Girl: 10,000 per book.

Customer: If you use the usual tape?

Girl:	7,000.
Customer:	In that case, just use the spiral. Will it take long?
Girl:	(Turns to her boss.) How long will it take for this?
Customer:	If I come pick it up at 12:00 can you do it?
Girl:	We can.

(Customer comes back.)

Girl:	It's ready sir.
Customer:	This copy isn't too good Miss. It's hard to read. Hmm, what should I do ... Can I get a small discount?
Girl:	Sorry sir, but I can't do that.
Customer:	But how will my students read it...? Oh well, I guess it's good enough. How much?
Girl:	One hundred eighty thousand. Thank you sir. This blank paper – it's free for you sir.
Customer:	(Laughs.) Alright. Thank you.
Girl:	Thank you. Please come again sir.

2. Request for the Office Boy

Teacher:	Hello. Can you photocopy this right away, before my next class?
OB:	Yes, I can.
Teacher:	Good. This one front and back. This other one not – copy just the front side (one-sided).
OB:	Okay. How many copies?
Teacher:	This one – 5 copies. The other one, 10 copies.
OB:	Which paper?
Teacher:	Oh, what paper... just A4 white. But this one, has to be colored card paper. Do we have green?

OB:	We're out of green. There's blue, red, yellow...
Teacher:	Blue is just fine.
OB:	What time is your class?
Teacher:	In ten minutes.
OB:	No problem. Hendri! Hey, this has to be copied right now. (To teacher): Okay, I'll bring it to your classroom after it's finished.
Teacher:	Thanks.

13. FAMILY

aunt (older)	bibi, tanté*	bu dé, bo dé
aunt (younger)	bibi, tanté	bu lik
bachelor	bujangan	legan
boy/girlfriend	pacar	s
brothers and sisters	saudara	sedulur
brother (younger)	adik	adhik
brother (older)	kakak, (a)bang*	(kang)mas
cousin	sepupu	misan
dear, darling	sayang, yang	tresna
divorce	cerai	pegatan
fiancé, fiancee	tunangan	—
grandfather	kakék	simbah/éyang kakung
grandpa	kék	mbah kung
grandmother	nénék	simbah putri
grandma/granny	nék	mbah uti, yang ti
honey	sayang	tresna
kid	nak, dék	lé (m) / nduk (f)
live together, unwed	kumpul kebo	s
love (n, v)	cinta, mencintai	tresna
married	menikah	mantenan, krama, nikah
nephew	keponakan	ponakan
niece	keponakan	ponakan
polygamy	poligami	s
pregnant	hamil	ngandhut
pregnant-slang	sudah isi	meteng
pregnant outside marriage	hamil luar nikah	meteng dhisik

161

second wife	isteri muda, isteri kedua	maru
separated, broken up	(udah) tpisah	putus
single	jomblo	joko (man)/ prawan (woman)
sister (older)	kakak (perempuan)	mbak yu
sister (younger)	adik perempuan	adhi wédhok
uncle (older)	paman, Om*	pak dhé, uwo
uncle (younger)	paman	pak lik
unregistered marriage	kawin bawah tangan	kawin siri
widow	janda	randa
widower	duda	duda

Language & Culture Notes

1. Although the term *Mas* as a generic term of address for younger men came from *kangmas* for older brother, it is used as a generic/general term of address for any young man (in Java) that one does not know, while the word *adik* or '*dik*' is not used in this way.

2. As in many Asian cultures, Indonesian children usually live with their parents until they get married and start their own home.

3. The terms *Om* and *Tante* are from the Dutch, but still sometimes used, especially by older Indonesians, or when Indonesians are addressing a Westerner and want to be polite, but are unsure of what term of address to use. In some areas or situations, *Om* is also used as slang for a 'sugar daddy' or the like.

4. *Kakak* is the country-wide term for older brother. However in a few places like Jakarta, *abang* is widely used. In Java, *Pak* and *Mas* are the terms of address for men, while in Jakarta, most young people using public transport will call a driver who is not really old '*bang*.' *(A)bang* is also slang in the Jakarta area for someone a woman is intimate with – a boyfriend or husband.

5. Polygamy is no longer common, but still exists. Many Indonesians see it as an excuse for a man to marry a young woman after his wife gets older, and many social groups in the country have called for its official end.

6. Not only are most Indonesian families closer than many Western families, but families within a single neighborhood are also expected to maintain close relations (on the surface), especially in Javanese culture. This results in plenty of gossip about what is happening in the 'Jones' family next door, and most families worry about what the neighborhood thinks of them. A reckless son or daughter often brings shame on the whole family.

7. Conversation 2 takes place at Idul Fitri, which comes at the end of Ramadan. It is the Islamic New Year, and most people travel to/visit their relatives, much like Christmas or American Thanksgiving. It is tradition and a common practice to ask others to forgive any wrongs you may have made against them during the previous year. The ritualistic phrase is: *Mohon ma'af lahir batin (atas kesalahan saya).* You can expect some of your Indonesian friends to greet you with this phrase during this time, and the appropriate reply is to say something like: '*Sama-sama, saya juga ya. (Kalau saya punya salah, tolong maafkan ya)*' as in conversation 2.

1. Chatting about Family

Mister: Apa Mbak Riani punya saudara?

Riani: Ya, satu adik dan dua kakak.

Mister: Adik perempuan atau laki-laki?

Riani: Perempuan.

Mister: Luar biasa! Ada empat putri ya? Adikmu masih di sekolah?

Riani: (Laughs.) Ya, di SMA.

Mister: Kalo kakak gimana? Sudah menikah?

Riani: Yang tua udah berkeluarga tapi yang kedua belum, dia masih mahasiswa.

Mister: Di mana?

Riani: Di UGM. Keluarga mister di sini?

Mister: Saya belum menikah. Ada satu adik perempuan aja. Dia sekarang ada di Amerika dengan orang tua. Ada satu nenek tinggal bersama paman dan bibi di California. Apa kakek, nenek Mbak masih hidup?

Riani: Di sisi ayah sudah meninggal, di sisi ibu masih hidup.

Mister: Mbak tinggal bersama orang tua dan adik kan?

Riani: Ya betul. Sama satu kakak juga. Apa Mister tidak rindu keluarga?

Mister:	Tidak terlalu. Saya pinda dari rumah keluarga saya sewaktu berumur 18 tahun. Sudah lama saya tidak tinggal bersama mereka. Tapi, setiap minggu kirim email dan pulang setiap tahun waktu liburan.
Riani:	Aduh! Saya pikir ibu pasti sangat merindukan Mister.
Mister:	Tentu saja – seperti semua Ibu-ibu ya.

2. With the Family at Idul Fitri

Tini:	Éyang, Tini mohon maaf lahir batin atas kesalahan Tini ya. (Tini kneels in front of and shakes hands with Grandma, who is sitting on the chair.)
Eyang Putri:	Sama-sama, Eyang juga ya. Kalau Eyang punya salah, tolong maafkan ya.
Tini:	Iya, Eyang.
Eyang Putri:	Semoga Tini jadi murid yang pintar di sekolah. Lalu besok besar jadi dokter.
Tini:	Iya, Eyang.
Eyang Putri:	Tini juga harus jadi anak yang berbakti dan menghormati orang tua. Jangan suka membantah nasehat orang tua, ya?
Tini:	Iya, Eyang. Tini akan jadi anak yang baik.
Eyang Putri:	Tini juga tidak boleh sering berkelahi dengan Mas Anton. Kalian harus baik dengan sesama saudara.
Tini:	Iya, Eyang.
Eyang Putri:	Ini Eyang ada hadiah uang untuk Tini. Tini bisa beli buku dengan uang ini. Jangan untuk jajan permen ya? Nanti gigi Tini sakit.
Tini:	Iya, Eyang, terima kasih.

3. Pak Santoso Takes a Second Wife

Yanti: Sar, kamu sudah dengar kabar belum ya, kalau Pak Santoso mau menikah lagi?

Sarwi: Menikah lagi? Terus Bu Santoso gimana?

Yanti: Ya masih suami-istri. Pak Santoso akan punya dua istri.

Sarwi: Waduh kasihan Bu Santoso...

Yanti: Kabarnya malah Bu Santoso yang minta Pak Santoso menikah lagi.

Sarwi: Lho, kok bisa?

Yanti: Iya, kabarnya karena Bu Santoso nggak bisa hamil, jadi dia minta Pak Santoso agar menikah lagi karena dia takut kalau keluarga Pak Santoso tidak punya keturunan. Pak Santoso kan kaya sekali. Nanti perusahaannya diwariskan ke siapa?

Sarwi: Wah, baik hati sekali ya Bu Santoso.

4. A Death in the Family

Grandma (Eyang Putri) dies and the family makes funeral arrangements. Marni is the daughter; Sita is a daughter of Marni.

Tetangga (Pak Sunu): Bu Marni, saya ikut bela sungkawa.

Bu Marni: Terima kasih, Pak Sunu.

Pak Sunu: Pemakamannnya jam berapa, Bu?

Bu Marni: Jam sebelas di dekat sini Pak.

Pak Sunu: Saya akan usahakan datang ke pemakaman Eyang Putri.

Bu Marni: Terima kasih, Pak Sunu.

(Sita approaches Bu Marni.)

Sita: Bu, Eyang Putri meninggal karena apa?

Bu Marni: Eyang meninggal karena sudah tua.

Sita: Berapa umur Eyang Putri, Bu?

Bu Marni: Umur Eyang Putri 89 tahun.

Sita: Kasihan Eyang, ya Bu?

Bu Marni: Tidak apa-apa. Oleh karenanya Sita harus terus berdoa supaya Eyang Putri senang di surga.

Sita: Iya, Bu. Sita akan berdoa untuk Eyang Putri.

1. Talking about Family

Mister: Apa mbak Riani duwé sédhérék?

Riani: Inggih, setunggal rayi kaliyan kaléh sedherek ageng.

Mister: Nuwun sewu, aku kurang ngerti basa krama....
                wédhok apa lanang?

Riani: Ésteri.

Mister: Artine ésteri apa?

Riani: Wédhok. (Mbak Riani at this point realizes that it would be useless to try to speak overly polite krama with Mister, and adjusts her level of speech down a bit.)

Mister: Walah! Ana papat wedhok ya? Adikmu ijih sekolah?

Riani: (Laughs.) Inggih, ing SMA.

Mister: Nék mbakyu? Wis nikah?

Riani: Mbakyu pertama sampun nikah, nanging ingkang nomer kali déréng, déwé(k)é taksih sekolah.

Mister: Néng endi?

Riani: Ing UGM. Kaluwargi Mister ing mriki?

Mister: Aku durung nikah. Ana adik wédhok siji wae tinggal neng Amerika karo wong tuwa. Ana siji mbah uti neng Amerika tinggal karo pak dé lan bu dé neng California. Apa mbah, lanang karo mbah putri isih ana?

Riani: Sederek bapak sampun sédo, sedérék ibu taksih sugeng.

Mister: Mbak ijih tinggal karo wong tuwa lan adik to?

Riani: Inggih leres kaliyan setunggal Mbah yu uga. Menapa
            Mister ora kangen kaluwargi?

Mister: Ora pati-pati. Aku pindah seka omah tatkala umur 18
            tahun. Wis suwe aku ora urip barang wong tua. Tapi saben
            minggu aku kirim email, lan tetep bali saben
            tahun – pas liburan.

Riani: Aduh, aku kinten Ibu Mister kangen kaliyan Mister.

Mister: Mestine, pada wae. Kaya ibu-ibu liyane ya.

2. At Idul Fitri

Tini: Éyang, Tini nyuwun pangapunten sedaya kelepatan Tini nggih...(Kneeling in front of and shaking hands with Grandma. Grandma is sitting on the chair.)

Eyang Putri: Pa̱dha̱-pa̱dha̱, Eyang uga̱ ya. Umpama Eyang dhuwe salah, tulung dipangapura̱ ya?

Tini: Inggih, Eyang.

Eyang Putri: Muga̱-muga̱, Tini dadi murid sing pinter neng sekolah. Trus sésuk gedhe dadi dokter.

Tini: Inggih, Eyang.

Eyang Putri: Tini uga kudu dadi anak sing berbakti lan ngregani wong tuwa̱. Aja seneng mbantah naséhat wong tuwa̱, ya?

Tini: Inggih, Eyang. Tini bakal dados lare ingkang sae.

Eyang Putri: Tini uga ora oleh kerep kerengan karo Mas Anton. Kowe sekaliyan kudu rukun karo pa̱dha̱-pa̱dha̱ sedhulur.

Tini: Inggih, Eyang.

Eyang Putri: Iki Eyang ana̱ hadiah duit kanggo Tini. Tini isa̱ tuku buku nganggo duit iki. Aja kanggo jajan permén ya? Mengko untune Titi loro.

Tini: Inggih, Eyang, matur nuwun.

3. Pak Santoso Takes a 2nd Wife

Yanti: Sar, kowe wis krungu kabar durung ya, Pak Santoso bakal nikah manéh?

Sarwi: Nikah maneh? Trus Bu Santoso piye?

Yanti: Ya isih gegarwanan. Pak Santoso bakal duwe garwa loro.

Sarwi: Waduh, mesakake Bu Santoso...

Yanti: Kabare malah Bu Santoso sing njaluk Pak Santoso nikah maneh.

Sarwi: Lho, kok isa?

Yanti: Iya, kabare marga Bu Santosa ora isa mbobot, dadine dhéwéké njaluk Pak Santoso nikah maneh amarga dheweke wedi menawa kaluwargi Pak Santoso ora duwe keturunan. Pak Santoso kan sugih tenan. Mengko perusahaane diwariske neng sapa?

Sarwi: Wah, apik tenan atine Bu Santoso.

4. A Death in the Family

Pak Sunu: Bu Marni, kula ndhérek béla sungkawa.

Bu Marni: Matur nuwun, Pak Sunu.

Pak Sunu: Pemakamanipun jam pinten, Bu?

Bu Marni: Jam sewelas, celak mriki, Pak.

Pak Sunu: Kula usahaken dumugi dhateng pemakaman Éyang Putri.

Bu Marni: Matur nuwun, Pak Sunu.

(Sita approaches Bu Marni.)

Sita: Bu, Eyang Putri séda lantaran menapa?

Bu Marni: Eyang seda lantaran wis sepuh.

Sita: Pinten yuswanipun Eyang Putri, Bu?

Bu Marni: Yuswanipun Eyang Putri 89 tahun.

Sita: Mesakaken Eyang nggih, Bu?

Bu Marni: Ora apa-apa. Mangkane Sita kudu terus ndonga supay
             Eyang bingah néng suwarga.

Sita: Inggih, Bu, Sita badhe ndonga kagem Eyang Putri.

Unit 13: English Translation of Conversations

1. Chatting about Family

Mr.:	Do you have any brothers or sisters?
Riani:	Yes, one younger and two older (sisters).
Mr.:	Younger sister or younger brother?
Riani:	Sister.
Mr.:	Wow! Four daughters. Is your younger sister still in school?
Riani:	(Laughs.) Yes, she's in high school.
Mr.:	How about your older sisters. Already married?
Riani:	The oldest already has a family, but the second not yet – She's still a student.
Mr.:	Where at?
Riani:	At UGM. Is your family here?
Mr.:	I'm not married yet. I just have one younger sister. She's in America with my parents. I have one grandma who lives with my uncle and aunt in California. Are your grandpa and grandma still alive?
Riani:	On my father's side, they're already dead, on my mother's side they're still alive.
Mr.:	You live with your parents and younger sister, don't you?
Riani:	Yes, that's right. With one older sister too. Don't you miss your family?
Mr.:	Not too much. I moved out of the family's house when I was 18. I haven't lived with them for a long time. But, every week I send an email and go home every year at vacation time.
Riani:	My goodness! I think your mom must really miss you.
Mr.:	Of course – like all mothers do.

2. With the Family at Idul Fitr

Tini: Grandmother, I beg your forgiveness for any wrongs I have done you/sins I have committed against you.

Grandma: The same too for me, yeah. If I have done anything wrong, please forgive me.

Tini: Yes, Grandma.

Grandma: I hope you are a student who's good/smart at school. Then later in the future, you can become a doctor.

Tini: Yes, Grandma.

Grandma: You also have to be a child who is devoted to and respectful of old people. Don't talk back to your elders, okay?

Tini: Yes, Grandma. I'll be a good kid.

Grandma: You also mustn't fight often with Anton. You two have to be a good brother and sister.

Tini: Yes, Grandma.

Grandma: Grandma has some money for you. You can buy a book with this money. Don't spend it on candy okay? It will ruin your teeth later.

Tini: Yes, Grandma. Thank you.

3. Mr. Santosa Takes a Second Wife

Yanti: Sar, have you already heard the news or not yet, that Mr. Santoso is going to get married again?

Sarwi: Married again? What will happen to Mrs. Santoso?

Yanti: Yes, they'll still be husband and wife. Mr. Santoso will have two wives.

Sarwi: Wow, poor Mrs. Santoso.

Yanti: They say that in fact it was Mrs. Santoso who asked Mr. Santoso to marry again.

Sarwi: How can that be? / What? – No way!

Yanti: Yeah, they say it's because Mrs. Santoso can't get pregnant, so she asked Mr. Santoso to marry again because she's afraid that Mr. Santoso's family won't have any offspring/heir. Mr. Santoso is very rich, you know. Later, who would his company be left to?

4. A Death in the Family

Grandma dies and the family makes funeral arrangements. Mrs. Marni is the daughter, and Sita is the granddaughter.

Neighbor: Mrs. Marni, I offer my condolences.

Mrs. Marni: Thank you Mr. Sunu.

Mr. Sunu: What time is the funeral Mam?

Mrs. Marni: Eleven o'clock. Near here.

Mr. Sunu: I will make an effort to come to your mother's service.

Mrs. Marni: Thank you Mr. Sunu.

(Sita approaches.)

Sita: Mom, why did Grandma Putri die?

Mrs. Marni: Grandma died because she was old.

Sita: How old was Grandma Putri Mom?

Mrs. Marni: Grandma Putri was 89.

Sita: Oh mother! Poor Grandma...

Mrs. Marni: It will be okay. But you have to always pray so that Grandma Putri is happy in heaven.

Sita: Yes, Mom. I'll pray for Grandma Putri.

14. LOVE

(have an) affair	(ber)selingkuh	(ber)selingkuh
bachelor	bujangan	legan, jaka
be forward (with someone)	gamblang	blak-blakan
betray	mengkhianati	cidra
bra	bh (bé ha- 'bust holder')	s
broken heart	patah hati	gerah manah
butterfly	kupu-kupu malam	lonthé
chick, girl	céwék	kenya
child	anak	bocah
cry	menangis	nangis
crazy about	tergila-gila	wuyung
crush (on someone)	naksir	tresna
curvaceous	montok*	semok/semuahhé
a date (regular appointment)	janji, ketemu dgn, apél	janjén
dear, darling	saying, yang	kangmas/nimas
dick, cock	burung	manuk, thithit
divorce	cerai	pegatan
a Don Juan, a beau	arjuna	arjuna
elopement	kawin lari	kawin lari
engaged	bertunangan	—
fiancé, fiancee	tunangan	—
a flirt/flirtatious	genit	menthél
flirt with	bercumbu-cumbu	andhon
fond of (thing)/want sex with	doyan	birahi
friend with benefits	TTM* (Té Té Ém)	—
girl/boyfriend	pacar	pacangan
trying to impress a girl/guy	ngegébét	gawé sengsem

176

love interest	gébétan	sir-siran
get/pick up women	merayu céwék	—
gigolo	gigolo	gemblak
guy, dude	cowok	joko
handsome	tampan	gantheng
hooker	ayam	ciblik
honey	sayang, gula-gula	kangmas/nimas
jealous	cemburu, iri	iri, dengki, srei
jerk off, masturbate	beronani	ngocok
live together, unwed	kumpul kebo	semanlevan
fall in love	jatuh cinta	gandrung
maiden (young, a virgin)	dara	kenyal
make eyes at someone	main mata	golék perhatian
make love, 'screw'	bercinta	andhon
married	menikah	manténan, nikah
'married by accident'	MBA*	meteng dhisik
match, fit	cocok	pas
miss someone	rindu, merindukan	kangen, kapang
ogling	melirik	plirak-plirik
over, finished	selesai	putus
panties	celana dalam	kathok njéro
playboy/womanizer	buaya darat	wédhokan
polygamy	poligami	poligami
pregnant	hamil	ngandhut
pregnant-slang	sudah isi	meteng
pregnant outside marriage	hamil luar nikah	meteng tanpa nikah
pretty	cantik	ayu
prostitute	pelacur	lonthé
puppy love	cinta monyet	—
rumor, gossip	gosip, kabar burung	kabar angin

177

second wife	isteri muda, isteri kedua	maru
separated, broken up	(udah) pisah	putus
single	jomblo	jaka/prawan
slut	pérék, WTS	lonthé
stud	pejantan	arjuna
sugar daddy	om-om, om senang	—
'sweetie pie'	gula-gula	tresna
tits	susu, payudara	téték
transvestite, lady boy	waria, béncong	wandu, banci
turned on (excited)	merangsang, mupéng	ngaceng
unregistered marriage	kawin bawah tangan	kawan siri
'up to you' (its up to you)	terserah anda	sakarepmu
whore	perempuan jalang	lonthé
widow	janda	randa
widower	duda	duda

Phrases/Sayings

absence makes the heart grow fonder (far to the eye, close to the heart)	jauh di mata, dekat di hati
love is blind	cinta itu buta
she's not *that* shy, she'll warm up to you (only as shy as a cat)	malu malu kucing
when the cat's away...(the mice will play) (when the eye's asleep the pillows ..)	mata tidur bantal terjaga

Language & Culture Notes

1. *Montok* refers to a curvy woman who would be considered slightly chunky in the rest of SE Asia – in other words, not a thin, curvy woman. For babies, it means chubby.

2. *MBA* is popular slang for married due to an unplanned pregnancy.

3. *TTM* stands for '*Teman Tapi Mesrah,*' and is used in the same way as similar terms in English (usually in gossip): 'more than just friends,' 'friends with benefits,' or 'sex buddies.'

4. Courting and marriage rituals vary greatly within Indonesia, depending on the ethnic group and religion. If you are a man courting a young Javanese woman, it is important to be respectful to her parents, and especially to get the mother on your side. Typically, when it is time to pop the question, the couple will sit together with both parents, and the man will ask permission for them to marry. It is common for the man to give the family a gift, such as batik, clothing, food, small household items - something useful. As in the West, jewelry, makeup, and clothing are common gifts given by a man to his bride-to-be. A Javanese (Muslim) wedding ceremony is a long, drawn-out affair, usually 2-3 days total, which includes pre-wedding rituals, the wedding itself, post-wedding rituals, and lots of idle socializing. As part of the wedding rituals, the groom gives the bride a dowry, which has been decided upon and accepted beforehand by the bride with the consideration of her family. The dowry is often money, but other things such as books, a house, land, a car, etc. are common.

5. The virtue of most daughters is carefully guarded in Indonesia as it is in good Christian families in America. Despite this, sex before marriage and unplanned pregnancies are also common problems, just as they are in the USA. Most daughters outside Jakarta live at home with their families until they are married. If a woman is well into her 20s and still not married, the family will encourage her to find someone soon.

6. Although Indonesia is predominantly Muslim, unplanned pregnancies and sex outside marriage are not uncommon. They are dealt with in a similar manner to such activity in a generally conservative USA in the past and present: the young couple usually gets married right away (*MBA*) in case of an unplanned pregnancy. Families often suspect but turn a blind eye to sexual activity outside marriage, as long as it isn't apparent and appearances of appropriate behavior are maintained. In other cases, the parents may find out about it and strongly encourage/order their child to stop seeing 'that boy/girl.'

7. Prostitution is common in Indonesia, as in most of Asia. In Jakarta, free-lance prostitutes or *ayam*, can be found anywhere and everywhere frequented by expats or rich Indonesians, and the city has a sordid nightlife scene that rivals Manila or Bangkok in many regards. Both Surabaya and Yogyakarta have large brothel only areas that cater to locals, and indeed every large city has a district where whore houses, karaoke bars, or extreme massage parlors can be found.

8. Mixed marriages between couples from two different religions is frowned upon in Indonesia; between a Muslim woman and a man of another faith it is illegal and generally not allowed. Given the cultural diversity of the islands with foreigners thrown into the mix, this legality issue is a commonly occurring problem. To circumvent this, the non-Muslim has to be willing to go to the *masjid* (mosque) and repeat the *syahadat* ('There is no God but Allah…') so as to become Muslim (usually in name only, with little expectation he'll be a good or practicing Muslim). Alternatively, the couple can get married overseas. By treaty, Indonesia has to recognize marriages from other countries, so by submitting the correct paperwork after returning to Indonesia, the marriage can then be legalized in Indonesia as well. The couple simply have to present their marriage certificate in-person to the registry, and pay the fee to have it made official in Indonesia.

9. For foreigners married to an Indonesian, the disregard with which their spouse's family comes to the house unannounced with plans to stay may cause friction. Family may ask for money for emergencies or personal business plans.

10. In Conversation 5, the husband works overseas. This is a common situation. Indonesia is second only to the Philippines in the sheer number of its citizens who work overseas – offshore in the oil industry, on cruise ships, in construction, or as maids to wealthy Muslims. These people sacrifice it all in order to send money to their families. A recurring news item in Indonesia and a headache for the government is the large number of Indonesian maids who are beaten or raped by their overseas employers each year. The government and various groups have tried to exert pressure on countries like Saudi Arabia to do something about the problem, but with little success.

1. Asking her out on a Date

Riani :   Mister punya pacar orang Indonesia?

Don: Tidak punya. Dulu sudah pernah, tapi kami sudah putus. Kalau Mbak Riani gimana?

Riani: Saya juga nggak punya.

Don: Masih tinggal bersama keluarga kan?

Riani: Ya, benar.

Don: Malam minggu ini mau bertemu di Kedai Kopi atau bagaimana?

Riani: Baik, tapi saya harus minta izin dari ibu dulu ya. Jam berapa?

Don: Ada jam malam kan?

Riani: Ya betul. Kalo setelah jam sepuluh tidak bisa.

Don: Ayo, kita jumpa jam delapan kalau begitu.

Riani: Baik. Nomer hp-mu berapa? Namamu mister John kan?

Don: Don. D-O-N. 0813........

2. Playing Pool, Talking about Chicks

Hendi :   Sudah lama ya kita tidak main bilyard seperti ini...

Joko: Iya, akhir-akhir ini aku sibuk dengan pekerjaanku.

Hendi :   Jadi bagaimana kabarmu akhir-akhir ini?

Joko:	Yah begitulah, sibuk. Tetapi aku sudah punya pacar sekarang.
Hendi:	Benarkah? Di mana kamu bertemu dia?
Joko:	Di kantor.
Hendi:	Wah, bagaimana dia?
Joko:	Ya, dia cantik, pintar, dan baik hati.
Hendi:	Berapa lama kalian berpacaran?
Joko:	Sekitar tujuh bulan.
Hendi:	Wah, selamat. Kalian pacaran serius untuk menikah?
Joko:	Ya, semoga. Aku sudah mantap dengan dia.
Hendi :	Jangan lupa undang aku di pernikahan kalian ya?
Joko:	Pasti!

3. Aunt Hani is Getting a Divorce

Monika finds out her sister, Hani, is getting a divorce because her husband is having an affair. Monika is talking with her husband.

Monika:	Mas tahu nggak kalau Mbak Hani rencananya mau cerai dengan suaminya?
Wawan:	Tidak. Kenapa kok cerai?
Monika:	Suami Mbak Hani ketahuan selingkuh dengan sekretaris kantornya.
Wawan:	Bagaimana Mbak Hani bisa tahu?

Monika:	Mbak Hani tidak sengaja ketemu dengan mereka berdua di rumah makan. Terus Mbak Hani marah-marah dan memutuskan untuk bercerai langsung saat itu juga.
Wawan:	Wah, Mbak Hani sepertinya butuh waktu lagi untuk memutuskan untuk cerai. Aku khawatir Mbak Hani sedang emosi sehingga langsung memutuskan cerai tanpa pikir panjang. Bagaimana nasib anak-anak mereka nantinya?
Monika:	Itu juga yang aku khawatirkan, Mas. Anak Mbak Hani kan masih kecil-kecil.
Wawan:	Sebaiknya kamu bicarakan baik-baik dengan kakakmu itu.
Monika:	Iya, Mas.
Wawan:	Anggota keluarga yang lain sudah tahu tentang ini?
Monika: takut	Sepertinya belum. Kami belum bicara dengan ibu. Kami penyakit jantung ibu kumat.
Wawan:	Ya, mémang sebaiknya begitu.

4. *Marriage Plans?*

Budhe:	Kapan, Ndi?
Andi:	Kapan apanya, Budhé?
Budhe:	Kapan nikahnya dong, Ndi?
Andi:	Wah, kalau itu masih harus saya pikirkan matang-matang.
Budhe:	Masih nunggu apa sih, Ndi? Kamu kan sudah punya pekerjaan dan umurmu itu kan sudah siap untuk menikah. Pacar kamu masih yang lama itu, kan?
Andi:	Iya, Budhe. Tapi saya dan Rina sekarang masih belum siap. Rina kan belum bekerja.

Andi: Mungkin setelah dia mendapat pekerjaan.

Budhe: Ya sudah Budhe doakan kalian agar segera menikah.
             Ibumu sudah pingin punya momongan.

Andi: Iya, Budhe, terima kasih.

5. When is Tuti's Husband Coming Back?

*Tuti's husband works on a cruise ship and he's been gone for two
months. The neighbors are having a conversation about when he might
come back and how lonely poor Tuti must be, and how glad they are
their husbands don't work away from home like that...*

Resti: Mah, saya sebenarnya kasihan dengan Tuti.

Umah: Kenapa, Res?

Resti: Mas Sumar, suami Tuti, itu kan kerja di kapal pesiar. Dia
             cuma pulang ke rumah dua bulan sekali. Pasti Tuti
             kesepian. Mereka kan pengantin baru.

Umah: Oh iya, ya. Tapi kan Mas Sumar selalu pulang bawa uang
             banyak.

Resti: Tapi apa gunanya uang banyak kalau kesepian?

Umah: Iya ya?

Resti: Memangnya kamu mau suamimu kerja jauh?

Umah: Ya nggak juga, Res.

Resti: Untung saja suami kita kerja di sini, meskipun gajinya
             tidak besar.

Umah: Iya, benar. Hidup sederhana lebih baik daripada hidup
             kaya tetapi berjauhan.

Javanese Conversations

1. Asking her out on a Date

Riani: Mister duwe pacar wong Indonesia?

Mister: Ora duwe. Mbiyén wis tau, tapi saiki wis putus.
            Menawa Mbak Riani piye?

Riani: Aku uga ora duwe.

Mister: Isih tinggal bareng kaluwargi, to?

Riani: Iya, bener.

Mister: Malem minggun iki meh ketemuan neng warung kopi
            apa piye?

Riani: Iya, tapi aku kudu njaluk ijin saka ibu sikik ya? Jam pira?

Mister: Ana jam bengi, to?

Riani: Iya bener. Nék setelah jam sepuluh ora isa.

Mister: Ayo, ketemu jam wolu nek ngono.

Riani: Ya wis, nomor hp-mu pira? Jenengmu mister John, to?

Mister: Don. D-O-N. 0813........

2. Playing Pool, Talking about Chicks

Hendi: Wis suwe ya awa(k)édéwé ora main bilyar kaya ngéné?

Joko: Iya, akhir-akhir ini aku sibuk karo gawéanku.

Hendi: Dadi, piye kabarmu akhir-akhir iki?

Joko: Yah, ngonolah, sibuk. Tapi aku wis duwe pacar saiki.

Hendi: Tenane? Néng endi kowe ketemu déwé(k)é?

Joko: Neng kantor.

Hendi: Wah, kaya piye deweke?

Joko : Iya, deweke ayu, pinter, lan apikan atine.

Hendi: Wis pirang suwe kowe padha sing pacaran?

Joko : Sekitar pitung wulan.

Hendi: Wah, selamat. Kowe padha pacaran serius kanggo nikah?

Joko : Ya, semoga. Aku wis mantep karo deweke.

Hendi : Aja lali undang aku ya neng kondanganmu.

Joko : Mestilah.

3. Aunt Hani is Getting a Divorce

Monika: Mas, ngerti ora menawa Mbak Hani rencanane arep cerai karo garwane?

Wawan: Ora. Kenapa ta kok cerai?

Monika: Garwane Mbak Hani ketauan selingkuh karo sekretaris kantore.

Wawan: Piye carane Mbak Hani isa ngerti?

Monika:	Mbak Hani ra sengaja ketemu wong loro kuwi neng omah makan. Trus Mbak Hani nesu-nesu lan mutusake cerai langsung pas kuwi uga.
Wawan:	Wah, Mbak Hani kayan butuh wektu manéh kanggo mutusake cerai. Aku khawatir Mbak Hani lagi emosi dadine langsung mutusake cerai tanpa mikir dhawa. Trus piye nasibe anak-anake?
Monika:	Kuwi uga sing aku khawatirke, Mas. Anake Mbak Hani kan isih cilik-cilik.
Wawan:	Becike kowe omongke apik-apik karo mbakyumu kuwi.
Monika:	Iya, Mas.
Wawan:	Anggota keluarga sing liyane ana sing ngerti tentang iki?
Monika:	Kayake durung. Awa(k)édéwé durung ngomong karo ibu. Awakedewe wedi penyakit jantunge ibu kumat.
Wawan:	Ya, pancén becike ngono kuwi.

4. Marriage Plans?

Budhe:	Kapan, Ndi?
Andi :	Kapan menapa, Budhé?
Budhe:	Kapan kawine ta ya, Ndi?
Andi:	Wah, menawi menika tasih kedah dipikir mateng-mateng.
Budhe:	Isih nunggu apa maneh ta, Ndi? Kowe kan wis duwe gawéan lan umurmu wis siap kanggo kawin. Pacarmu isih sing lawas kaé to?

Andi:	Inggih, Budhe. Tapi kula kaliyan Rina sakmenika taksih déréng siap. Rina kan dereng ga̲dh̲ah̲ pegawéan. Mungkin setelah Rina angsal pegawean.
Budhe:	Ya̲ wis, Budhe dongake kowe pa̲dha̲ gek endang is̲a̲ nikah. Ibumu wis péngén duwe momongan.
Andi:	Inggih, Budhe, matur nuwun.

5. When is Tuti's Husband Coming Back?

Resti:	Mah, aku sakjane mesakake karo Tuti.
Umah:	Kena̲pa̲ ta̲, Res?
Resti:	Mas Sumar, garwane Tuti, kuwi kan kerja neng kapal pesiar. Déwé(k)é mung bali néng ngomah rong wulan sepisan. Mesti Tuti kesepian. Deweke loro kan mantén anyar.
Umah:	Oh iya ya. Tapi kan Mas Sumar mesti bali gawa duit akéh.
Resti:	Tapi a̲pa̲ gunane akeh duit nék kesepian?
Umah:	Iya, ya?
Resti:	Emangne kowe gelem garwamu nyambut gawe adoh?
Umah:	Ya uga, ora Res.
Resti:	Untung wae garwane awakedewe padha nyambut gawe neng kéné, meski gajine ora gedhe.
Umah:	Iya̲ bener. Urip sakanane luwih becik ketimbang sugih nanging uripe adoh-adohan.

Unit 14: English Translation of Conversations

1. Asking Her out on a Date

Riani: Do you have an Indonesian girlfriend?

Don: I don't. I had one before, but we've already broken up.
            And how about you?

Riani: I don't have a boyfriend either.

Don: You still live with your family, don't you?

Riani: Yes, I do.

Don: This Saturday night would you like to meet at Kedai Coffee
            Shop, or something . . . ?

Riani: Okay, but I have to ask permission from my mother first. What
            time?

Don: You have a curfew, right?

Riani: That's right. If it's after 9:30 I can't.

Don: Well, let's meet at 8 in that case.

Riani: Okay. What's your mobile phone number?
            Your name is John, isn't it?

Don: Don. D-O-N. 0813...

2. Playing Pool, Talking about Chicks

Hendi: We haven't played pool like this for a long time...

Joko: Yeah, lately I've been busy with my work.

Hendi: So what's up/how's it going with you these days?

Joko: Just busy you know. But I've got a girlfriend now.

Hendi: Really? Where did you meet her?

Joko: At the office.

Hendi:	Well, what's she like?
Joko:	Yeah, she's pretty, smart, and nice.
Hendi:	How long have you been seeing each other?
Joko:	Around seven months.
Hendi:	Well, congratulations. Are you thinking about getting married?
Joko:	Yeah, I hope. We already have a steady relationship/We're already going steady /been seeing each other for a long time.
Hendi:	Don't forget to invite me to your wedding okay?
Joko:	Definitely.

3. Aunt Hani is Getting a Divorce

Monica:	Do you know that Hani is planning to get a divorce from her husband?
Wawan:	No. How come she's getting divorced?
Monica:	Her husband was found having an affair with the secretary in his office.
Wawan:	How did Hani find out?
Monica:	Hani happened to bump into the two of them in a restaurant. Then she got mad and decided to divorce him right then at that moment.
Wawan:	Well, it seems like Hani needs more time to decide on a divorce. I'm worried Hani is so emotional that she immediately decided to get a divorce without thinking it over. What will happen to their children later?
Monica:	That's what I'm worried about too dear. Hani's kids are still small.
Wawan:	It would be good for you to have a long talk with your sister about it.
Monica:	Yes dear.
Wawan:	Do the other members of the family already know about this?

Monica:	Probably not yet. We haven't spoken with mother. We are afraid it would make mom have a relapse with her heart condition/have another heart attack. (This could be literal or figurative.)

4. Marriage Plans?

Aunt:	When Andy?
Andy:	When what, Aunt?
Aunt:	When will you get married? – of course.
Andy:	Oh, if that's it, I still have to think it over carefully.
Aunt:	What is it you're waiting for Andy? You already have a job and your old enough to get married. Your girlfriend is still the one you've had a long time, isn't she?
Andy:	Yes Aunt. But Rina and I aren't ready yet. Rina isn't working yet you know. Maybe after she gets a job.
Aunt:	Okay then. I'll pray that you two get married soon. Your mother wants to have a grandchild.
Andy:	Yes Aunt. Thank you.

5. When is Tuti's Husband Coming Back?

Resti:	Mah, I really feel sorry for Tuti.
Umah:	Why, Res?
Resti:	Tuti's husband, Sumar, you know – he works on a cruise ship. He only comes back home once every two months. Tuti must be lonely. They're newlyweds right.
Umah:	Yes, yes, but you know Sumar always returns with a lot of money.
Resti:	But what's the use of (having) lots of money if you're lonely?
Umah:	I suppose/Yeah, I guess so.
Resti:	Would you really want your husband to work far away?
Umah:	No, I wouldn't either Res.

Resti: We're just lucky our husbands work here, although their
            paychecks aren't big.

Umah: Yeah, that's true. A simple (modest) life is better than being rich
            but being far apart.

15. MORE USEFUL VERBS

Where possible, the Indonesian verbs are listed in their base noun/verb root form. The Javanese, however, are listed as commonly used.

English	Indonesian	Javanese
advance	maju	maju
be afraid	takut	wedi
annoy, bother, harass	ganggu	mbebéda
attack	serang	s
become	jadi	dadi
beat, win	menang	s
bite	gigit	cokot
believe, trust	percaya	percaya
build, make	buat	gawé
build, construct, erect, put up	bangun	mbangun
burn, roast	bakar	obong
bribe	suap/sogok	sogok
catch (a person/criminal)	tangkap	cekel
cause	sebab	s
change, switch	ganti	s
chat	ngobrol/omong	s
check	periksa	mriksa
check in/deposit/leave	titip	s
choose, pick, vote	pilih	s
come back/return, return an item	kembali	bali, mulih
confirm, make sure	pasti	mesthi
continue, keep doing	terus	s
close, cover	tutup	s
compete	berlomba	tanding
cut, do surgery	potong	s
decide to/on	putus	putuské
die, kill/extinguish	mati	mati, modhar
drop, fall	jatuh	tiba
dream	mimpi	ngimpi
drive	setir	s
fail	gagal	s
find	temu	s
finish	selesai	rampung
fix, repair, improve	memperbaiki*	ndandani
fit, match, suit	cocok	s
fly	terbang	mabur
forget	lupa	lali

193

gather/get together	kumpul	ngumpul
get married	menikah	nikah
get ready, prepare	siap	siap, cumawis
get well, recover	sembuh	waras, mari
go back, give back	kembali	bali
go around	keliling	mubeng
go down, get off, lower	turun	mudun
go up, get on, ride	naik	munggah
go to the bathroom	ke kamar kecil/belakang	néng pekiwan
guard	jaga	jaga
handle, manage	urus	s
hang up (on wall)	gantung	s
happen	terjadi	kelakon
heat up	memanaskan	ngangeti
hear	dengar	krungu
hit	pukul	nuthuk, geblok
hold a load	muat	momot
invite	ajak, undang*	s
in charge of	pimpin	s
kiss	cium	ambung
let	biarkan	gawé
let know, tell	memberitahu*	ngabari
lie	bohong	goroh
lie down	berbaring	teturon
line up	antri	s
listen, listen to	dengarkan	ngrungoké
live	tinggal, hidup	urip
look for	cari	golék
loosen, exhale, untie	lepaskan	kendho
make a mistake, be wrong	salah	s
make sure	pasti	mesthi
mix together	campur	s
move	gerak*	obah
order, command	perintah	préntah
perform Islamic prayer	solat, sholat	s
pick someone up	jemput	methuk
pee/piss	pipis, kencing, buang air kecil*	s, nguyuh
play	main	dolan
posted, stationed, assigned duty	tugas	—
practice, train	latihan	s
pray (general)	doa	donga
press (a button)	tekan	pencét
promise	janji	s
pull	tarik	s
push	dorong	surung

put, place a bet	taruh	séléh
raise	angkat	s
remember	ingat	éling
repeat	ulangi	baléni
report	lapor	s
rest	istirahat	s, ngaso
retreat	mundur	s
ride	naik	munggah
run	lari	playu
say	kata + person*	jaré
shoot	tembak	s
shit (take a ..)	buang air besar	ngising
show (movie), play (a song)	putar	puter
smile	senyum	mésem
speak	berbahasa	wicara
stand	berdiri	ngadeg
start	mulai	s
start a vehicle	slah	s
steal	curi	nyolong
step	langkah	s
stink	bau	ambu
stop, halt	henti	lérén, sérén
store	simpan	s
succeed	sukses, berhasil	kasil
supply/be complete	lengkap	ganep
be sure	pasti	mesthi
swim	renang	lumban
take time	habiskan waktu	—
take someone somewhere	antar	terké
try	coba,usaha	s
used to, accustom to	terbiasa	kulina
used up/to use up	habis	enthék
visit	kunjung	tilik
wait	tunggu	enténi
walk	jalan kaki	mlaku
waste time	buang waktu	—
witness	saksi	seksi
win	menang	s
wish that, hope	harap, semoga*	moga-moga
worry	khawatir	kuwatir
wrap	bungkus	wungkus

Language Notes 1

1. *Memperbaiki*, from the root *baik*, is a useful, active verb (having an object) that can be used generally for 'fix,' 'repair,' 'improve,' or 'make better.' *Mereka belum memperbaiki atap*. They haven't repaired the roof yet. For passive voice, *diperbaiki* is also common: *Jalan itu udah diperbaiki*. The road has been repaired. *Aku memperbaiki motorku sendiri*. I fixed my motorbike myself. *Ada rencana memperbaiki taman kota*. There are plans to improve the city park.

2. The difference between *ajak* and *undang* for 'to invite': *ajak* is broader in meaning, and can be 'invite, urge to do, or challenge,' depending on the situation. *Undang* is restricted to inviting to an event, such as a party or dinner.

3. *Gerak* means to move physically, for example: The old man moved quickly. *Laki-laki tua itu bergerak dengan cepat*. Or, to make something move, as in 'The cat moved the ball.' *Kuncingnya menggerakkan bola*.

4. As in English, there are a number of words for 'pee/piss.' *Pipis* is the word used by/when speaking to little kids, like 'pee' or 'pee-pee' in English. *Kencing* equates more to 'piss' or 'take a piss' and has the same slightly crude or rough connotation. Finally, *buang air kecil* is more formal and is what you would hear in a hospital or more polite settings, like the word 'urinate' in English.

5. *Memberitahu*, from the root *tahu* and *beri* – to give, means to let someone know. Its object can be either first-person or third-person. For example, 'Let me know as soon as possible.' *Memberitahu ku secepatnya*. 'If you see her, please let her know.' *Kalau anda ketemu dia, tolong memberitahunya*.

6. 'He said/She said…': In bahasa, the most common way to convey reported speech is to use the word *kata* as in *Kata Doni dia tidak mau begitu*. 'Donny said he didn't want to do that.' Or simply *Katanya tidak mau gitu* – 'He said he didn't want to do that.' You can use the verb *bilang* for 'say' as well: *Donny bilang dia tidak mau gitu*. Or, *Dia bilang apa?* – What did he say? However, using the word *kata* for reported speech is more common.

7. The difference between *harap* and *semoga*: Harap is the general verb for 'to hope.' It can be used in a wide range of situations: *Aku berharap kamu cepat sembuh*. I hope you get well soon. *Tiada harapan* – there's no chance/hope and *harapan hidup* – life expectancy. Semoga is limited to commonly occurring phrases of well-wishing, as in *Semoga sukses*. – 'I wish you success.' *Semoga hal yang kamu inginkan berhasil* – I hope that the things you want come to pass. *Semoga* is typically not preceded by a subject noun or pronoun in such phrases.

16. MECHANICAL AND BUILDING

Places

parts store/hardware store	'TB' - Toko Bangunan	s
shop/garage	béngkél motor	s
parts store	toko suku cadang	s
(car) dealership	dealer (mobil)	s
body shop/repair (dents, etc.)	kenténg magic	s
car wash	cuci motor/mobil	s
streetside tire repair spot	tambal ban	s

Tools, Parts, & Materials

allen wrench/keys	kunci L	s
axe	kapak	kampak
bolt	baut	s
bracket (for shelves)	siku rak	s
bushing	bos, metal	s
cable	kabel	s
cap	tutup	s
clamp	klém	s
clamp - adjustable band	klem selang	s
concrete/cement	semén	s
cord	kabel, tali	s
copper	tembaga	tembaga
drill	bor	s
drill bit	mata bor	mata bor
file	kikir	s
glue	lém	s
hammer	palu	pukul
hoe	cangkul	pacul
hook	huk, hak	cangkolan
hose	selang	s
jack (tire/car)	dongkrak	s
level (carpenter's)	waterpas	s
level (brick layer's)	pélpén	s
lock (door)	kunci laci	s
material	bahan	s
metal	logam	wesi

197

nail	paku	s
nut	mur	s
padlock	(kunci) gembok	s
paint brush	kuas cat	kuas cét
plane (wood)	ketam	pasah
plastic	plastik	s
pliers	tang	s, cathut
pliers - needle nose	tang lancip	s
plug-electric	stop kontak	s
plug - stopper	sekang	s
pipe/plumbing tape	pléster pipa	s (pip<u>a</u>)
plywood	triplék	s
power strip	stop kontak empat/enam	s
putty knife/scraper	kap cat	s
pvc	pvc	s
rag	lap	s
rake	penggaruk	s/garuk
regulator	regulator	s
rope/cord	tali	s
saw	gergaji	graji
screw	sekrup	s
screwdriver	obéng	dréi
screwdriver-Phillip's head	obéng bintang	s
shovel	sekop	s
socket	(anak) sok	s
socket wrench	kunci sok, gagang ratchet	s
soldering iron	solder	s
stainless steel	sténlés, baja anti karat	s
tape measure	rol méter	méteran
tow rope	tali derek	s
T (socket) wrench	kunci (sok) T	s
vice grips	tang buaya	tang b<u>aya</u>
wire	kawat	s
wire cutters	tang potong	s
wood	kayu	s
2 x 4	*batang kayu	s
wrench- box/closed end	kunci ring	s
wrench - open end	kunci pas	s
crescent/adjustable wrench	kunci Inggris	s

axle	as	s
belt (fan)	ban, tali	sabuk sténg
blacksmith/metalsmith	tukang besi	tukang wesi
breaker/kill switch	saklar pemutus	saklar mateni
bushing	bos	s
caliper	jangka	<u>j</u>ang<u>ka</u>
carpenter	tukang kayu	s
carburetor	karburetor	s
chain (on motorcycle)	rantai roda	ranté rod<u>a</u>
coil (in a fridge, heater)	dinamo, kumparan	s
clutch	kopling	s
extension cord	rol kabel	s
electrical plug	steker, colokan	s
exhaust pipe	pipa kenalpot	s
flat tire	ban kemps	ban gembos
fix flat tire	tambal ban	s
filter (n - air, oil)	saringan, penyaring	s
fuse	sékering	s
gauge	méteran	s
gear (1st, 2nd, ...)	persnéling	s
gear, sprocket	roda, gigi	s
generator	génerator	s
hole	lubang	bolongan
igniter (on furnace)	penyalaan	s
ignition	kontak	s
leak	bocor	s
maintenance	pemeliharaan	s
mechanic	montir	s
("dude at the shop")	mas bengkel	s
mason/brick layer	tukang batu	s
muffler	kenalpot	s
be (is) on	hidup	urip
outlet/socket	stopkontak	s
piston	piston, lantak	séker
piston rod	pelantak	stang séker
reserve	cadangan	s
resistance - electrical	hambatan	s
shocks (absorber-car)	sok (bréker)	s
spark plug	busi	s

spring (n)	pér	s
starter	starter, kontak	s
supply (n)	persediaan	s
switch- push button	tombol	s
switch (knob)	kenop	s
switch - electric	saklar	s
transformer	step up/step down, trafo	s
valve	katup	klép

Mining & Heavy Equipment

(conveyor) belt	ban (pembawa barang)	s
crusher	mesin penghancur	s
dump truck	truk katrol	s
loader	truk/mesin pemuat	s
explosives, blasting material	(bahan) peledak	mesiu
pit	lubang	bolongan
raw material	bahan baku	s
extracted ore	bahan galian	s
waste matter	bahan buangan	ampas

Structures

arch	lengkungan	s
bridge	jembatan	s
building	gedung	gedong
ramp	jalur landai (on road)	s
stairs	tangga	ondo

Actions & States

add	tambah	imbuh
adjust	menyétel, setel	s
backfire (v)	meledak	njeblug
bent	bengkok	bengkong
blocked	hambat,macet	s
break down	ngadat	mogok
bring	bawa	gawa

broken	rusak	s
change	ganti	ijol
charge/recharge	mengisi	ngisi
collapse	bobol	jebol
cut in and out (engine)	pincang, terus mau mati	mbrebet
cut off (electric, supply)	memutuskan	maténi
die/stop	mati	s
dig	menggali	ngeduk
fix/repair	memperbaiki	mbenaké
hit	pukul	thuthuk
install	pasang	s
kill/shut off	matikan	paténi
loosen	lepaskan	culké
measure precisely/with calipers	berjangka	jongko
missing/not running on 4 cylinders	mbrebet	s
on (is on)	hidup	urip
replace	ganti, pasang	ijol
run/work	jalan, berfungsi	urip
short circuit	korsléting	s
start an engine	menghidupkan	nguripké
stall out, quit	mogok	s
stuck, jammed	macét	s
squeaks, squeaky	derit	s
tear down (a building)	bobol	jebol
tighten	mengetatkan	ngencengi
turn	putar	puter
turn on (engine, electrical)	hidupkan	nguripké
turn to/set (a switch, tv)	pasang	masang
use	pakai/gunakan	nganggo
won't start (engine)	mogok, macet/ tak mau hidup	s s

At the Dealership/Service Station

semir ban	polish tires	s
tukar tambah	a trade-in	s
servis ringan	a quick service	s
kampas rém	drum brake	s
rém cakram	disc brake	s

Language & Culture Notes

1. Small *bengkel motor* (repair shops) are everywhere, and cheap. Most are honest, and only very rarely will one try to overcharge you for parts and labor because you are a *bulé*. Compared to shops/garages in Western countries, they are wonderful. Something that would take days and hundreds of dollars to fix in the USA usually costs a few dollars and takes a half hour in Indonesia. And they'll always discuss a cheap option that will keep it running for a little while longer ... (I've had a shop use epoxy cement to glue a carburetor back together, which lasted for another 8 months before it had to be replaced.) For a larger repair, if you do not get your bike into the *bengkel* until near closing time (early evening 5-7pm usually), you can simply leave it with them overnight and pick it up the next afternoon. For major repairs, you may have to spend from 200-500.000 rupiah ($20-55 USD) - worst case scenario.

2. *Toko Bangunan* or TB is the correct term for a store carrying building supply and hardware materials, but I have also heard it referred to as simply *béngkél* (without the 'motor') in Yogya, and have also heard other people refer to such stores as *Toko Ahong*, because in many smaller cities in Indonesia, it is almost always a Chinese who owns and runs such a store.

3. *Saringan* is more common for a smaller air or oil filter, such as on a car or motorcycle engine. *Penyaring* would be used for a much larger filter in a factory, such as a water filter/filtration system.

4. The term "2 x 4" to refer to one of the most common sizes of cut lumber for building in the USA, does not exist in Indonesia (nor in the rest of the world). If you are working in wood, you will have to go to a lumber supply - *toko kayu* and have wood cut to the measurements you want (in centimeters obviously).

5. Chances are that any house you move into will be poorly built. This becomes an issue with the country's massive amounts of rainfall (see Unit 8: Home Sweet Home). If you hire builders to have your (dream/retirement) home built, be prepared to insist on an agreed set of specs before building starts, and then be physically present on a daily basis to ensure that shortcuts are not taken and the workmanship meets your standards. Otherwise, you will be looking at constant revisions (and having to negotiate for more money to have it finished).

6. For the most part, houses on Java are made of poor quality concrete, that never sets properly due to rain. It will easily crack and crumble when a nail is hammered into it. This presents great challenges when trying to make any additions, like shelves or cabinets, to the house. You will need to use special screws with plastic inserts, available at the building supply store, to do the job.

7. The quality of brick used in portions of homes that are not concrete is usually very poor. Often, one can break the bricks in half easily with bare hands. It is this poor quality that led so many houses to completely collapse in the Bantul area, south Yogyakarta, when the big earthquake struck there in 2006. If you are having brick work done, inspect the quality of brick.

8. In the conversations in this unit, notice the widespread use of more colloquial Indonesian, such as the word *lanjutin* for *lanjutkan*. Also, *gak* for *tidak*, *trus* for *terus*, *tuker* for *tukar*, *ngabisin*, *gantungin*, etc.

9. In Conversation 2, notice the young men's use of *Ahong* or *Hong* for the store owner/clerk and the hardware store itself. The store owner is obviously Chinese-Indonesian, and this can be considered a derogatory way to refer to that fact. The use of *TB* or *Pak TB* in place of *Ahong* or *Hong* would be more politically correct. On the other hand, these terms for Chinese Indonesians are not uncommon, and the young men themselves probably do not think anything of them.

Indonesian Conversations

1. Building a New Home

Suami:	Pak Harso, kok tembok rumah ini jadi satu sama tembok tetangga sebelah. Kenapa kok gitu?
Pak Harso:	Ya, karna lebih mudah buatnya.
Suami:	Aduh Pak. Saya kan udah bilang, harus terpisah.
Istri:	Lagian itu kan jadi ngerusak tembok tetangga.
Pak harso:	Lha..terus gimana?
Suami:	Tembok harus dibangun ulang, sesuai rencana semula.
Istri:	Memang tanah ini gak luas, supaya terlihat lebih luas, buat tembok yang gak terlalu tinggi, bahan nya tetap pake beton, jangan batu bata.
Pak Harso:	Nanti di plester gak Bu?
Istri:	Ya haruslah pak, kan udah dibilangin. Kalo bapak lupa terus, nanti rumah ini kapan jadinya.
Suami:	Pak, plafon yang di dapur juga dibenerin yah.
Pak Harso:	Iya. Lha emangnya kenapa Pak?
Suami:	Plafon banyak yang retak, kalo yang retak jangan dipasang pak. Nanti minta tukar ke toko si Ahong aja. Saya sudah telfon dia tadi pagi.
Istri:	O iya, sama pintu kamar mandi di belakang salah pasang, bukan pintu kayu, tapi pintu alumunium. Nanti itu juga diganti ya Pak.

Pak harso:	Iya Bu, Iya Pak. Nanti langsung saya ganti.

Suami:	Ya udah, sekarang lanjutin kerjanya.

2. Doing Some Home Repair

Ali:	Ampun deh, kok dari tadi kita masang paku, gak bisa-bisa yah?

Bambang:	Padahal waktu kita beli paku ini, si Ahong bilang, bisa buat tembok beton juga.

Ali:	Terus gimana nih?

Bambang:	Ya udah, kita ke toko Ahong aja lagi, minta tuker paku yang cocok buat tembok.

Ali:	Paku yang kayak gimana sih?

Bambang:	Yang bisa juga buat tembok beton lah. Aku tau kok. Bentuknya kayak paku payung gitu, tapi lebih besar.

Ali:	Atau mungkin, jenis paku yang harus di bor yah?

Bambang:	Bisa jadi sih, tapi ntar deh, kita tanya lagi ke Ahong

(Ali & Bambang go back to the hardware store.)

Ali:	Hong, paku ini gak bisa dipasang.

Pemilik Toko:	Ooohhh..sini aku ganti aja.

Bambang:	Ganti paku apa Hong?

Pemilik Toko:	Paku khusus tembok beton, tapi cara masangnya harus pake bor dulu. Yang kayak gini.

(The store owner shows them the special concrete nails.)

Ali:	Oh yang ini, bilang kek dari tadi, biar kita gak bolak balik kesini. Ngabisin waktu aja.
Bambang:	Tau ni si Ahong. Oke lah gpp. Yang penting, dapet paku yang cocok buat nggantungin rak.

(Ali and Bambang go back home.)

Bambang:	Ambilin bor dong. Sekalian sama rak nya yah?
Ali:	Oke, ini bornya.
Bambang:	Udah jadi deh, bisa nempel pakunya di tembok. Lebih kuat juga buat gantungin rak ini.

3. Getting the Motorcycle Fixed

Dedi:	Mas, motorku ni sering mati. Padahal baru aja aku servis di béngkél resmi Honda. Kenapa ya mas?
Montir:	Waktu itu, servis aja ato skalian semuanya di cék?
Dedi:	Hanya servis aja sih Mas.
Montir:	Berarti gak ganti oli dong?
Dedi:	Gak mas, karna baru aja ganti oli, tapi gak waktu di servis.
Montir:	Udah di cek businya belum?
Dedi:	Belum Mas.
Montir:	Akinya?
Dedi:	Mmm..belum juga Mas.
Montir:	Ya udah, saya cek nya sekarang. Kuncinya mana Mas?
Dedi:	Ini Mas.

Montir:	Mas, ini businya harus ganti. Akinya juga harus diisi lagi. Pantesan aja motornya mati terus.
Dedi:	Ya udah Mas, sekalian aja semuanya diganti. Businya sama akinya. Kira-kira berapa ya Mas?
Montir:	Businya mau yang asli Honda atau yang biasa aja?
Dedi:	Kalo yang asli Honda berapa mas?
Montir:	Kalo yang asli 25 ribu, kalo yang biasa, cuma 10 ribu aja. Gimana? Mau yang mana?
Dedi:	Yang bagus aja lah mas. Yang asli aja.
Montir:	Oke.

4. Oil Change & Service

Mister:	Motorku perlu ganti oli
Mas Bengkel:	Oli apa Mister?
Mr.:	Yang mana ya...
Mas:	Castrol?
Mr.:	Tidak perlu yg begitu mahal. Yg lebih murah tapi bagus aja.
Mas:	(Hands Mister a liter of Pertamina). Mau servis juga Mister?
Mr:	Ya, sama servis, oli ini cukup bagus. Lagi, ada masalah reting nih. Nggak hidup. (Shows them left blinker.) Masalahnya mungkin kabel di dalam ya?
Mas:	(Looks at left blinker.) Nggak, Mister. Sepertinya lampunya mati.

Mr:	Di sini jual kan?
Mas:	Ya, ada.
Mr:	Baik. Ganti itu juga ya. Saya datang kira-kira dua jam lagi ambil motor. Terima kasih.
Mr:	(Comes back 2 hrs later, walks up to Mas.) Sudah?
Mas:	Sudah. (Hands Mr. the bill.) Lima puluh ribu, lima ratus.
Mr:	(Pulls out a 50.000 note.) Lima puluh pas gimana?
Mas:	Ya, nggak papa. Terima kasih mister.
Mr:	Sama sama.

5. Broken Pump in the Rice Paddies

While working in his rice field, Pak Samijo finds the irrigation is not working properly. Apparently, a pump is broken.

Pak Samijo: Pak, ini pompanya rusak lagi, nggak mau hidup. Nggak tau kenapa.

Tukang pompa: Biar saya lihat dulu, Pak. (Checks the pump.) Oh, katupnya yang rusak. Harus diganti.

Pak Samijo: Kira-kira berapa lama memperbaikinya?

Tukang: Kalau bahannya ada, tidak lama. kira-kira 1-2 jam sudah selesai.

Pak Samijo: Di mana beli itu?

Tukang:	Bisa beli di toko bangunan di kota, tapi kalau mereka habis, harus dipesan atau dibeli di Semarang. Kalau titip saya saja, nanti saya belikan.
Pak Samijo:	Ya, begitu juga baik. Pergilah sekarang aja. Kalau tidak ada, pergi sampai Semarang. Klep itu penting sekali.
Tukang:	Iya. Saya sms dari kota beritahu Pak kalau saya harus ke Semarang.
Pak Samijo:	Baik. Aku tunggu sms mu.

Reading Sample: Repair Receipt (*Nota Bengkel*)

Tanggal, 4/5 200 00

Kepada Yth, b. Honda
B. 3340. KO

TARUNA MOTOR
BERDAGANG ALAT2 SEPEDA MOTOR
JL. RAYA PONDOK GEDE NO. 11
TELP. 87799453 - 9130792
JAKARTA - TIMUR

NOTA PENJUALAN

BANYAK	NAMA BARANG	HARGA SATUAN	JUMLAH
1 x	Bongkar Carburator + Ongkos		25.000
1 Set	Reparkit Tiger		15.000
	Baut		5.000

LUNAS
0 4 MAY 2010

PERHATIAN
Barang[2] yang sudah dibeli
tidak dapat dikembalikan / ditukar.

TOTAL 45.000

Tanda Terima

Hormat Kami,

(..........................)

(..........................)

Javanese Conversations

1. Building a New Home

Suami:	Pak Harso, kok tembok omah iki dadi siji karo temboke tanggane? Kok ngono ki piye?
Pak Harso:	Inngih, kan langkung gampil ndamelipun.
Suami:	Waduh, Pak. Aku kan wis ngomong, kudu dipisah.
Istri:	Lagian kuwi isa ngerusak tembokke tanggane.
Pak Harso:	Lha terus pripun?
Suami:	Temboke di baleni kaya rencana wingi.
Istri:	Pancen lemahe iki ora jembar, bén kétok luwih jembar digawe témbok sing aja dhuwur-dhuwur, bahane tetep nganggo beton, dudu bata.
Pak Harso:	Mangkih dipun pléster nggih, Bu?
Istri:	Lha kudu no, Pak. Kan uwis dikandhani wingi. Nék Pak Harso kesupén terus, kapan dadine omah iki?
Suami:	Pak, plafone sing néng dapur didandani ya?
Pak Harso:	Nggih, lha wonten menapa ta Pak?
Suami:	Plafone akéh sing retak, nek retak aja di pasang, mengko njaluk ijol neng tokone koh Ahong wae. wae. Aku wis telpon mau ésuk.
Istri:	Oh ho oh, karo pintu kamar mandi mburi salah pasang –dudu lawing kayu, ning lawang almunium. Mengko di ganti ya Pak?

| Pak Harso: | Nggih Bu, mangke kula gantos. |
| Suami: | Ya wis, ditutugke anggone nyambut gawe. |

2. Doing Some Home Repair

Ali:	Walah, ket mau awa(k)édéwé masang paku ora isa-isa ya?
Bambang:	Padahal pas awakedewe tuku paku iki, Ahong ngomong nek isa nggo maku beton ya.
Ali:	Terus piye iki?
Bambang:	Ya wis, awakedewe bali néng nggone Ahong manéh, njaluk ijol paku kanggo témbok.
Ali:	Pakune kaya ngapa to?
Bambang:	Paku sing isa nggo maku tembok lah, aku ngerti kok bentuke . . . kaya pines ngono ning luwih gede.
Ali:	Apa mungkin jenis paku sing kudu di bor ya?
Bambang:	Isa uga, ning mengko takon sik karo ahong wae . . . (Ali & Bambang go back to the hardware store.)
Ali:	Hong, pakune ora isa di enggo.
Ahong:	Oh kéné tak gantine wae.
Bambang:	Di ganti paku apa Hong?
Ahong:	Paku sing khusus nggo tembok beton, tur sing masang kudu nganggo bor sikik – sing kaya ngéné loh [karo nduduhi paku tembok khusus].

Ali: Walah sing iki ta, ngomong ket mau ta, dadi ora marahi
        aku bolak balik ndéné . . . ngenték-entékké waktu wae.

Bambang: Mbuh ki si Ahong, ya wis, sing penting entuk
            paku sing cocok nggo nggantungke rak.
            (Ali & Bambang return home.)

Bambang: Tulung jukukke bor ya, sisan karo rake ya..

Ali: Iya iki bore.

Bambang: Wis dadi ki, pakune isa némpel néng témbok.
            Luwih kuwat kanggo nggantung rak iki.

3. Getting the Motorcycle Fixed

Dedi: Mas, motorku ki kok kérép mati, padahal bar tak serviske
        neng béngkél resmi Honda loh. Ngapa ya Mas?

Montir: Pas servis, mung servis thok apa sisan karo di cék kabéh?

Dedi: Mung servis thok sih Mas.

Montir: Berarti ora ganti oli, no?

Dedi: Ora Mas, soale lagi wae ganti oli, tapi ora ganti pas
        diservis.

Montir: Wis di cek busine durung?

Dedi: Durung Mas.

Montir: Akine?

Dedi: Mmm, koyone uga durung Mas.

Montir: Ya wis, tak cek saiki, kuncine endi, Mas?

Dedi: Iki Mas.

Montir: Mas, iki busine kudu ganti. Akine ya kudu di isi manéh. Pantesan wae motore mati terus.

Dedi: Ya wis Mas, sisan wae kabéh diganti. Busi karo akine. Kira-kira pira ya Mas?

Montir: Busine arep sing asli Honda apa sing biasa wae?

Dedi: Nek sing asli Honda pira, Mas?

Montir: Nek sing asli Honda selawé éwu, ning nek sing biasa mung sepuluh éwu. Piye? Arep sing endi?

Dedi: Sing apik wae lah, Mas – sing asli wae.

Montir: Iya.

4. An Oil Change

Mister: Motorku perlu ganti oli.

Mas Bengkel: Oli apa Mister?

Mr.: Sing endi ya?

Mas: Castrol?

Mr: Ora perlu sing larang. Sing murah ning apik wae.

Mas: (Hands Mister a liter of Pertamina). Arep karo servis ora Mister?

Mr: Ya, karo servis, oli iki cukup apik. Trus, iki uga ana masalah reting, ora murup. (Shows Mas left blinker.) Masalahe mungkin kabel néng njero ya?

Mas: (Looks at left blinker). Dudu, Mister. Ketoke lampune mati.

Mr: Néng kéné dodol to?

Mas: Ya, ana.

Mr: Ya, diganti sisan ya. Aku teka kira-kira rong jam engkas njupuk motore ya. Matur nuwun.

Mr: (Comes back 2 hrs later, walks up to Mas.) Uwis?

Mas: Uwis. (Hands over the bill.) Séket éwu limang atus.

Mr: (Pulls out a 50.000 rb note.) Seket ewu pas wae, piye?

Mas: Ya, ra papa. Matur nuwun, Mister.

Mr: Padha-padha.

5. Broken Pump in the Rice Paddies

While working in the field, Pak Samijo finds the irrigation is not working properly. Apparently, a pump is broken.

Pak Samijo : Pak menika pompanipun rusak malih mboten purun murup. Mboten ngertos kenging napa.

Tukang: Kula tiliki rumiyin Pak. (Checks pump.) Oh, klépipun risak. Kedah dipun gantos.

Pak Samijo: Kinten kinten dangu mboten ndandosipun?

Tukang: Menawi wonten bahanipun, mboten dangu. Kinten-kinten 1-2 jam sampun rampung.

Pak Samijo : Tumbasipun wonten pundi?

Tukang: Saged tumbas wonten dhateng toko bahan bangunan éng kutha, ing menawi sampun telas, kedah pesen men<u>apa</u> tumbas ing Semarang. Saged titip kul<u>a</u> mangke kul<u>a</u> tumbasaken.

Pak Samijo: Nggih mekaten nggih langkung sae. Budhal sakmenik<u>a</u> kémawon. Menawi mboten wonten, tindak ngantos Semarang. Klép menik<u>a</u> penting sanget.

Tukang: Nggih, mangke kul<u>a</u> sms saking kutha ngabari menawi Kul<u>a</u> kedah dhateng Semarang.

Pak Samijo: Nggih, Kul<u>a</u> tengg<u>a</u> sms-ipun panjenengan.

English Translation of Conversations

1. Building a New Home

Husband: Mr. Harso, You're making the wall of this house so it's the same as the next door neighbor's. Why are you doing that?

Harso: Yes, because it's easier to build.

Suami: Look! I've already told you, they have to be separate.

Wife: Besides, it will also cause the neighbor's wall to break.

Harso: Oh... What should I do now?

Husband: The wall has to be built over again, according to the original plan.

Wife: This land isn't that spacious/large. So that it looks more open, make the wall so that it isn't too high, out of concrete not brick.

Harso: Then covered in plaster-cement isn't it Mam?

Wife:	Yes, as I've already told you, that's what you need to do. If you keep forgetting, when will this house ever be done?
Husband:	The ceiling in the kitchen – do it right too, okay.
Harso:	Yes sir. Why is that again?
Husband:	Many of the ceiling tiles are cracked; if they're cracked they can't be installed/fit. Just ask the clerk later at the Chinese hardware store. I already telephoned him earlier this morning.
Wife:	Oh yeah, the same with the bathroom door in the back... you installed it wrong – it's not a wood door, but an aluminum door. That has to be changed later too.
Harso:	Yes Mam, Yes sir... I'll fix everything/make the changes right away.
Husband:	Okay then, get back to work now.

2. Doing Some Home Repair

Ali:	Oh Good Lord!, How come since we started using these nails, they won't work huh?
Bambang:	But actually, when we bought these nails, the Chinese clerk/owner said they could also be used for concrete walls.
Ali:	So, what should we do now?
Bambang:	I've had it. Let's just go to the hardware store again and ask someone who knows, for nails that can be used for concrete walls.
Ali:	Hmm, nails like what?
Bambang:	Ones that can also be used on concrete walls. I know which — they're shaped like tacks/flathead nails, except bigger.
Ali:	Or maybe, the kind of nails that have to be screwed/drilled in, yeah?
Bambang:	It could be, but go ahead and bring them (these nails we already have), we'll ask again at the hardware store.

Ali:	Chinaman, these nails can't be put in.

Ali: Chinaman, these nails can't be put in.

Shop Owner: Oh, (I see). I'll just exchange them.

Bambang: Exchange them for which nails?

Shop Owner: Special nails for concrete walls. But to use them, you have to use a drill first. Ones like this. (The owner shows them the special concrete nails.)

Ali: Oh, these. You could've told us before so that we didn't have to come back and forth. What a waste of time.

Bambang: Look here, Chinaman, it's fine – I don't care. What's important is that we get the right nails for hanging a shelf.

(Ali and Bambang go back home.)

Bambang: Dude, bring the drill. And the shelf along with it.

Ali: Okay, here's the drill.

Bambang: All right, it's done. We can put the nails into the wall. It's stronger for hanging the shelf too.

3. Getting the Motorcycle Fixed

Dedi: Hi. My motorcycle here keeps dying (stalling out). Actually, I just got it serviced at the official Honda shop. (I wonder) Why huh?

Mechanic: Right now, do you want to just have it serviced/get a tune-up, or have everything checked?

Dedi: Only a service I think…

Mechanic: Are you sure you don't want an oil change?

Dedi;   No, because the oil was just changed, just not at the time it was serviced (last).

Mechanic: Have you checked the spark plug yet or not ?

Dedi: Not yet.

Mechanic: The battery?

Dedi:	Hmm, No, that neither.
Mechanic:	Very well, I'll check them now. Where is the key sir?
Dedi:	Here it is.
Mechanic:	Sir, the spark plug has to be changed. The battery also needs recharged. No wonder why your motorcycle keeps dying.
Dedi:	Okay then, go ahead and change them both – the spark plug and the battery. About how much will it be?
Mechanic:	Do you want an original/genuine Honda plug or just an imitation one?
Dedi:	How much for a genuine Honda one?
Mechanic:	For a genuine 25 thousand, for an imitation, only 10 thousand. How about it? Which one do you want?
Dedi:	Just give me the good one – the genuine one, okay.
Mechanic:	Okay.

4. At the Repair Shop

Foreigner:	My bike needs an oil change.
Shop Kid:	Which oil?
Foreigner:	Hmm, which one yeah…
Shop Kid:	Castrol?
Foreigner:	I don't need one that expensive. One that's cheaper but still good.
Shop Kid:	(Hands him a liter of Pertamina.) Do you want it serviced/a tune-up too?
Foreigner:	Yeah, with a tune-up – this oil is good enough. Also, there's a problem with this turn signal. It doesn't come on. Could the problem maybe be the wire inside?
Shop kid:	No, it looks like the lamp/bulb is burned out.
Foreigner:	You sell them here, right?

219

Shop Kid:	Yeah, we've got em.
Foreigner:	Good. Change it too, okay. I'll come back in about two hours to pick up the bike. Thank you.
Foreigner:	(Comes back.) Is it done?
Shop Kid:	It's ready. Fifty thousand, five-hundred.
Foreigner:	(Pulls out a fifty-thousand note) How about fifty thousand exact?
Shop kid:	Yep, no problem. Thank you, sir.
Foreigner:	Thank you.

5. A Broken Pump

Mr. Samijo	This pump is broken again, it doesn't want to start.. I don't know why.
Pump Man:	Let me take a look at it first sir. (Checks the pump.) Oh, the valve is what's broken. It has to be changed.
Mr. Samijo:	About how long will it take to fix it?
Engineer:	If they have the part, not long. About 1 or 2 hours is all.
Mr. Samijo:	Where can you buy it?
Repair Man:	It can be bought at the hardware store in town, but if they're out, It will have to be ordered or bought in Semarang. If you'll just let me take care of it, I'll buy it later.
Mr. Samijo:	Yes, that's just fine. But go now. If they don't have it, go on to Semarang. That pump is very important.
Repair Man:	Okay. I'll sms you from town and let you know if I have to go to Semarang.
Mr. Samijo:	Good. I'll wait for your sms.

17. ENVIRONMENT

This unit does not contain a 'Javanese Conversations' section

English	Indonesian	Javanese
air	udara*	s
beach	pantai	kisik
cave	gua	s
earth	bumi	jagat
grass	rumput	suket
hill	bukit	s
land	darat	lemah
moon	bulan	wulan
Mother Earth	Ibu Pertiwi	s
mountain	gunung	s
nature	alam	s
plants	tanaman	tanduran
river	sungai	kali
sea	laut	segara
sky	langit	s
star	bintang	lintang
sun	matahari	srengéngé
tree	pohon	uwit
water	air	banyu
weather	cuaca	s

Terrain & Conditions

alleyway	gang	s
cold	dingin	adhem
clear/sunny	terang	padhang
cloudy	berawan	mendhung
curvy (river)	bengkang, meliuk	bengkong
desert	padang/gurun pasir	s
dry	kering	garing
dusty	berdebu	nglebu
flat	datar	rata
flooded	dibanjiri	s

221

forest/jungle	hutan	alas
hilly	berbukit	saputhuké
hot	panas	s
humid, damp	lembab	s
lightning	kilat	s
muddy	berlumpur	jeblok
noisy, festive	ramai	ramé
paved street	jalan aspal	dalan aspal
dirt road	jalan tanah	dalan lemah
distance	jarak	elét
quiet	sepi	s
rainy	ada hujan	udan
rice fields	sawah	s
river	sungai	kali
rugged	berat, terjal	njulék
sandy	pasiran	wedhi
snowy	ada salju	ana salju
snowing	turun salju	s
steep	curam	njulek
stifling hot/sultry	gerah	sumuk
thick jungle	hutan lebat	alas rimba
thunder	guntur	gludhug, bledhég
thunderstorm	badai petir	lésus gludhug
valley	lembah	s
wet	basah	teles
winding (road, river)	berliku-liku	kélok-kélok
wavy/hilly-up & down	naik turun	munggah-medhun
windy	berangin	s
wind is blowing	angin berhembus	s

Time of day

dawn	fajar /
	subuh-word for prayer same time
sunrise	matahari terbit
dusk	magrib (prayer at same time) /senja
sunset	matahari terbenam
middle of the night	tengah malam
pre-dawn (2:30-4:00)	dini hari

Animals & Bugs (Binatang dan Serangga)

ant	semut	s
bat	kelelawar	lowo
bear	beruang	s
bee	lebah	tawon
bird	burung	manuk
butterfly	kupu-kupu	kupu
camel	onta	s
chameleon	bunglon	bunglon
cockroach	kecoak	coro
crab	kepiting	yuyu
cricket	jangkrik	s
crocodile	buaya	baya
dog	anjing	asu
dove	merpati	dara
dragonfly	capung	s
elephant	gajah	s
firefly	kunang-kunang	s
flying white ant	laron*	s
fly	lalat	laler
frog	katak	kodhok
gecko	cicak	cecak
goldfish	ikanmas	s
goose	angsa	banyak
grasshopper	belalang	walang
hornet/wasp	lebah penyengat	s
horse	kuda	jaran
large house lizard	tokek	s
lion	singa	singa
monkey/ape	monyet/kera	kethék
mosquito	nyamuk	s
moth	ngengat	s
myna bird*	beo	s
owl	burung hantu	s
parrot	parkit, parrot	s
peacock	merak	s
phoenix (mythical bird)	*garuda	s
pigeon	burung dara	dara
rabbit	kelinci	s

rat	tikus	s
seagull	camar	kuntul
scorpion	kalajengking	ka<u>l</u>ajengking
shrimp	udang	urang
snake	ular	ulo
snail	siput	bekicot
sparrow	pipit	s
swallow	burung walet*	s
spider	laba-laba	onggo-onggo
squirrel	tupai	bajing
tiger	harimau	macan
turtle	kura-kura	s
worm	cacing	s

Animal Slang

anjing/asu	about the worst name one can be called in Indonesian, like "you yellow-bellied cur" in the American wild west.
babi	like a 'pig' in English, but for a Muslim, much worse and similar to being called *anjing*
tikus	like "rat" in English, a sneaky slimebag who steals money or takes bribes
tikus negara	a government worker on the take
seperti ayam melihat musang	like a deer frozen in headlights dumbstruck, dumbfounded

Actions

cross/go across	menyeberang
climb (a mountain)	mendaki
climb up	naik
climb down	turun
camp	berkéma, kamping

Language & Culture Notes

1. *Udara* refers only to air, as in the sky or atmosphere. Air that is moving, from a compressor or your lungs is *angin*, the same word as wind.

2. '*Tokek*' is also onomatopoeia for the deep, bird-like call the lizards make.

3. *Laron* typically fly into houses when it rains and die in large numbers, so that you have to sweep the floor afterward. They are very small and fragile.

4. A Myna bird is a brown or black bird of the starling family common in Indonesia and throughout Asia. They often have some bright coloring on their beaks, heads, or wings. They are much smaller than a parrot, but similarly, mimic sounds they hear, and are often trained to talk.

5. *Garuda* is obviously not the same as the Phoenix, but similar in many regards. Some Indonesians will translate *Garuda* as eagle, but it is a mythical, rather than real bird. It is a popular name for hotels, express services, and of course, the only Indonesian domestic airline that also operates internationally.

6. Indonesians have come up with an interesting way to profit from the nest-building preferences of the swallow, or *burung walet*. They use concrete block buildings, which have holes in them, and speakers that play recorded bird sounds. The swallow are lured into the holes to build nests, which are then harvested and sold at hight prices to the Chinese market.

7. As in most other developing Asian countries, most Indonesians are still not concerned about where they throw wrappers, bottles, etc. and beautiful natural sites that receive lots of visitors are usually also degraded by lots of litter.

Indonesian Conversations

1. Camping Trip

Toni: Kita dirikan ténda di sini saja, ya?

John: Di sana lebih baik (points to a spot). Tempatnya
             datar dan dekat sungai. (They walk over to the spot.)

Bambang: Ya, di sini cocok untuk kémping. Kita berkémah di bawah
             pohon besar itu saja.

(Toni, John, and Jarwo put up the tent while Bambang and Andrew find
firewood. When they return a half hour later, the tent has been set up.)

Andrew: Apakah kita bisa berenang di sungai itu?

Jarwo: Ya, bisa. Tapi airnya dingin sekali.

Andrew: Arus sungai tidak deras?

Jarwo: Oh, tidak. Kalau hujan arusnya deras.

Andrew: Kalau begitu, ayo kita berenang!

(All of them go swimming except Bambang, who is tasked with guarding
their camp spot. Since it's already dark, Bambang calls them to come
cook dinner.)

Bambang: Woiii! Kalian nggak kedinginan ya? Ayo cepat naik, kita
             masak makan malam.

Jarwo: Oke, kami juga sudah lapar.
             (In a little while, they all return to camp to make dinner.)

Toni:	Aku bawa mi instan dan juga panci untuk masak.
John:	Tunggu sebentar, aku nyalakan api dulu. Di mana korék api?
Andrew:	Ini! (Hands the matches to John.)
John:	Oh, kayunya agak lembab.
Jarwo :	Coba taruh daun-daun kering juga, supaya apinya cepat menyala.
Bambang:	Kita buat ikan bakar, ya. Aku bawa ikan.
John:	Aku juga bawa kentang. Kita juga bisa buat kentang bakar.
Jarwo:	Hah? Kentang bakar, sepertinya enak juga!

2. Insects and snakes in the house!

Ibu Dibyo:	Aaaaa! (Screaming, frightened)
Pak Dibyo:	Ada apa, Bu?
Ibu:	Itu, Pak. Ada ular besar masuk rumah.
Pak:	Mana ularnya? Nggak ada.
Ibu:	Itu! Di bawah rak piring.

(Mrs Dibyo hides behind her husband, but without warning nearly steps on a large spider and gets scared again.)

Ibu: Aaaa…. Apa itu? Hiiiy, laba-laba! Buang jauh-jauh, Pak!

Pak: Ah, hanya laba-laba saja. Tidak mengganggu. Usir saja pakai sapu.

(Mrs. Dibyo sweeps the spider out while Mr. Dibyo catches the snake in a sack.)

Ibu: Pak, ularnya sudah ditangkap?

Pak: Sudah, Bu. Itu hanya ular tikus, tidak berbahaya. Ularnya sudah saya masukkan ke dalam karung, nanti saya buang jauh-jauh.

(A short while later, a house lizard falls onto Mrs. Dibyo's shoulder. She lets out a scream and brushes her shoulder, knocking the lizard off.)

Ibu: Pak, tolong Pak! Ada tokék di bahu saya! Tidak mau lepas juga.

Pak: Sini, biar saya ambil. (Pak Dibyo takes the lizard outside.)

Ibu: Ini pasti karena rumah kita paling ujung, dekat dengan hutan jadi banyak binatang kesasar ke sini.

3. Rafting Trip - near Magelang

Leni: Permisi, Mas. Kami mau arung jeram/rafting).

Mas Sukoco: Oh, kamu yang dari Jogja itu, ya?

Leni: Iya, benar.

Mas Sukoco: Berapa orang yang mau ikut rafting?

Jarwo: Kami semua, lima orang. Bayar sekarang atau nanti?

Mas Sukoco: Bayar sekarang saja. (Jarwo pays.) Kamar ganti di sana, ya
             (pointing). Yang perempuan di kiri dan yang laki-laki di
             kanan.

Andrew: Oh, terima kasih banyak, Mas.

(After changing clothes, they all head to the river with the guide. They
can see the river has a strong current and white-water in the distance.)

Sinta: Sungainya dalam, Mas? Saya nggak bisa berenang.

Pemandu: Ya, cukup dalam. Tapi tenang saja, nanti saya bantu.

John: Berapa lama kita akan rafting di sungai ini?

Pemandu: Kira-kira 2,5-3 jam. Tidak terlalu lama. Itu perahu yang
             kita pakai (pointing to a yellow raft). Jangan lupa pakai
             pelampung dan helm!

4. Reading a Topography Map

A squad of soldiers is on patrol in the jungle

Sersan: Ayo, kita berhenti! Aku mau lihat peta sebentar lagi. (Takes out map.)

Prajurit: Iya, baik. Aku capék sekali.

Sersan: Sial! terlalu gelap. Serahkanlah sénter mu.
Ya, kita sekarang pas di mana sih.. Iya, korporal! Ke sini.

Korporal: Ya Sersan.

Sersan: Korporal pikir berapa kilo sejak kita menyeberang sungai?

Korporal: Tidak tahu ya...kira-kira sembilan, sepuluh... mungkin.

Sersan: Baik, aku juga pikir gitu. Dan jaraknya sampai gunung itu?

Korporal: Sekitar 5 kilo?

Sersan: Baik, (uses compass to take bearing) arah empat puluh derajat utara timur. Mari, lihat péta. Jadi gitu, kita seharusnya ada disekitar di sini kan... Jadi, jika kita terus jalan dua, tiga kilo lagi ada jalan tanah yang melewati sawah.

Korporal: Kita bisa ikuti sehingga mencapai kamp médan platon.

Sersan: Kalo cepat, kita bisa di sana sebelum gelap sekali. Instruksikan prajurit maju cepat. Aku mau melihat jalur di depan dulu.

Korporal: Iya, sersan. Pasukan! Siapkan bergerak. Sersan mau coba berjalan sampai kamp malam ini.

Prajurit1: Masih berapa jauh?

Korporal: Nggak jauh. Kira-kira satu jam setengah kita udah di sana.

Prajurit2: Bagus! Aku mau mandi dan makanan yang énak.

Prajurit1: Aku juga. Aku bosan sekali makan bekal.

5. Jungle Survival Training (Pelatihan Ketahanan Hutan)

Sertu: Aku Sertu Siregar. Minggu depan kalian semua akan belajar bagaimana bertahan hidup dalam hutan. Hutan Papua bukan desa, dan bukan juga kampung, itu pasti akan membunuh kamu kalau kamu tidak menyadari betapa berbahayanya kehidupan di dalam hutan itu.

Sertu: Selalu awas terhadap keadaan sekeliling! Lihat, pikir, dan rencanakan. Korporal, kalo kamu sedang patroli, dan saat itu hampir magrib, kamu melihat ada awan gelap seperti jika akan turun hujan. Apa yang kamu lakukan?

Korporal: Cari tempat kering untuk berkemah malam.

Sertu: Benar. Tempat yang di dataran tinggi atau di lembah?

Korporal: Di dataran tinggi, sersan.

Sertu: Luar Biasa! Mungkin kamu bisa jadi Sersan yang baik.

Sertu: Selama dua minggu, kalian akan belajar cara menyeberang sungai deras, memasang perangkap, menghindari perangkap, dan kecakapan lain yang diperlukan di dalam hutan. Kalian akan tahu bahwa golok dan daun-daun pisang adalah teman terbaik. Bahkan serangga-serangga kecil bisa membunuhmu. Periksa sepatu boot setiap kali sebelum memakainya dan jangan pakai bot sepanjang waktu. Kaki tidak akan kering. Bersandal aja kalau tidak sedang patroli. Makanan, sampah, kotoran harus dibuang; kalau tidak, nanti ada masalah dengan semut dan nyamuk. Kalau air senimu kuning itu artinya kamu dehidrasi. Minum air sebanyak-banyaknya. Dehidrasi membuat kamu tidak bisa berpikir jernih dan kamu bisa terbunuh karena itu.

17. English Translation of Conversations

1. Camping Trip

Toni: Let's just put up the tent here, okay?

John: Here is better (as he points to a spot.) The spot is level and near the river. (They walk to the spot that John indicates.)

Bambang: Yeah, here is good for camping. Let's camp under that big tree.

(Tony, John, and Jarwo set up the tent, while Bambang and Andrew find wood. A half hour later, the tent has been set up.)

Andrew: Can we swim in the river?

Jarwo: Yeah, we can, but the water is really cold.

Andrew: The current isn't too strong?

Jarwo: Oh no. When it rains, it's strong.

Andrew: Okay then, let's go swimming!

(All of them go swimming except Bambang because he's tasked with guarding the tent. Because it's already nighttime, he calls them all to cook dinner.)

Bambang: Woah! Aren't you freezing? C'mon get up here, let's cook supper.

Jarwo: Okay, we're hungry too.

(Not long after, they all come up to camp and get things ready to cook dinner.)

Tony: I brought instant (ramen) noodles and a pan for cooking.

John: Wait a second, I'll light the fire first. Where are the matches?

Andrew: Here! (handing the matches to John).

John: Oh, the wood is rather/kind of wet.

Jarwo: Try putting dried leaves on too, so that the fire lights fast(er).

Bambang: We're making grilled fish. I brought fish.

John: I brought potatoes too. We can make baked/grilled potatoes too.

Jarwo: Huh? Baked potatoes sound good too!

2. Insects and Snakes in the House!

Mrs. Dibyo: Aaaah!

Mr. Dibyo: What is it Dear?

Mrs: That. There's a big snake in the house.

Mr.:   Where is it? There isn't one.

Mrs: There! Under the dish rack. (Mrs. Dibyo hides behind Mr. Dibyo,
                however, without warning she nearly steps on a big spider, and
                she's scared again.)

Mrs: Aaaa,, what's that? Eeeek! A spider! Throw it out!

Mr: Ah, it's only a spider. It won't bother anyone. Just use the broom
                to chase it out.

(Mrs. Dibyo sweeps the spider out of the house while Mr. Dibyo catches
thesnake and puts it in a sack.)

Mrs: Dear, have you already caught the snake?

Husband: Yes, I have. It was only a jungle snake, not dangerous. I've
                already put the snake in a sack and later I'll throw it out far
                away.

(Not long after, a big house lizard falls on Mrs. Dibyo's shoulder. Being aware of
this, she lets out a scream while brushing her shoulder so the lizard falls off.)

Wife: Help dear! There's a lizard on my shoulder. I don't want it to get
                away too.

Husband: Here. Let me get it. (Mr. Dibyo takes the lizard and throws it
                outside.)

Wife: This must be cause our house is on the edge of the jungle, so
                lots of lost critters/animals find their way here.

3. Rafting Trip near Magelang

Leni: Excuse me... We want to go white water rafting.

Sukoco: Oh, you're the ones from Jogja, right?

Leni: Yeah, that's right.

Sukoco: How many people are there who want to go rafting?

Jarwo: We're five all together. Should we pay now or later?

Sukoco: Go ahead and pay now. (Jarwo pays.) The changing rooms are over there (as he points). The women's on the left and the men's on the right.

Andrew: Oh I see, thanks a lot.

(After changing clothes, they all go to the river together with the guide. They arrive at a river with white-water (rapids) and a strong current. With the help of the guide, they get onto the raft.)

Sinta: Is the river deep? I can't swim.

Guide: Yeah, deep enough/pretty deep. But relax, I'll help you.

John: How long will we be rafting on this river?

Guide: About 2 ½ or 3 hours. Not too long. That's the raft we'll use (pointing at a yellow, rubber, raft.) Don't forget to wear your life jackets and helmets.

4. Reading a Topography Map

A squad of soldiers is on patrol in the jungle

Sergeant: Everyone hold up. I want to look at the map again for a moment.

Private: Good. I'm so tired.

Sgt: Shit! It's too dark. Hand over your flashlight. Okay, where exactly are we... Yep. Corporal, come here!

Corporal: Yes, Sergeant.

Sgt: Corporal, how many klicks/kms do you think it's been since we crossed the river?

Corporal:	I'm not sure.. about 9 or 10 maybe.
Sgt:	Good. I think so too. And the distance to that mountain?
Corporal:	Around 5 km?
Sgt:	Good. (Uses compass to take a bearing.) 45 degrees NE. C'mon, let's look at the map. So, if that's right, we should be just around here, right.. So, if we keep on this road for two or three more klicks, there will be a trail that runs through the paddies.
Corporal:	We can follow it until we reach the platoon's (field) base camp.
Sgt:	If we hurry, we can be there before it's too dark. Instruct the men to quick-time march/pick up the pace. I want to take a look at that trail ahead first.
Corporal:	Yes, Sergeant. Troops! Get ready to move out. The sergeant wants to make it to camp tonight.
Private 1:	How far is it still?
Corporal:	Not far. We'll be there in about 1 ½ hours.
Private 2:	Good! I want a shower and some good food.
Private 1:	Me too. I'm so tired of eating MRE's/rations.

5. Jungle Survival Training

MSgt/First Sgt:	I am Master Sergeant Siregar. This next week all of you are going to learn how to survive in the jungle. The jungle of Papua isn't the village, nor is it the countryside. It will surely kill you if you don't realize how dangerous living in the jungle is.
MSgt:	Always pay attention to your surroundings! Look, think, and plan. Corporal, if you are on patrol and it's nearly dusk, you see there are dark clouds that look like they might turn to rain. What do you do?
Corporal:	Find a dry place to camp for the night.
Msgt:	That's right. Someplace on high or low ground?
Corporal:	On high ground, Sergeant.
MSgt:	Outstanding! Maybe you will make a good sergeant yet..

MSgt: For two weeks, all of you are going to learn how to cross strong rivers, set traps, detect/avoid traps, and other skills that you need in the jungle. All of you will come to know that a machete and banana leaves are your best friends. On top of that, small insects can kill you. Check your boots every time before putting them on and don't wear them all the time. Your feet won't dry out. Just wear sandals when you aren't on patrol. Food, trash, and waste have to be disposed of; if not, there will be a problem with ants and mosquitoes. If your urine is yellow it means you are dehydrated. Drink plenty of water. Dehydration makes you unable to think clearly and you can die because of it.

18. MEDICAL

Please review the Medical section of Unit 1: Words You Already Know, before continuing. Only the vocabulary words most likely to occur/be needed in Javanese have been included.

Instruments

English	Indonesian
bandage	perban
clean cloth	handuk/lap bersih
gauze	kasa
I.V. (Intravenous drip)	I.V. (ii vé), intra vaskulér
(infusion)	alat infus
knife	pisau
forceps	pinsét, catut
needle	jarum
pincers	pengsér
razor	(pisau) cukur
splint (n./v.)	bidai/membidai
stretcher	brankar/brangker
syringe	semprot/semprit
tube	pipa
tweezers	pinsét/catut kecil
wet cloth	lap basah

Anatomy

blood vessels	nadi, urat nadi
bone	tulang
heart	jantung
intestines	usus, isi perut
kidneys	ginjal
liver	hati
lungs	paru-paru
spleen	limpa (kecil)
stomach	perut
vein	véna

Facilities & Hygiene

antiseptic	antiséptik, détol (brand name)
bleach	bayclin (brand), pemutih
clean	bersih
clinic in village	puskesmas
clinic/lab	laboratorium
dirty	kotor
disinfectant	disinféktan
diseased	yang sakit
cold	dingin
health	keséhatan
healthy	séhat
hot, flushed	panas
hospital	rumah sakit
infected	kejangkitan, ada inféksi
iodine	bétadine (brand name)
midwife	bidan
nutritious	bergizi
nurse	perawat, suster
pee, urine	air seni
sanitation (cleanliness)	kebersihan
soap	sabun
tampons	softéx (brand name), pembalut wanita
toothbrush	sikat gigi
toothpaste	odol, pasti gigi
unsanitary (unclean)	tidak bersih
substance, mineral	zat
vitamin	vitamin
zinc	séng

Sicknesses & Specific Conditions

'have' → *'ada'* 'suffer from' → *'derita'*	*Indonesian*	*Javanese*
anemia	kurang darah	s
appendicitis	usus buntu, sakit apéndik	s
bleeding gums	gusi berdarah	s
bloody stool	bérak darah	s
a broken bone	tulang patah	s
bruised-black & blue	memar	s

238

bumps/spots on skin	bintik bintik	s
chills (with fever)	demam/panas dingin	s
a cold	masuk angin	s
congested, stuffed up	ingus	s
conjunctivitis (pink eye)	bélékan	s
contagious	menular	s
crippled	béngkok	s
a cough	batuk	watuk
a cut	luka	s
dandruff	ketombé	s
dengue fever	DB (Dé Bé, demam berdarah)	s
dehydration	dehidrasi, kekurangan cairan	s
diabetes	penyakit gula/manis	s
diarrhea	diaré	mencrét
a fever	demam	mriang, adhem panas
the flu	flu	pilek
gonorrhea	sakit sabun	s
a headache	pusing, sakit kepala	s
heat stroke	panas stép	s
high blood pressure	(tekanan) darah tinggi, hiperténsi	
infect someone	*menjangkiti, menulari	s
infected by	tertular, terjangkit	s
kidney stones	batu ginjal	s
lice	lih	s
liver problems	masalah hati	s
malaria	malaria	s
mal/under-nourished	kurang gizi	s
measles	campak	s
not healing well (wound)	luka kotor	bonyok
rash	ruam	biduren
red spots (as with dengue)	bintik-bintik merah	s
runny nose	pilek	s
outbreak	wabah, serangan penyakit	s
salmonella typhoid	salmonela tipus	s
serious/hurt badly	parah	s
an STD/VD	penyakit kelamin/kotor	s
spread, has spread	terjangkit	s
stomachache/sick stomach	sakit perut	loro weteng
swollen, puffy	bengkak	s
thyroid condition	penyakit baguk/gondok	s (beguk)
toothache	sakit gigi	loro untu
typhoid fever	tifus/tipus *	s
typhus	tifus/tipus	s
wheezing	mendesah	s

'Need' → *'perlu/butuh'* + *following vocabulary:*

a cast	gips
to drink water	minum air putih/aqua
rest	istirahat
to stay in bed	berbaring di tempat tidur
stitches	(setik) jahitan
to take medicine	minum obat

Describing How You Feel (Indonesian-Javanese-English)

(me)rasa = feel, *ada* = have/there is, *gejala* = symptom

Indonesian	*Javanese*	*English*
balgam	s	mucus, phlegm
berbengang	s	ringing in ears
biasa	s	normal
capai/capek	s	tired
dingin	s	feel cold
keringat dingin	s	break out in (cold) sweat / (when a fever breaks)
keringat	s	sweaty
lemah	s	weak
muntah	mutah	vomited/puked
nyeri	s	painful/a pain
nyeri menusuk	s	stabbing pain
nyeri yang hilang timbul	senut-senut	throbbing
nyaris	s	faint, going to faint
panas	s	hot
panas dalam	adem	have a fever
pusing kepala	s	dizzy
nyeri separo	s	migraine
pening	s	headache
pingsan	s	fainted/going to faint
pusing	s	headache
sakit kepala	s	headache
sakit perut	s	stomachache/sick to stomach
tidak apa-apa	s	I'm okay, it's nothing

Treatments in Indonesia

fogging, pengasapan — fogging against mosquitoes

pasir Abate — powder that kills mosquito eggs in water

jus jambu — to help recover from dengue fever

Redoxon — vitamin C + zinc, in tube, effervescent

Vermint ('vermen') — for typhus and other infections

daun keji beling and
daun kumis kucing — to get rid of kidney/urinal tract stones

daun sirih (boiled) + salt, — for getting rid of conjunctivitis (pink eye)
used as an eyewash/saline

Yakult (yogurt drink) — for good bacteria, nutritional supplement

losien anti-nyamuk, Autan — mosquito lotion

Instructions & Advice

Your going to be fine	Kamu akan baik baik saja
Take this medicine	Minum obat ini
Once a day	Satu kali sehari
Open wide	Buka mulut
Three times a day	Tiga kali sehari
Lie down	Berbaring
Sit still/don't move	Jangan bergerak
Lift up your shirt	Angkat kaos

Language & Culture Notes

1. The root *jangkit* refers to infection from an insect to a person, whereas the root *tular* refers to infection spread from person to person.

2. Dengue fever, typhus, and malaria are common in Indonesia, for a variety of reasons. In Indonesian, these are referred to as *débé (DB)*, *tifus*, and *malaria*, respectively. If you live in Indonesia for several years, chances are you'll get one or more of them.

3. Regarding '*tifus*,' there is some confusion in the way the word is used in Indonesia and the West. There are two separate, unrelated diseases, both of which are called *tifus* in Indonesia. The first is what is usually called 'typhoid fever' by Westerners. It is a bacterial infection that wreaks havoc with your GI tract, from salmonella bacteria in feces spread through (dirty) water. It is very common in Indonesia, and if you live there for any amount of time, you can expect to get it. A special blood test (*Widal*) will tell you what type(s) of bacteria and their count. If the bacteria count is too high, hospitalization and an antibiotic drip and special diet (plain foods) are required. If not, most people will opt to treat it on their own, with oral antibiotics (Azithromycin or Ciprofloxacin) and rest, which can take a very long time. If you decide to treat *tifus* this way, make sure to get a *Widal* blood test every week to make sure the bacterial count is going down, and be sure to eat yogurt or supplements containing pro-biotics, so that you can continue to digest normal food. The 2nd type of *tifus* is a bacterial disease people get from fleas, ticks, mites, or lice. It has many of the same symptoms as typhoid fever and other tropical diseases: a high fever, muscle and joint pain, rash, stomach pain, and delirium.

4. There are several classes and types of clinics & hospitals:
Klinik Labaratorium in cities are quick, convenient places to go and get any kind of blood test, from a full range of tests, to see if you have a viral or bacterial infection and what kind it is. Regular checks (blood pressure, sugar) and shots are also given there. Pharmacies have a doctor or even a dentist on site for consultation for limited hours daily (mornings or evenings), with hours posted outside.

5. Results of blood tests (*hasil*) from labaratories/clinics are easy to read. Normal ranges are given (*harga normal/biasa*) so you can compare. WBC = white blood cells, RBC = red blood cells, PLT = platelets; each of these is usually broken down into the various types. Widal = the bacteria in your blood, which is broken down into type and count.

5. (cont.) If you've got a debilitating fever, feel weak, and are sweating rivers, tell the clinic you want *"pemeriksaan darah komplit berisi widal, malaria, db, tifus"* and you will know what you have and how serious it is by the end of the day. The doctor or staff at the clinic can tell you if you need to go to the hospital for treatment. If the bacteria count is not high in case of tifus (1/80 for example or 1-2 on a scale of 1-5), you can remain as still as possible for a few days and take antibiotics yourself to treat it, then get another blood test, which will tell you if/when you are back to normal. You are probably looking at a week or two of antibiotics, no physical activity, and a diet that consists of clean, non-irritating food, followed by plenty of good bacteria - the kind found in yogurt and cheese. Since the quality of care in many Indonesian hospitals is uncertain, specialists aren't always on shift, and tests can take longer to get. These clinics/labs are a quicker, cheaper way to find out what's going on. If you have a disease that requires hospitalization, simply bring the lab results with you to the hospital – it saves a lot of time and most tests won't need to be redone.

6. Be aware that at chain pharmacies where more female clerks than are needed are hanging around inside, these salesgirls are commonly paid a commission and will inevitably try to offer you the most expensive (usually herbal) treatment for any condition you have, rather than the cheapest, most effective one. You just have to tell them it's too expensive, and ask for the inexpensive and/or generic medicine.

7. *Masuk angin* is most accurately translated as 'have/caught a cold.' As in the West, any condition/illness that cannot be accurately identified, will commonly be ascribed by people (or doctors) as 'having a cold,' or *masuk angin*.

8. One practice found in the *kampung* for a baby that is *ingus* - has a lot of snot and a runny nose, is for the mom to put her mouth over the baby's nose and suck the snot out. (Needless to say, this is a rather strange sight, the first time one witnesses it.)

Indonesian Conversations

1. I Feel Sick

Patient:	Selamat pagi.
Perawat:	Selamat pagi.
Patient:	Sudah dua hari saya sakit perut.
Perawat:	Di bagian mana yang sakit?
Patient:	Perut saya kanan bawah.
Perawat:	Silahkan Anda tiduran.
Patient:	Iya . . .
Perawat:	Sakit perut kanan bawah? Anda sakit usus buntu.
Patient:	Masih bisa di obati?
Perawat:	Ini harus dioperasi.
Patient:	Operasi di sini bisa?
Perawat:	Bisa.

2. At a Pharmacy

Pembeli:	(Walks into store, starts looking around.)
Mbak Apotek:	Bisa saya bantu?
Pembeli:	Saya mencari antiséptik dan pléster.
Mbak:	(Shows customer where it is in store.) Di sini Mas.

Pembeli:	(Picks up items, one by one, holding them.) Ini berapa?
Mbak:	Itu dua puluh lima ribu.
Pembeli:	Kalo ini? (Picks up other item.)
Mbak:	Enam-belas.
Pembeli:	Ya. Cukup, dua-duanya. (Gets out a 100.000 rupiah bill.)
Mbak:	Ada yang kecil?
Pembeli:	Tidak ada.
Mbak:	Ada seribu?
Pembeli:	(Reaches into pocket or wallet.) Ya, ada (Hands money to the clerk.)
Mbak:	Kembalian enam puluh lima ribu. Terima kasih.

3. At the Village Clinic

Bidan:	Selamat pagi Ibu.
Patient:	Selamat Ibu Bidan.
Bidan:	Bisa saya bantu Bu?
Patient:	Saya mau periksa kehamilan...
Bidan:	Sudah berapa lama Anda terlambat datang bulan/ menstruasi?
Patient:	Dua bulan
Bidan:	Periksa urin dulu ya Bu. Biar tahu Anda hamil atau tidak.
Patient:	Iya Bu.

| Bidan: | Selamat hasil urin positif. Anda hamil. |
| Patient: | Terima kasih Ibu Bidan. |

4. School/Village Children Immunizations

Anak2:	Selamat pagi Ibu. [Anak2 = anak-anak]
Perawat:	Selamat pagi juga. Hari ini anak-anak akan dapat imunisasi campak, imunisasi agar sehat dan tidak mudah sakit.
Anak:	Suntiknya sakit tidak?
Perawat:	Suntiknya tidak sakit.
Anak:	Suntiknya dimana Ibu Perawat.
Perawat:	Di lengan saja.
Anak:	Baik Ibu. Saya tidak takut di suntik.
Perawat:	Anak pintar. Sekarang satu persatu Ibu suntik, ya?
Anak2:	Iya Ibu. (At end of visit): Terima kasih suster.

Reading Sample 1: Optician Business Card

OPTIK "SUN'S"

GRATIS !

* PEMERIKSAAN MATA
* CUCI / SERVICE KACAMATA
* MENERIMA RESEP DOKTER

Tamini Square Lantai Dasar GS 16 No. 8-9
Jakarta Telp. (021) 877 86046

Reading Sample 2: A Doctor's Note

Jalan Ring Road Utara No. 160
Condong Catur Depok Sleman Yogyakarta 55283
Telp. 0274- 446 3535 (Hunting) Fax. 0274-4463 444
E-mail:info@rs-jih.com

007/PSM/22/01124/04
No. Revisi : 00

Surat Keterangan Sakit

Yang bertanda tangan di bawah ini menerangkan bahwa :

Nama   : Donald Eldon

Umur   : 38 tahun

Alamat   : Jln. Kayen Raya, Gg Sibert 3 E- 67

Pekerjaan : ....

Dari hasil pemeriksaan yang saya lakukan, yang bersangkutan dalam keadaan sakit,

dan membutuhkan istirahat selama .... 7 .... (Tujuh ....) hari.

Dari tanggal ... 2 Maret '09 ... s/d tanggal ... 8 Maret '09 .....

Demikian, surat keterangan ini agar dapat dipergunakan sebagaimana mestinya.

Jogjakarta, 2 Maret 20 09

Dokter pemeriksa,

(....)

248

Reading Sample 3: Laboratory Clinic Blood Test Results
(followed by author's notes)

Laboratorium Klinik
Namanya Klinik

Laboratorium, Foto Rontgen dan EKG dilayani setiap hari
Senin-Jumat: 06.00 - 21.00 WIB, Sabtu: 06.00 - 19.00 WIB

Peduli Hidup Sehat *Praktek Dokter Umum, Praktek Dokter Internis*

Konsultasi Gizi - Senin dan Kamis: 14.00 -16.00 WIB

Jl. Kalimantan (R. Road Utara)
Catur X, Sleman Yogyakarta Telp. (0274) XXXXXX, Fax. (0274) xxxxxx

Minggu/Libur Nasional: Tutup

No.Per   :032168
Nama   :Donald Hobbs. Tn./ 39 th/ L
Alamat   :Gg Siberut, No E 7
Dokter/Inst :

No. Reg :   018459
Tgl   : 28/03/2010

Hasil Pemeriksaan

Jenis	Hasil	Nilai Rujukan
KIMIA KLINIK		
Ureum	28.9	L.19.2-42.8 P.14.9-36.3
Creatinin	1.06	L.0.8-1.5 P.0.7-1.2
As. Urat	7.8	L.3.5-8.5 P.2.5-6.2
SGOT/AST	16	6 - 30 u/l
SGPT/ALT	30	7 - 32 u/l
HEMATOLOGI		
Darah Rutin Automatic	Terlampir	
-HB	14.7	L. 13-17 P. 11-15
-Leukosit	7.300	4-11 ribu
-DIFF		
-Eosinofil	1	1-3%
-Basofil	0	0-1%
-Batang	1	2-5%
-Segmen	57	50-65%
-Limfosit	37	20-45%
-Monosit	4	2-8%
-LED		
-1 Jam	2	-
-2 Jam	10	-

-Eritrosit	4.92	L. 4.5-6.2 P. 4-5.4
-Trombosit	262.000	150-400 ribu
-Hematokrit	45	L. 40-50 P. 35-47
-MCV	89.7	76-96
-MCH	29.6	27-31
-MCHC	33.0	30-35

OR:

WBC	6.0 x 10^9/L	4.0 - 10.0
Lymph#	2.4 x 10^9/L	0.8 - 4.0
Mid#		

IMUNO - SEROLOGI

HBsAg (Elisa)	Negatif : 0.27	Negatif bila < 1.0
Anti HCV	Negatif : 0.10	Negatif bila indek < 1.0
HIV	Negatif	Negatif

Widal

Salmonella typhi O	Negatif	Negatif
Salmonella typhi H	Positif: 1/320	Negatif
Salmonella paratyphi A-O	Negatif	Negatif
Salmonella paratyphi A-H	Positif: 1/80	Negatif
Salmonella paratyphi B-O	Positif: 1/80	Negatif
Salmonella paratyphi B-H	Negatif	Negatif
Salmonella paratyphi C-O	Positif: 1/80	Negatif
Salmonella paratyphi C-H	Negatif	Negatif

*Bila Ada Keraguan Atas Hasil, Harap Menghubungi Laboratorium Klinik

* Terimakasih atas Kepercayaan Anda

[STAMP HERE]   [SIGNATURE]

Arfiatul Jannatun   P. Noor , dr, M.Kes, Sp.PK
Analis   Dokter Penanggung Jawab

Author's Notes About the Blood Test Results

1. This is a composite sample test based on several blood tests at several different clinics. Expect each clinic's report to look slightly different but have the same basic parts: (1) Parts of blood (*Hematologi*) and count for each type of cell (red, white, leukocytes, etc. –often known as CBC) and (2) Bacteria count (*Widal*). In this test, I had kidneys and liver functions tested, which shows under the heading *KIMIA KLINIK*. The first three sub-items are related to kidneys, the last two (*SGOT* and *SGPT*) to liver function. Notice too that this test included tests for HIV and Hepatitis, with results shown under the heading *IMUNO-SEROLOGI*.

2. For every item, a normal range is given (*Nilai Rujukan* or *Nilai Normal/Biasa*). The 'L' in this particular test stands for *Lelaki* - Men, and the 'P' for *Perempuan* - Women. Not all clinics will show the normal range of results by sex in this manner. (The normal ranges for men and women for most items are slightly different, as you can see.)

3. Learning to read a blood test like this is an important basic skill essential for any expat living in Indonesia. Being able to read one will help you diagnose an illness quickly and cheaply. Relying solely on Indonesian doctors' advice through consultations is a foolish way to deal with trouble because doctors sometimes have little experience or practical training and tend to generalize when it comes to expats, thinking they just ate something wrong and prescribe the usual antibiotics before sending you home. (Or perhaps, like a friend of mine, you could be told you have cancer or you need something removed when you don't.)

Reading Sample: Dengue Fever & Typhoid

Pada tahun 2007, saya tinggal di rumah di utara Yogyakarta dekat sunai dan ada tanah kosong di belakang rumah. Jadi, ada banyak nyamuk di sana. Di Indonesia, orang-orang terjangkit DB dengan mudah dan setiap tahun ada banyak kasus, khususnya ketika musim berganti - dari musim hujan ke musim kemarau.

Dalam beberapa hari saya lemah sekali sampai tidak bisa berdiri atau bergerak tanpa merasa akan pingsan. Saya mau terus tidur saja sepanjang hari dan waktu bangun, ada banyak keringat (seperti banjir), dari leher dan bahu-bahu saya.

Setelah tiga hari, saya kembali kerja. Masih ada demam dan merasa lemah, tapi lebih baik dari sebelumnya. Seorang guru yang lain, waktu dia melihat saya, suruh saya pergi ke klinik/labaratorium yang berada di jalan yang sama dengan sekolah bahasa kami. Di sana, saya bilang kepada pegewai bahwa saya pikir mungkin ada sakit parah seperti malaria, dan saya mau dapat pemeriksaan darah komplit.

Beberapa jam kemudian, saya pergi balik ke klinik mengambil hasilnya. Menurutnya, saya ada tifus salmonella, atau 'tifus.' Juga, hasilnya antibodi DB sedikit tinggi, tapi tidak pasti jika saya kena DB juga, atau tidak. Melihat hasilnya, saya langsung pergi ke rumah sakit nanti harinya. Seorang Suster mengambil hasil dari klinik yang saya bawa ke rumah sakit dan langsung saya diberi tempat tidur dengan infus.

Setelah R.S. periksa asuransi saya, saya harus memilih kamar yang saya inginkan. Asuransi keséhatan sekolah kami cukup untuk kamar pribadi standar, jadi saya memilih kamar itu. Besok paginya, dokter datang. Katanya saya harus tinngal di R.S. beberapa hari sampai satu minggu, tergantung. Dia juga memberikan tes lain agar tahu kalau hasilnya memang positif DB.

Hasilnya tes itu positif, jadi dokter tahu masalah saya serius - punya tifus maupun DB kedua-duanya. Tiga hari kemudian, saya menerima IV antibiotik, dan harus makan makanan yang tidak ada bumbu sama sekali, seperti roti, kentang, dan sayuran. Akhirnya, setelah empat hari dan hasil tes lebih normal, saya bisa keluar dari R.S. dan pulang ke rumah. Saya merasa bahagia sekali.

Javanese Conversations

1. I Feel Sick

Pasien:	Sugeng énjang.
Perawat:	Sugeng énjang.
Pasien:	Sampun kalih dinten kula sakit padharan.
Perawat:	Bagian pundi ingkang gerah?
Pasiean:	Padharan kula ingkang bagian tengen ngandhap.
Perawat:	Mangga panjenengan saréan.
Pasien:	Inggih.
Perawat:	Gerah padharan tengen ngandhap? Panjenengan gerah usus buntu.
Pasien:	Taksih saged dipun obati?
Nurse:	Menika kedah dipun operasi.
Pasien:	Operasi ing mriki saged?
Perawat:	Saged.

2. At the Pharmacy

Mbak: Saged dipunbiyantu?

Pembeli: Kula pados antiséptik lan plaster.

Mbak: Wonten mriki Mas (shows buyer where they are).

Pembeli: (Picks items up one by one.) Menika pinten?

Mbak: Menika selangkung éwu.

Pembeli: Menawi menika?

Mbak: Nembelas.

Pembeli: Nggih cekap. Kalih-kalihipun. (Gets out a 100.000 bill.)

Mbak: Wonten ingkang alit?

Pembeli: Mboten wonten.

Mbak: Wonten setunggal éwu?

Pembeli: (Reaches into pocket.) Nggih wonten. (Pays clerk.)

Mbak: Matur nuwun. Susukipun sewidhak gangsal éwu.

3. At the Village Clinic

Pasien: Sugeng énjang, Ibu.

Bidan: Sugeng énjang, bidan.

Pasien: Kula badhé periksa kehamilan.

Bidan: Sampun pinten wulan panjenengan telat menstruasi?

Pasien: Kalih wulan.

Bidan: Kula periksa urin rumiyin nggih Bu. Supados mangertos panjenengan menika mbobot menapa mboten.

Pasien: Inggih Bu.

Bidan: Selamat, hasil urin positif. Panjenengan hamil.

Pasien: Matur nuwun, Bu Bidan.

4. School/Village Children Immunizations

Anak2: Sugeng énjing, Bu.

Perawat: Sugeng énjang, anak-anak. Dinten menika, anak-anak badhe pikanthuk imunisasi campak, imunisasi supaya séhat lan mboten gampil sakit.

Anak: Suntikipun sakit mboten?

Perawat: Suntikipun mboten sakit. Ampun ajrih.

Anak: Suntikipun ing sisih pundi Bu?

Perawat: Ing asto kémawon.

Anak: Inggih, Bu, kula mboten ajrih dipun suntik.

Perawat: Lare pinter. Sakmenika, setunggal mboko setunggal Ibu suntik, nggih?

Anak2: Inggih Ibu.

Anak2: (At end of visit) Matur nuwun, Bu.

1. I Feel Sick

Patient:	Good morning.
Nurse:	Good morning.
Patient:	My stomach has hurt now for two days.
Nurse:	Which part is it that hurts?
Patient:	My lower right stomach.
Nurse:	Please lie down.
Patient:	Okay.
Nurse:	Your lower right stomach? You have appendicitis.
Patient:	Can I still take medicine for it?
Nurse:	You have to have an operation.
Patient:	Can you do the operation here?
Nurse:	We can.

2. At a Pharmacy

Customer:	(Walks into store.)
Pharmacy Gal:	Can I help you?
Customer:	I'm looking for antiseptic and bandaids.
Gal:	Here they are sir.
Customer:	How much is this?
Gal:	It's twenty-five thousand.
Customer:	And this?
Gal:	Sixteen.
Customer:	Okay. Good enough. Both of them.

Gal:	Do you have anything smaller?
Customer:	I don't.
Gal:	Do you have a thousand?
Customer:	Yeah, here.
Gal:	Your change is sixty-five thousand. Thank you.

3. At the Village Clinic

Midwife:	Good morning Mam.
Patient:	Good morning.
Midwife:	Can I help you?
Patient:	I'd like a pregnancy test …
Midwife:	How long has it been since you had your period/menstruation?
Patient:	2 months.
Midwife:	Let's check your urine first, okay? It will let us know if you're pregnant or not.
Patient:	Okay.
Midwife:	Congratulations, the urine test is positive. You're pregnant.
Patient:	Thank you.

4. School/Village Children Immunizations

Children:	Good morning Nurse.
Nurse:	Good morning to you too. Today you children are going to get a measles immunization/shot, so that you are healthy and don't get sick.
Child:	The shot hurts, doesn't it?
Nurse:	The shot doesn't hurt.

Child:	Where will we get the shot nurse?
Nurse:	Just in the arm.
Child:	Okay nurse. I'm not afraid to get a shot.
Nurse:	Smart kid. Now I'll give you each a shot, one by one, okay?
Children:	Okay nurse. Thank you nurse.

Reading Sample 4: Dengue Fever & Typhoid

In 2007, I was living in a house in north Yogyakarta close to a river and which had some empty land behind it. So, there were a lot of mosquitoes there. In Indonesia, it is easy to catch Dengue Fever, and every year there are many cases, especially during the change in seasons – from the rainy season to the dry season.

For several days I was very weak until I couldn't stand or move without feeling like I was going to faint. I just wanted to sleep all day long and when I woke up, there was a lot of sweat (like a flood), from my neck and shoulders.

After three days, I returned to work. I still had a fever and felt weak, but better than before. Another teacher, when she saw me, got me to go to the clinic which was on the same street as our language school. There, I told the worker that I thought maybe I had a serious disease, like malaria, and I wanted to get a complete blood test.

A few hours later, I went back to the clinic to get the results. According to the test, I had Typhus Salmonella, or 'Tifus.' Also, the results for the antibody for dengue fever were a little high, but it wasn't certain if I had dengue too or not. Seeing the results, I went straight to the hospital later that day. A nurse took the results from the clinic which I had brought to the hospital and I was immediately given a bed with an infusion (I.V. drip).

After the hospital checked my insurance, I had to choose the room I wanted. Our school's health insurance was enough for a standard private room, so that's the room I chose. The next morning, the doctor came. He told me that I had to be in the hospital from a few days to a week, depending. He also did another test that would tell us if I was really positive for dengue fever.

The results of the test were positive, so the doctor knew my problem was serious – I had typhoid fever and dengue fever both. For the next 3 days, I received an antibiotic drip and had to eat food that didn't have any seasonings/spices, like bread, potatoes, and vegetables. Finally, after four days and test results that were fairly normal, I could check out of/leave the hospital and return home. I felt very happy.

19. STUDENT LIFE

Review the Academic - School section of Unit 1: Words You Already Know, before continuing. A wordlist for Javanese is present only where such words are commonly used.

accepted (into a school, program)	diterima
Bachelor's degree	S1 (és satu)
boy/girl scouts	Pramuka
camp (band, training)	outbound
cheat (on an exam)	conték
class	kelas (general), kuliah (at university)
college	universitas, sekolah tinggi
College (College/Faculty of Law)	fakultas
curfew	jam malam
dean	dékan
Department, School, Faculty	fakultas
didn't get accepted (to a school)	tidak diterima
drop out/quit school	berhenti
boarding house	kost, kos
dormitory	asrama, graha
elective	mata kuliah pilihan
exchange student program	pertukaran pelajar
exchange student	siswa pertukaran
expelled from	dipecat dari
field trip	field trip, darma wisata/widyawisata
financial aid*	—
grades	nilai
GPA	IP (i pé), index préstasi
graduate	lulus
graduation ceremony	wisuda
'hell week' (freshman initiation)	ospék
infractions/demerits	pelanggaran
lecture	kuliah
major (field of study)	jurusan
Master's degree	S2 (és dua)
merits	pujian
minimum passing score	KKM
new student admissions	PMB - penerimaan mahasiswa baru
payment plan/deferred tuition*	—
principal / headmaster	kepala sekolah

professor	dosén*	
lecture	kuliah	
requirement (class)	mata kuliah wajib	
Registrars Office/Admissions	tempat pendaftaran	
research	penelitian	
scholarship	béasiswa, darmasiswa	
Social Rural Internship	KKN*	
student	siswa, mahasiswa (m) mahasiswi (f)	
student affairs office/head	wakasék	
student council	OSIS, déwan mahasiswa	
study tour	widyawisata	
subject	mata kuliah, mata pelajaran (h.s.)	
summer semester	semester pendek	
take a class	masuk kelas	
thesis	skripsi, tésis*	
tuition	SPP, uang sekolah	
uniform	seragam	
work-study (university)	widyakarya	

School Supplies/Materials

backpack	ransel	s
bag	tas	s
ballpoint	bolpoin	bolpén
blackboard	papan tulis	blabak
chalk	kapur	s
eraser	penghapus	setip
felt tip marker (permanent)	spidol	s
glue	lém	s
liquid paper (white out)	tipéx (brand name)	s
notebook	buku catatan, blok note	s
paper clip	klip kertas	s
pen	péna	pén
pencil	pénsil	potlot
pencil case	tempat pénsil	dusgrib
rubber band	karét gelang	s
ruler	penggaris	garisan
scissors	gunting	s
whiteboard	papan tulis	blabak
whiteboard marker	spidol	s

Language & Cultural Notes

1. *Skripsi* is used for thesis that undergraduates have to complete at the end of their studies; *tesis* is used for the thesis that graduate students do.

2. The school year for K-12 usually starts in July, and ends in June. There is about a month vacation between school years. University start dates differ, but classes always start sometime between August and October.

3. There is quite a mix of good private and public universities across Indonesia, but nothing like the disperse, state university system found in the USA. The most famous/prestigious universities tend to be located on Java, and include: UI (Universitas Indonesia) public and located in Jakarta, Trisakti (a private wealthy college in Jakarta), UGM (Universitas Gaja Madah) a public uni in Yoygakarta, Atma Jaya (a private Catholic University in Jakarta), Sanata Dharma (a private Catholic university in Yogyakarta), ITB (Institut Teknologi Bandung) a public technical uni in Bandung, IPB (Institut Pertanian Bogor) a public agricultural uni in Bogor, and UNPAD (Universitas Padjadjaran) a public uni in Bandung, among others.

4. Money for university, besides outright scholarships (*beasiswa*), does not exist. There are no student loans or grants, so putting a child through university becomes a family responsibility.

5. There are 3 routes to public university: (1) regular = pay high tuition and bribes, which is what most students do. (2) jalur khusus = attend on scholarship, for really smart kids who did well in high school. (3) SPMB = national tests, like SAT/ACT in the USA; if you pass them, tuition is cheaper than it is for students on route number 1.

6. There are two types of students at private university: regular paying, and '*préstasi*' which is used to refer to those who are on scholarship.

7. It should not be surprising that the environment of corruption taints universities in Indonesia, as it does so many aspects of life. The amount of money that students pay in order to attend a university varies, and professors with control or influence over admissions often take bribes or charge families in order to let their kid get into the school.

8. The names and corresponding student number of students who have been accepted into university for an upcoming school year are commonly publicly posted in the newspaper or online, or announced via the newspaper and posted at the school. Other universities send letters similar to colleges in the USA.

9. Most universities do not have dorms; instead, a large number of cheap kost/kos, or boarding houses, are located in neighborhoods surrounding a university. Many are exclusively for men or women, but others are mixed. Students usually have their own rooms and share a bath and central TV room & kitchen. Regulations vary widely depending on the kost, from having strict curfews and no visitors of the opposite sex, to having relatively no regulations at all.

10. Yogyakarta and Bandung are known as student cities, because they both have a large number of colleges and students, from all over Indonesia, relative to the population.

11. Universities in Indonesia do not have fraternities and sororities like U.S. colleges; a word to describe such a thing would be *persatuan* brotherhood, or *kelompok*, group; an accurate translation requires a full sentence in Indonesian.

12. Cheating is more common among young people in schools in Indonesia than in Western countries due to an environment of corruption where cheating is commonplace and rewarded in many aspects of life, as well as a collective mentality towards doing assignments. Unless punishment is severe, most students feel no compulsion not to cheat simply because 'it's wrong,' as many of their counterparts in the North America would, or because they want to earn a grade for themselves or learn the material.

13. Many Indonesians have trouble translating the word *dosen* into English; those who do inevitably translate it as 'lecturer.' The word 'professor' as used in the USA, generally for any teacher at university regardless of status, makes it an equally good translation for *dosen*; 'instructor' is another.

14. *KKN – Kuliah Kerja Nyata* is a mandatory and important part of nearly every student's undergraduate university program. During their final year of university, students spend one month doing a social work experience project full-time, to help a rural/isolated community.

15. *Semester pendek* is about the same as summer term/semester at universities in North America. It's usually a bit shorter (hence the name), with a smaller selection of various or special courses. Much fewer students attend, usually to bring up their grades or repeat a course they failed.

16. There are a number of professional degrees, for those who attend specialized business or vocational colleges – *Pendidikan Profesi*: DI is a one-year degree – for stewardesses, ship workers, etc. DII is a two-year degree, and DIII a three-year degree – common for secretaries. D IV is a four-year degree from a *Sekolah Tinggi* (specialized Academy or College), such as STIE - the Academy of Economics.

Indonesian Conversations

1. Getting into Uni

Ayah: Kamu udah dengar dari UGM?

Putra: Ya, Pak.

Ayah: Hasilnya apa? Diterima atau nggak?

Putra: Syukurlah Pak, saya diterima.

Ayah: Waaahhh..bapak senang sekali dengarnya. Selamat ya nak.
           (Dad kisses his son on the cheek and hugs him.)

Putra: Terimakasih ya Pak. Ini semua karena doa Bapak sama
           Ibu.

Ayah: Yang pasti, karna kamu serius belajar sebelum ujian masuk
           UGM. (Dad calls Mom in.) Ibu! Putra diterima di UGM.

Ibu: (Comes from the kitchen.) Waaahh..selamat ya Nak.
           Gives her son a hug.)

Putra: (Emotionally touched) Iya Ibu, terimakasih banyak ya, ini
           semua karna doa Ibu dan Bapak.

Ibu: Ini harus dirayain ya Pak.

Ayah: Iya Bu, harus. Acara syukuran aja. Ngundang tetangga.

Ibu: Acaranya hari apa ya Pak?

Ayah:	Besok minggu depan saja, pas hari Minggu.
Putra:	Gak usah dirayain Pak, Bu. Lebih baik, uangnya buat nambahin uang kuliah aja. Gimana?
Ayah:	Lha..Kenapa gitu Nak? Maksud Bapak, supaya tetangga tau, kalo anak Bapak diterima kuliah di UGM.
Putra:	Gak usah lah Pak, saya gak mau dirayain.
Ibu:	Ya sudah lah Pak. Gak jadi aja.
Ayah:	Terus, kapan mulai kuliahnya Nak?
Putra:	Dua minggu lagi Pak. Pas hari Senin.
Ibu:	Harus pendaftaran ulang gak Nak?
Putra:	Iya Bu. Besok saya mau ke kampus untuk daftar ulang, sekalian lihat jadwal untuk orientasi mahasiswa baru.
Ayah:	Besok Bapak anter ke kampus ya Nak?
Ibu:	Iya, Ibu juga mau ikut ya Nak?
Putra:	Gak usahlah Pak, Bu. Biar nanti saya sendiri saja datang ke kampus.
Ayah:	Oh, iya jadinya kamu diterima fakultas apa Nak? Biologi atau Pertanian?
Putra:	Seperti harapan saya Pak, saya diterima di fakultas Biologi.
Ayah:	Baguslah Nak.
Ibu:	Pesan Ibu..belajar yang rajin ya Nak, biar nanti nilai kamu bagus dan cepat selesai kuliahnya.
Putra:	Iya Bu, pasti. Terima kasih ya Bu, terima kasih ya Pak.

Ayah:	Iya Nak.
Ibu:	Iya Nak. Ibu selalu doakan kamu.

2. New student on Campus

Siswa Lama:	Halo. Apa kabar?
Siswi Baru:	Hi. kabar baik aja...
S. Lama:	Mbak siswi baru kan?
S. Baru:	Iya. Mas juga?
S. Lama:	Aku udah tahun kedua.
S. Baru:	Di Fakultas Psikologi?
S. Lama:	Bukan. Jurusan ku Sastra.
S. Baru:	Kelas ini pilihan atau wajib?
S. Lama:	Untuk siswa jurusan astra ini mata kuliah pilihan.
S. Baru:	Untuk saya ini wajib ya.
S. Lama:	Kedengarannya Mbak tidak mau ikut . . .
S. Baru:	Ya, betul.
S. Lama:	Kenapa? Dosen ini terkenal dan bagus, menarik. semua siswa senang di kelasnya. Mungkin semester nanti kamu akan suka juga.

S. Baru:	Saya gak begitu suka sama materi kuliahnya. Buat saya ini membosankan.
S. Lama:	Belum pernah masuk kuliah ini kan Mbak?
S. Baru:	Udah Mas, ini yang kedua kali. Mungkin saya kurang memahami materinya.
S. Lama:	Bisa jadi kayak gitu. Kalo Mbak mau, saya punya beberapa buku catatan dan modul yang bisa mbak baca di rumah.
S. Baru:	Terima kasih. Nanti saya fotokopi atau beli aja di Gramedia.
S. Lama:	Gak usah Mbak. Mbak bawa aja bukunya, karena saya punya dua buku, yang satu punya teman saya. Dia berikan buku itu untuk saya.
S. Baru:	Kapan saya bisa dapat bukunya?
S. Lama:	Nanti setelah selesai kuliah ini ya Mbak.
S. Baru:	Oke deh. Makasih ya Mas.
S. Lama:	Iya, Mbak sama-sama.

3. Student Caught Cheating on a Test

Andi:	(Andi is busy looking for answers on his mobile phone.)
Dosen:	(Catches Andy red-handed and approaches Andy's desk.) Eehhmmm…Ngapain kamu?
Andi:	(Afraid) Ah, tidak apa-apa, Pak. Ini ada sms masuk.
Dosen:	Mana? Saya mau lihat.

Andi:	Jangan Pak. Ini sms dari pacar saya.
Dosen:	Yang benar? Soalnya dari tadi saya lihat kamu selalu pegang hp sedangkan kamu lagi ujian.
Andi:	Ah, Bapak bias aja deh. Saya tidak apa-apain kok Pak.
Dosen:	Makanya itu, kalo mémang kamu gak ngapa-ngapain, saya mau liat hp kamu sekarang. Mana?
Andi:	(Afraid he's been caught.) Aduh! Mati aku.
Dosen:	Nah..kan? Kamu ketahuan nyontek. Semua jawaban ada di hp kamu.
Andi:	Tidak Pak. Saya tidak ada maksud nyontek waktu ujian.
Dosen:	Gak ada maksud gimana? Udah jelas kamu tulis semua di hp kamu tentang materi ujian hari ini.
Andi:	Tidak Pak. Bapak salah.
Dosen:	Udahlah! Kamu nggak boleh lagi mengerjakan ujian hari ini, dan kamu nggak lulus untuk mata kuliah ini.
Andi:	Pak...Maaf Pak. Saya nyontek karena saya tidak sempat belajar Pak. Saya banyak kerjaan dirumah. Maklumlah Pak..
Dosen:	Gak bisa. Kamu nggak lulus mata kuliah ini. Nanti kamu bisa ulang di seméster péndék. (Takes Andy's test.)
Andi:	(Andy leaves the classroom.)

4. Talk with a Professor

Linda talks with her professor about a paper

Dosen: Linda, topik buat tugas akhir kamu mana?
Saya belum terima.

Linda: Aduh Prof, maaf banget yah, saya masih bingung nih.

Dosen: Bingung kenapa?

Linda: Karena ada beberapa topik yang menarik buat saya.

Dosen: Waah.. bagus Linda. Berarti kamu serius dan benar-benar memahami apa yang akan menjadi bahan penelitian kamu.

Linda: Iya Prof, tapi saya masih sulit untuk menentukan mana yang paling tepat.

Dosen: Coba berikan dulu beberapa topik itu ke saya. Nanti kita bisa berdiskusi untuk memilih topik apa yang paling tepat.

Linda: Iya Prof, saya akan kirim lewat email siang ini.

Dosen: Setelah itu, saya akan beri saran supaya mempermudah kamu dalam memilih.

Linda: Sebenarnya, sudah ada yang paling saya inginkan. Tetapi saya pikir agak sulit untuk mengumpulkan data-datanya Prof.

Dosen: Kamu gak usah khawatir, karna saya yakin, tidak ada data-data yang tidak mungkin untuk di dapat.

Linda: Selain itu, ada juga beberapa teman yang topiknya agak sama dengan topik yang akan saya kerjakan ini Prof.

Dosen:	Itu gak masalah. Topik bisa aja sama, tetapi, metode dan hasilnya berbeda. Yang diperoleh pasti bisa berbeda. Yang jelas, kamu harus bisa memberikan bukti-bukti nyata dalam penelitian kamu nantinya.
Linda:	Oo..Begitu. Mohon bantuannya ya Prof.
Dosen:	Pasti saya akan bantu kamu, karena saya paham benar potensi kamu dalam bidang studi ini.
Linda:	Baik kalau begitu. Saya kirimkan sekarang ya Prof.
Dosen:	Iya Lin. Saya tunggu.
Linda:	Terima kasih Prof.

5. We've Almost Graduated...

Two students are nearly finished with their S1 degrees, and are talking about what they will do after they graduate.

Adhonk:	Hey, gak terasa yah, udah 4 taun kita kuliah disini.
Budi:	Iya nih..kuliah jauh-jauh dari orangtua..eh..sekarang udah mau lulus. Seneng banget rasanya.
A:	Ngomong-ngomong ntar pas udah lulus, mau ngapain?
B:	Mmm..rencananya banyak. Tapi ada satu yang paling penting.
A:	Apaan tuh?
B:	Aku rencana mau lanjutin kuliah S2 di OZ.
A:	Wow, keren tuh..emangnya kamu mau kuliah dimana? Trus jurusannya apa?
B:	Rencananya sih di Australian National University, karena memang ayah ku ada rélasi disana. Aku ambil Teknik juga.

A: Bagus banget tuh.

B: Tapi itu kan baru rencana. Aku maunya langsung kerja. Tapi orangtuaku pengen aku kuliah lagi S2.

A: Setauku, kalo kita kuliah S2 di luar negri bisa sambil kerja paruh waktu kan?

B: Bisa sih, tapi bidang kerja nya terbatas.

A: Yang penting kan kerja, ada pengalaman baru dan dapet duit juga kan, hehehehe…

B: Iya bener juga yah.

A: Udahlah terusin aja kuliah S2 nya. Paling gak kita bisa nambah relasi, nambah pengetahuan, bisa banyak temen dari berbagai negara dan pastinya pengetahuan kita jadi lebih luas lagi kan?

B: Bener juga yah. Ngomong-ngomong kalo rencana kamu apa?

A: Aku sih péngén langsung kerja karena aku harus bantu orangtuaku untuk sekolahin adek ku yang paling bungsu.

B: Rencana kamu mau cari kerja dimana? Jakarta? Atau malah luar Jawa?

A: Aku rencana mau cari kerja di Jakarta aja. Aku sudah mulai ngirim2 CV ku ke beberapa perusahaan asing di Jakarta.

B: Waaahh, kerén banget tuh. Udah ada hasil belum?

A: Sudah. Minggu depan aku mau ke Jakarta untuk interview. Aku ngelamar di posisi Management Trainee, karna nantinya kalo lolos bisa langsung jadi junior manager.

B: Siiipp..lah. semoga kamu lolos yah.

A: Iya lah. Makasih ya.

Javanese Conversations

1. Getting Into Uni

Ayah: Kowe wis krungu saka UGM?

Putra: Sampun, Pak

Ayah: Hasile apa? Ketampa apa ora?

Putra: Alhamdulillah Pak, Kula ketampi.

Ayah: Waaahh Bapak seneng banget krungu kabar kuwi. Selamat ya Nak. (Dad kisses his son on the cheek and hugs him.)

Putra: Matur nuwun nggih Pak, Menika sedaya amargi saking donganipun Bapak kaliyan Ibu.

Ayah: Sing mesthi, merga kowe sinau tenanan sakdurunge ujian masuk UGM...(Dad calls Mom to come.) Ibu! Putra ketampa néng UGM.

Ibu: (Comes in from kitchen.) Waaah selamat ya Nak. (Mom hugs her son.)

Putra: (Emotionally touched) Nggih Ibu, matur nuwun sanget, menika sedaya saking donganipun Bapak lan Ibu.

Ibu: Iki kudu dirayakake,Pak.

Ayah: Iya Bu. Acara syukuran wae. Ngundang tangga-tangga.

Ibu: Acarane dina apa ya Pak?

Ayah: Sésuk minggu ngarep wae, pas dina minggu.

Putra: Mboten isah dipunrayakaken Pak, Bu. Langkung sae artanipun kagem nambahi biaya kuliah mawon, pripun?

Ayah: Iha ngapa kok ngono, Nak? Maksude Bapak bén tangga-tangga ngerti, nék putrane Bapak ketompo kuliah néng UGM.

Putra: Mboten kémawon lah Pak, kula mboten purun dirayaaken.

Ibu: Ya wis lah Pak, ora sida wae.

Ayah: Terus kapan mulai kuliahe Nak?

Putra: Kalih minggu malih Pak. Pas dinten Senin.

Ibu: Kudu daftar ulang ora Nak?

Putra: Nggih Bu, mbénjang kula badhe dhateng kampus kangge daftar ulang, sekaliyan ningali jadwal orientasi mahasiswa énggal.

Ayah: Sésuk Bapak ngeterke néng kampus ya, Nak?

Ibu: Ibu ya péngén melu ya Nak.

Putra: Mboten usahlah Pak, Bu. Kersanipun mbenjang kula piyambak wonten kampus.

Ayah: O iya, sidane kowe ketampa neng Fakultas apa Nak? Biologi apa pertanian?

Putra: Kadhos kersanipun Bapak, kula ketampi wonten fakultas Biologi.

Ayah: Ya apiklah Nak.

Ibu: Pesene Ibu.. sinau sing sregep ya Nak, bén mengko bijimu apik lan cépét rampung kuliahe.

Putra: Nggih Bu. Matur nuwun nggih Bu, matur nuwun nggih Pak.

Ayah: Iya, Nak.

2. New Student on Campus

Siswa Lama:	Hei, piye kabare?
Siswi Baru:	Hei, kabarku apik-apik wae.
S. Lama:	Mbak, mahasiswa anyar ta?
S. Baru:	Iya. Mas uga?
S. Lama:	Aku wis taon keloro.
S. Baru:	Néng Fakultas Psikologi?
S. Lama:	Dudu. Jurusanku Sastra.
S. Baru:	Kelas iki pilihan utawa wajib?
S. Lama:	Kanggo murid jurisan sastra iki pelajaran pilihan.
S. Baru:	Kanggoku iki wajib ya.
S. Lama:	Kesanne Mbak ora gelem mélu.
S. Baru:	Ya, betul.
S. Lama:	Kenapa? Dosen iki kondang lan apik, menarik. Kabeh murid seneng neng kelase. Mungkin semester mengko kowe uga seneng.
S. Baru:	Aku ora pati seneng karo materine. Kanggoku iki mboseni.
S. Lama:	Durung tau melbu kuliah iki ta, Mbak?
S. Baru:	Uwis, Mas. Iki sing kaping loro. Mungkin aku kurang paham materine.

S. Lama:	Is<u>a</u> uga kaya ngono. Men<u>awa</u> Mbak gelem, aku dhuwe catetan lam modal sing is<u>a</u> diwoco neng omah.
S. Baru:	Matur nuwun. Mengko aku ngopi ut<u>awa</u> tuku wae neng Gramedia.
S. Lama:	Ora usah Mbak. Mbak gowo wae bukune merga aku duwe loro bukune, sing siji dhuwéké k<u>anca</u>ku. Dhéwé(k)é ngenehake buku kuwi kanggo aku.
S. Baru:	Kapan aku is<u>a</u> oleh bukune?
S. Lama:	Mengko setelah rampung kuliah iki ya, Mbak.
S. Baru:	Ya wis. Matur nuwun y<u>a</u> Mas.
S. Lama:	Y<u>a</u>, Mbak p<u>a</u>dh<u>a</u>-p<u>a</u>dh<u>a</u>.

3. Caught Cheating

(During a test, Andy is busy looking on his mobile phone.)

Dosen:	(Having caught him red-handed, he approaches Andy's desk.) Eeehhmmm... isih ng<u>apa</u> kowe?
Andi:	(Afraid) Oh mboten men<u>apa</u>-men<u>apa</u> Pak. Menik<u>a</u> wonten sms mlebet.
Dosen:	Endi? Aku péngén ndelok.
Andi:	Sampun, Pak. Menik<u>a</u> sms saking pacar kul<u>a</u>.
Dosen:	Sing Bener? Soale két mau aku ndelok kowe mesti nyekel hp padahal kowe isih ujian.

Andi:	Ah, Bapak menika. Kula mboten menapa-menapa kok Pak.
Dosen:	Mugakna nék kowe ora kenapa-kenapa aku pengen ndelok hpmu saiki, Endi?
Andi:	(Afraid because he's been caught) Aduh, modar aku.
Dosen:	Nah, tenan to kowe ketauan nyonto. Kabeh jawaban ana neng hpmu.
Andi:	Mboten, Pak. Kula mboten gadhah maksud nyonto pas ujian.
Dosen:	Ora nduwe maksud kepiye? Wis cetho kowe nulis kabéh neng hpmu bab materi ujian dina iki.
Andi:	Mboten Pak. Bapak klentu.
Dosen:	Wislah. Kowe ora oléh ngerjakake ujian iki manéh, lan kowe ora lulus pelajaran iki.
Andi:	Pak, nyuwun pangapunten Pak. Kula nyonto amargi mboten sempet sinau, Pak. Kula wonten kathah pedamelan ing griya. Mohon dipunmaklumi, Pak.
Dosen:	Ora isa. Kowe ora lulus pelajaran iki. Mengko kowe isa ngulang neng semester péndék. (Takes Andy's test.)
Andi:	(Leaves the classroom.)

4. Talk with a Professor

Prof: Linda, topik kanggo tugas akhirmu endi?
Aku durung nampa.

Linda: Aduh Prof, nyuwun pangapunten, kula taksih bingung menika.

Prof: Bingung kenapa?

Linda: Amargi wonten topik-topik ingkang menarik kangge kula.

Prof: Waah, apik Linda. Berarti kowe serius lan bener-bener paham apa sing meh dadi bahan penelitianmu.

Linda: Inggih, Prof. Nanging kula taksih kesulitan kagem milih topik pundi ingkang paling cocok.

Prof: Coba kowe wenehke topik-topik kuwi néng aku. Mengko awa(k)édhéwé isa diskusi kanggo milih topik apa sing paling cocok.

Linda: Inggih Prof. Kula enggal ngirim email siang menika.

Prof: Setelah kuwi, aku uga arep ngenéhi kowe naséhat supaya kowe luwih gampang milih.

Linda: Sejatosipun sampun wonten topik ingkang paling kula raosi. Ananging kula pikir radi sulit kagem ngempalakén data-datanipun, Prof.

Prof: Kowe rasah kuatir, merga aku yakin ora ana data-data sing ra mungkin digoléki.

Linda: Sakliyanipun menika, uga wonten réncang ingkang topikipun radi mirip kaliyan topik ingkang kula badhe garap menika, Prof.

Prof:	Kuwi ora masalah. Topik isa wae padha, nanging metode lan hasile bédha. Sing jelas, kowe kudu isa ngenehi bukti nyata neng penelitianmu.
Linda:	Oo, mekaten. Nyuwun tulung dipunbiyantu, Prof.
Prof:	Aku mesti nulungi kowe merga aku ngerti tenan potensimu neng bidang iki.
Linda:	Inggih menawa makaten. Kula kirimaken dhateng Prof sakmenika nggih?
Prof:	Iya Lin, tak tunggu.
Lin:	Matur sumbah nuwun, Prof.

5. Almost Graduated

Aldri:	Hei, ora kerasa ya, wis 4 tahun awa(k)édhéwé néng kéné.
Bambang:	Iya ki . . . kuliah adho-adoh saka wong tuwa je..ee..saiki wis méh lulus. Seneng banget rasane . . a . . .
Aldri:	Ngomong-ngomong mengko pas wis lulus meh ngapa?
Bambang:	Mmm.. rencanane akéh. Tur ana siji sing paling penting.
Aldri:	Apa kuwi?
Bambang:	Aku rencanane meh ngelanjutake kuliah S2 neng Australia.
Aldri:	Wow. Kerén kuwi...emange kowe méh kuliah néng endi? Trus, jurusane apa?
Bambang:	Rencanane sih neng Australian National University, merga pancen bapakku duwe relasi neng kono. Aku uga njukuk Teknik.

Aldri:	Apik banget kuwi.
Bambang:	Tur kuwi kan isih rencana. Aku sih geleme langsung nyambut gawe. Tur wong tuwaku péngén aku kuliah manéh S2.
Aldri:	Sakngertiku, nék awa(k)edhewe kuliah S2 neng luar negeri isa karo kerja paruh waktu ta?
Bambang:	Isa sih, tur jenis kerjane terbatas.
Aldri:	Sing penting kan kerja, ana pengalaman anyar lan uga oleh duit.. he he he..
Bambang:	Iya, bener kuwi.
Aldri:	Wis lah, terusna wae kuliah S2-né. Paling ora kowe isa nambah relasi, nambah pengetahuan, nambah kanca akeh saka macem-macem negara, lan mestine wawasan awa(k)edhewe dadi luwih jembar ta?
Bambang:	Bener kuwi. Ngomong-ngomong nek rencanamu dhewe piye?
Aldri:	Aku sih pengen langsung nyambut gawe merga aku kudu mbantu wong tuwaku nyekolahke adikku sing paling ragil.
Bambang:	Rencanamu meh golek gawean neng endi? Jakarta? Apa malah luar Jawa?
Aldri:	Aku renacanane pengen golek gawéan neng Jakarta wae. Aku wis mulai ngirim-ngirim CV-ku neng perusahaan asing neng Jakarta.
Bambang:	Waaahh..kerén tenan kuwi. Wis ana hasile durung?

Aldri: Uwis. Minggu ngarep aku meh neng Jakrta kanggo tés wawancara. Aku ngelamar posisi Management Trainee, merga mengko nék wis lolos isa langsung dadi junior managér.

Bambang: Siiipp..lah. Muga-muga kowe lolos yah.

Aldri: Iyo lah. Matur nuwun ya.

19. English Translations of Conversations

1. Getting into College

Dad:	Did you hear yet from UGM?
Son:	Yes, Dad.
Dad:	What's the news/verdict? Have you been accepted or not?
Son:	Thank God I was accepted.
Dad:	Woo hoo.., I'm very happy to hear that. Congratulations, son. (Dad kisses his son on the cheek and hugs him.)
Son:	Thanks, Dad. It's all because of you and Mom's prayers.
Dad:	It's certainly because you studied hard before the UGM entrance exam. (Dad calls Mom.) Mom/Dear! Your son was accepted into UGM.
Mom:	(Coming from the kitchen) Wow, congratulations, Son.
Son:	(Touched) Yes, Mom. Thank you so much. It's all because of you and Dad's prayers.
Mom:	We should celebrate this Dear.
Dad:	Yes, dear we should. Just a little get-together to give thanks – we'll invite the neighbors.
Mom:	What day will it be, Dear?
Dad:	Sometime next week – on Sunday.
Son:	There's no need to celebrate Mom. It would be better to use the money to help pay for tuition. How about it/Don't you think?
Dad:	Now why do you say that Son? I want one so that the neighbors know that my son was accepted into UGM.
Son:	Don't bother Dad. I don't want a celebration.
Mom:	It's settled Dear. We won't have one.
Dad:	Well then, when do you start college/classes Son?
Son:	In two weeks Dad – on Monday.

Mom:	Don't you have to go back for registration?
Son:	Yes Mom. Tomorrow I'm going to campus again for registration, and to look at the schedule for new student orientation.
Dad:	Tomorrow I'll take you to campus okay?
Mom:	Yes, and I'll go with you.
Son:	There's no need Dad, Mom. Let me just go to campus later by myself.
Dad:	Okay fine. So what Faculty were you accepted into Son?
Son:	Like I had hoped Dad – I was accepted by the Faculty of Biology/Biology Department.
Dad:	That's great, Son.
Mom:	My message/advice is to study hard so that later your grades are good and you finish college quickly.
Son:	Yes, Mom. For sure. Thank you Mom, thank you Dad.
Dad:	Okay, Son.
Mom:	Yes, Son. I'll always pray for you.

2. New Student on Campus

Old Student:	Hello. How's it going?
New Student:	Hi. Just fine.
Old:	You're a new student, aren't you?
New:	Yes. You too?
Old:	I'm already in second year.
New:	In the Faculty of Psychology?
Old:	No. My major is art.
New:	Is this class an elective or required?

Old:	For students majoring in art this is an elective course.
New:	For me it's a requirement.
Old:	It sounds like you don't want to take it...
New:	Yeah, that's right.
Old:	Why? The professor is famous, good, and interesting. All the students like the class. Maybe later in the semester you'll like it too.
New:	I don't really like the material in the lectures. It makes me bored.
Old:	You haven't taken this course before have you?
New:	I have. This is my second time. Maybe I don't understand the material very well.
Old:	It could be like that. If you want, I have a few notebooks and modules that you can read at home.
New:	Thank you. Later I'll photocopy or buy them at Gramedia.
Old:	There's no need. You can just borrow the books, because I have two (sets), one are my friend's. He gave them to me.
New:	When can I get the books?
Old:	Later after the class is finished, okay?
New:	All right then. Thanks, yeah.
Old:	Don't mention it.

3. Student Caught Cheating on a Test

Andi:	(Andi is busy looking for answers on his mobile phone.)
Professor:	(Catches Andi cheating red-handed, and approaches Andy's desk.) Uuuhh huum, What are you up to?
Andi:	(Afraid) Uh, nothing sir. I got an sms.
Professor:	Where? I want to see.
Andy:	Don't sir. It's an sms from my girlfriend.

Professor:	Oh really? The thing is, from before, I've seen you always hold your phone while you are taking the test.
Andy:	Ah, c'mon professor, just let it go. I wasn't doing anything.
Professor:	In that case, if you really weren't doing anything, I want to see your mobile phone now. Where is it?
Andy:	(He's afraid because he's been caught). Crap, I'm dead.
Professor:	Well now, you've been caught cheating. All of the answers are on your mobile phone.
Andy:	No professor. I wasn't going to cheat during the test.
Professor:	You weren't going to do what? It's already clear you put everything about the material on today's exam on your phone.
Andy:	No professor. You're wrong.
Professor:	It's over! You are not allowed to re-take today's test, and you won't receive credit for this course.
Andy:	Professor. I'm sorry sir. I cheated because I didn't have time to study. I had a lot of work to do at home. Please understand.
Professor:	I can't. You won't receive credit for this course. Later you can repeat it during summer semester. (Takes the test.)

4. Talk with a Professor

Professor:	Linda, where is the last topic/paper I assigned? I haven't received it yet.
Linda:	Oh Professor, I'm so sorry, but I'm still confused.
Professor:	Why are you confused?
Linda:	Because there are several topics that I'm interested in.
Professor:	Wow, that's great Linda. It means you are serious and really understand what it is that will be the material for your research.
Linda:	Yes professor, but it's still difficult to determine what (topic) is most appropriate.

Professor :	Try to give me the several topics first. Then, we can discuss choosing one that is the most appropriate.
Linda:	Yes professor. I'll send them by email this afternoon.
Professor:	After that, I'll give you suggestions so that it makes it easier for you to choose.
Linda:	Actually, there's already one that I want to do the most, but I think it will be quite difficult to collect the data, Professor.
Professor:	You shouldn't worry because I am sure there isn't any data which is impossible to get.
Linda:	Besides that, there are also several friends whose topics are really similar to this topic that I would do, Professor.
Professor:	That's not a problem. The topics can be the same, but, the methodology and results different. The data which is obtained will certainly be different. What's clear is that you have to be able to provide evidence/obvious proof in your research eventually.
Linda:	Oh, I see. I'll really need your help, okay Professor?
Professor:	I'll certainly help you, because I truly appreciate your potential in this field of study.
Linda:	That's good. I'll send it to you now, Professor.
Professor:	Okay, Lin. I look forward to it.
Linda:	Thank you Professor.

5. We've Almost Graduated ...

Adhonk:	Hey. You know, it doesn't feel like we've been here for 4 years.
Budi:	Yeah, here.. going to college far away from our parents, shit. Now we're already going to graduate. It feels real good.
Adhonk:	By the way, what are you going to do after we've graduated?
Budi:	Hmm... I've got lots of plans. But there's one that's most important.
Adhonk:	What is it?

Budi:	I plan to continue studying a Master's degree in Australia.
Adhonk:	Wow. That's cool…Do you know for sure where you're going to school or what your major will be?
Budi:	My plan is for Australian National University, because my dad has connections there. I'm going to take engineering too.
Adhonk:	That's great.
Budi:	But it's just a plan you know. I want to work right away. But my parents want me to go get a Master's.
Adhonk:	As far as I know, if we go to get our Master's overseas, we can do it while we work part-time, right?
Budi:	You can, but the kinds of jobs are very limited.
Adhonk:	What's important, you know, is that it's work. You'll have a new experience and get paid too, ha ha…
Budi:	Yeah, that's true.
Adhonk:	Just go on and get your Master's. What's important is you can gain connections, knowledge, and have lots of friends from different countries.
Budi:	That's true too. By the way, what are your plans?
Adhonk:	I want to work right away because I have to help my parents put my brother, who's the youngest in our family, through school.
Budi:	Where do you plan to find work? Jakarta? Or outside Java instead?
Adhonk:	I just plan to find work in Jakarta. I've already started sending my CV to a few foreign companies in Jakarta.
Budi:	Great/Right on. I hope you graduate.
Adhon:	Yeah, for sure. Thanks.

20. NGO LIFE

Please review Unit 1: Words You Already Know before continuing. The units Village Life, Medical, and Military will also be of particular interest to NGOs.

(go) according to plan	(berjalan) menurut rencana
after action report	laporan setelah kegiatan
agriculture	pertanian
aid (food, medical)	bantuan
AID	Badan Pembangunan Internasional
amputee	orang yg dipotong lengan atau kakinya
area of responsibility	daerah tanggung jawab
artificial arm	lengan palsu
artificial leg	kaki palsu
beneficial	manfaat
beneficiary	ahli waris
bio-degradable	barang yang mudah terurai alami
blind	buta, tuna nétra (formal)
broken/broken down	rusak
builder	tukang bangunan
busy/peak period	sibuk/masa sibuk
commercial sex worker	PSK-pekerjaan seks komersial
community involvement (in a work project/bee)	gotong-royong
convention (agreement)	perjanjian, persetujuan
consumption	pengunaan
contractor, sub contractor	kontraktor
contribution	sumbangan
cooperative (co-op)	(toko) koperasi
course of action	tindakan
cultivate	menanami
damaged	kerusakan
deadline	batas waktu
deal with	berhadapan dengan
deaf	tuli

debris	reruntuhan, puing
delay, delayed	tunda, tertunda
destroyed	musnah, dimusnah
disabled (person)	difabel
dispose (throw away)	membuang
donations	derma, sumbangan
down (system is down)	tidak berfungsi
earthquake	gempa bumi
emergency	darurat
energy	tenaga
environment	lingkungan
environmentally friendly	ramah lingkungan
evacuation	pengungsian
evacuee	pengungsi
farming cooperative	Koperasi petani
fee, charge	biaya
fire extinguisher	alat pemadam kebakaran
first aid kit	P3K/PPPK (pé tiga ka)
flexible (schedule, attitude)	fleksibel
flood(ed)	(di)banjir(i)
food aid	bantuan makanan
fund-raising	penggalangan dana
fumes	asap, uap
garbage, trash	sampah
go-ahead, green light	restu, izin
handicapped	cacat
handicrafts	pertukangan, kerajinan tangan
high standards	standar tinggi
(we work to high standards; we expect high standards from our staff)	
horticulture	hortikultura, ilmu perkebunan
hire	séwa (menyewa)
interview	wawancara
insurance	asuransi
incineration plant	pembangkit listrik tenaga sampah
in operation/working	dalam tugas, berfungsi

in the field	di lapangan
integrated farming system	sistem pertanian terpadu
land mine	ranjau
lay the foundation (for)	peletakan batu pertama
local hire (n)	pekerja lokal
logistics	logistik
livelihood	mata pencaharian
marketing	pemasaran
measure	tindakan (as in a step taken to prevent X)
medical aid	bantuan médis
memo	memo (same pron.)
mute	bisu
mutual cooperation/aid	gotong-royong (GR), kerjasama
natural disaster	bencana alam
natural resources	sumber daya
NGO	LSM
notice (on board, in office)	pengumuman
note - reminder	catatan pengingat
on the safe side	di sisi yang aman
on schedule	sesuai jadwal
on-site	di lokasi
on stand-by	siap sedia
orphanage	panti asuhan
orthopedic center	pusat bedah tulang
overtime	lembur
over budget	melebihi anggaran
phase (of a project)	tahapan
physical rehabilitation	pemulihan fisik
pilot project	proyek percontohan
POC (point of contact)	perwakilan
pollution	pencemaran, polusi
priority	prioritas
proposal	pengajuan
prosthetic	prostétik

ranching	peternakan
recommend	menyarankan
reconstruction	rékonstruksi
recycled	didaur ulang
refugee camps	tempat pengungsian
restoration	pemulihan
resume/curriculum vitae	daftar riwayat hidup
safety procedures	(tata)cara/prosedur keselamatan
seek refuge	cari/minta suaka
service call	layanan panggilan
sewage	kotoran, limbah
SITREP	laporan keadaan
staff meeting	rapat pegawai
standards (govt, int'l)	standar
suffering	penderitaan
supplier	pemasok
target (goal, aim)	sasaran, tujuan
target group (people)	sasaran kelompok
task force	gugus tugas
temporary	sementara
track record	rekam jejak
translator	penerjemah
volunteer	sukarélawan
volunteer work	kerja sukaréla
warranty, under warranty	garansi, masa garansi
waste water	limbah
water purification plant	instalasi penjernihan air
water table	air permukaan bawah tanah

Language & Culture Notes

1. Some of the most common NGOs operating in Indonesia include: Oxfam, Handicap International, Ausaid, the Red Cross, and Plan International.

2. Indonesia is prone to a number of natural disasters each year due to its geology, including volcanic eruptions, floods, tsunamis, earthquakes, and mudslides. Some of the most famous events in recent years include the tsunami of 2004, which devastated Aceh, the earthquake in Bantul, Yogyakarta in 2006, the eruptions of Mount Merapi in 2006 and 2010, and an earthquake that hit Padang in 2010. A major disaster caused by a combination of natural geology together with the gas industry's drilling practices are the mud geysers/hot mud flows that have wreaked havoc in eastern Java and continue to displace thousands of people around the Sidoarjo region of East Java, with no sign of abating. Needless to say, there will always be an abundance of work in Indonesia for relief/aid workers.

3. There is an ugly side to disaster relief that most expats and NGO hands are familiar with. People will try to get food aid and supplies for their neighborhoods, even when they don't really need them and other areas are in dire circumstances, going so far as to set up road blocks to vehicles delivering aid, and to harass Western associates for it. The UN (or an NGO) arrives on the tail of a disaster, and its workers proceed to drive around in their new one hundred thousand dollar SUVs on daily per diem rates and a budget that is grossly at odds with local conditions (of poverty). NGOs have to conduct needs assessments and interview potential recipients of aid projects and medical aid because if left to local government or the people themselves, there would be far too much fraud and abuse of the system.
For these reasons, it is important for an NGO field worker to have a grasp on the political, social and cultural dynamics in play in the region they will be working in, in order to be able to source correct and real data for aid dispersion.

4. Even a rudimentary knowledge of the local language will improve a foreigner's standing in the eyes of locals and establish trust much more quickly than using an interpreter. If one goes to a Javaneses village and says just a few words in Javanese, the local villagers suddenly open up and celebrate that you have taken the time to learn about their language and culture.

Indonesian Conversations

1. Prospective Aid Recipient

An amputee has already been selected from an initial interview with an NGO for a prosthetic arm. The man is now talking with the doctor.

Rudi: Dokter sekarang setelah tangan saya diamputasi, saya harus bagaimana?

Dokter: Saya minta Anda bersabar. Kami akan mencarikan tangan palsu untuk Anda.

Rudi: Apakah tangan palsu itu bisa berfungsi normal seperti tangan saya yang diamputasi, Dok?

Dok: Dengan tangan palsu itu Anda akan beraktivitas seperti biasa. Tetapi sebelumnya Anda harus latihan cara menggunakannya dengan benar.

Rudi: Seperti apa cara latihannya, Dok?

Dok: Nanti akan ada programnya. Anda akan mulai dari gerakan mudah dulu.

Rudi: Apakah harga tangan palsu mahal?

Dok: Jangan khawatir, Anda tidak perlu membayar tangan palsu itu.

Rudi: Lalu bagaimana, Dok?

Dok: Ada LSM yang nanti akan bantu membeli tangan palsu itu. Tangan palsu itu gratis bagi semua korban gempa bumi di Yogya.

Rudi: Jadi, kami tidak harus keluar uang, ya, Dok?

Dok: Tidak, Pak, tidak.

Rudi: Alhamdulillah.

2. Water Purification Project

An NGO worker meets with the Pak RT to discuss a water purification project for kampung.

LSM: Permisi, Pak. Saya datang kemari untuk membahas proyek air bersih bagi warga kampung ini.

Pak RT: Wah kebetulan, karena gempa bumi menyebabkan sumur di desa ini jadi kering.

LSM: Jadi biasanya di mana warga mencari air resik, Pak?

Pak RT: Ya di sekitar sini ada sungai kecil. Tapi ya airnya tidak begitu bersih. Banyak warga yang diare. Tapi ya bagaimana lagi, itu sumber air bersih yang hanya ada di dekat sini.

LSM: Jadinya kami akan membantu warga di sini agar punya persediaan air bersih, kalau diijinkan.

Pak RT: Oh pasti, Mas. Lalu bagaimana caranya mencari air bersih?

LSM: Kami akan membangun bak penampungan air di RT ini. Lalu air bersih akan disalurkan dari sumber mata air di gunung dengan saluran.

Pak RT: Kira-kira butuh waktu berapa lama, ya?

LSM: Paling lambat satu bulan untuk menyelesaikan bak penampungan air itu. Tapi kami butuh bantuan warga RT juga dalam pembangunan bak itu.

Pak RT: Warga sini siap membantu.

3. After the Quake

NGO workers visit Bantul after an earthquake to assess the damage and see what is needed.

LSM: Mas saya dari LSM, mau tanya kira-kira warga kampung ini masih membutuhkan bantuan apa, ya?

Warga: Wah, kalau bantuan kami menerima apa saja yang Mas beri. Tapi kalau disuruh memilih, kami butuh bahan material untuk membangun rumah.

LSM: Kalau makanan sudah tidak butuh ya?

Warga: Kebetulan kalau makanan kami sudah punya persediaan yang cukup dari LSM lain, Mas. Ya cukup lah untuk persediaan satu bulan.

LSM: Jadi butuh bahan material seperti misalnya pasir, semen, kayu, seperti itu ya Mas?

Warga: Iya, dan juga alat-alat pertukangan seperti sekop, palu, dan cangkul.

LSM: Kira-kira warga di sini akan membangun berapa rumah ya?

Warga: Di desa ini ada sekitar 40 rumah yang rusak dan bangunan sekolah kami runtuh.

LSM: Kalau kondisi jalan, rusak tidak?

Warga : Jalan di sini masih baik, Mas.

LSM: Kalau begitu mungkin sekitar tiga hari lagi kami akan datang membawa bahan material yang dibutuhkan.

Warga: Terima kasih, Mas. Saya tunggu bantuannya datang.

Javanese Conversations

1. Prospective Aid Recipient

Rudi: Dokter, sakmenika saksampunipun aksa kula dipunamputasi, kula kedah pripun?

Dok: Kula nyuwun panjengan ingkang sabar. Kawula sedanten badhe madosaken aksa palsu kagem panjenengan.

Rudi: Punapa aksa palsu menika saged kados normalipun aksa kula sakderengipun diamputasi, Dok?

Dok: Mawi aksa palsu menika, panjenengan saged ngelajengaken aktivitas kados biasa. Ananging sakderengipun panjenengan kedah latihan cara migunakakén ingkang leres.

Rudi: Kedah menapa latihanipun, Dok?

Dok: Mangke wonten programipun. Panjenengan mulai saking gerakan ingkang gampil rumiyin.

Rudi: Punapa reginipun aksa palsu awis?

Dok: Sampun kuatir, panjenengan mboten perlu maringi arto kagem aksa palsu menika.

Rudi: Lajeng pripun, Dok?

Dok: Wonten LSM ingkang mangke kedah mbiyantu mundhut aksa palsu menika. Aksa palsu menika gratis kagem korban gempa bumi ing Yogya.

Rudi: Dadosipun, kula mboten kedhah medhal arta, Dok?

Dok: Mboten, Pak, mboten.

Rudi: Alhamdulillah.

2. Water Purification Project

LSM: Nuwun séwu, Pak. Kula tindak dhateng mriki kagem bahas proyek pengadaan air bersih kagem wergi kampung menika.

Pak RT: Wah kaleresan, amargi gempa bumi nyebabaken sumur ing desa menika dados asat.

LSM: Dados, biasanipun ing pundi wergi madosi toya resik?

Pak RT: Nggih, ing sekitar mriki wonten kali alit. Ananging toyanipun mboten resik sanget. Kathah wergi ingkang pikantuk sakit diare. Ananging kados pundi malih, menika namung wontenipun sumber toya resik ingkang celak mriki.

LSM: Dadosipun, kawula sedanten badhe mbiyantu wergi mriki supaya gadhah persediaan air bersih, menawi dipun paringi ijin.

Pak RT: Oh, menika mesti, Mas. Lajeng pripun caranipun supados toya resik?

LSM: Kawula sedanten badhe mbangun tandon toya ing RT mriki. Lajeng toya resik kedhah dialiraken saking sumber toya ing wredi ngagem saluran.

Pak RT: Kinten-kinten perlu wektu pinten dangu nggih?

LSM: Paling dangu setunggal wulan kagem ngerampungaken tandon toya menika. Ananging kawula sedanten betah bantuan saking wergi RT kagem pembangunan tandon menika.

Pak RT: Wergi mriki siap mbiyantu, Pak.

3. After the Quake

LSM: Mas, aku s<u>aka</u> LSM, arep takon kira-kira warga kampung kéné isih butuh bantuan <u>apa</u> ya?

Warga: Wah, nék bantuan <u>apa</u> wae ditampa, Mas. Tapi nek oleh milih, awa(k)édhéwé néng kene butuh bahan material kanggo bangun omah.

LSM: Nék panganan wis ora butuh ya?

Warga: Nek panganan, awakedhewe wis duwe persediaan sing cukup s<u>aka</u> LSM li<u>ya</u>, Mas. Ya cukuplah kanggo persediaan sewulan.

LSM: Dadi butuhe bahan material k<u>aya</u> misale pasir, semen, kayu, kaya ng<u>ana</u> kuwi ya, Mas?

Warga: Iyo, lan ug<u>a</u> alat-alat tukang kaya sekop, palu, lan pacul.

LSM: Kir<u>a</u>-kir<u>a</u> warga neng kene arep mbangun pirang omah y<u>a</u>?

Warga: Neng ndes<u>a</u> iki <u>ana</u> sekitar 40 omah sing rusak lan gedung sekolah sing ambruk.

LSM: Nek kondisi dalan, rusak ora?

Warga: Dalan neng kene isih apik, Mas.

LSM: Nek ngono mungkin sekitar telung dine manéh awakedhewe tek<u>a</u> mréné ngg<u>awa</u> bahan material sing dibutuhke.

Warga: Matur nuwun, Mas. Taktunggu bantuane tek<u>a</u>.

20. English Translation of Conversations

1. Prospective Aid Recipient

Rudi: Doctor, now that my arm is amputed, what do I have to do?

Doctor: I ask you to be patient. We are going to find a prosthetic arm for you.

Rudi: Will the arm be able to function normally like my arm that was amputed, Doc?

Doc: With the arm you will take part in activities like usual. But before that you have to practice how to use it correctly.

Rudi: Like what kind of practice, Doc?

Doc: Later there will be a program. You will start with simple movement first.

Rudi: Is the price of a false limb expensive?

Doc: Don't worry, you don't need to pay for it.

Rudi: Then how will it be paid for?

Doc: There is an NGO that will help you buy the false limb. These false limbs are free for all the earthquake victims in Jogja.

Rudi: So, we don't have to spend money, right Doc?

Doc: No, no.

Rudi: Thank God.

2. Water Purification Project

NGO: Excuse me, Sir. I came here to discuss the clean water project for the people of this village/neighborhood.

Village Head: Oh it's perfect timing, because the earthquake caused the wells in the village to run dry.

NGO: So usually where do the people get clean water?

Head: Well there's a small river around here. But you know the water isn't that clean. A lot of people have diarrhea. But what else can we do? —It's the only clean well/watering spot there is near here.

NGO:	That's why we're going to help the people here to have a clean water supply, if it is approved.
Head:	Oh sure. Then how exactly will we get clean water?
NGO:	We'll build a water (collection) tank at your place. Then, clean water will channeled from the headwaters/source in the mountains with canals.
Head:	And about how much time will you need?
NGO:	At most one month to finish the water tank. But we'll need the help of the villagers too for the building of it.
Head:	The people here are ready to help.

3. After the Quake

NGO:	Sir, I'm from an NGO. I want to ask what kind of help you think the people of this area/village still need?
Villager:	Oh, as far as help, we'll take anything that you give us. But if I was forced to choose, we need building materials to make houses.
NGO:	As for food, you don't need it anymore, right?
Villager:	(Coincidentally), we happened to have received a sufficient supply of food from another NGO. It's enough for a month's supply.
NGO:	So you need materials, for example like sand, cement, wood – like that right?
Villager:	Yes, and also (builders') tools like shovels, hammers, and hoes.
NGO:	About how many houses will the people here build do you think?
Villager:	In this village there are around 40 houses that are damaged and the school building collapsed.
NGO:	Are the streets damaged or not?
Villager:	The streets here are still good sir.

NGO: In that case, maybe in around three days we'll come again and bring the building material that you need.

Villager: Thank you sir. I'll wait for the help to arrive.

21. MILITARY LIFE

Please review the military vocab in Unit 1: 'Words You Already Know,' before continuing. A Javanese word list is not included in the following vocabulary section, other units in the text contain Javanese useful for some military ops.

INDIVIDUAL & SQUAD GEAR

ammo/bullets	peluru
BDUs	*PDL (Pé Dé éL)
backpack	ransél
bayonet	sangkur
belt	kopel
beret	barét
binoculars	teropong, verkeker (Dutch)
boots	sepatu bot
bullet proof vest	rompi anti peluru
canteen	pélplés
compass	kompas
dress uniform	*PKL (pé ka él)
fatigues	*PDLT (Pé Dé él Té)
field jacket	jakét tempur
first aid kit	PPPK (pé tiga ka)
flashlight	sénter
gas mask	masker
gloves	sarung tangan
GPS	GPS
grenade	granat
handgun	senapan tangan
helmet	hélm
jungle hat	topi rimba
machete	golok
magazine (rifle)	magazin
magazine pouches	tas magazin
map	péta
mosquito net	kelambu
mosquito lotion	losion anti nyamuk, autan (brand)
poncho	ponco
radio	radio
rations	ransum
rifle	senapan, senjata
ropes	tali
shoe polish	semir sepatu
sling	tali sandang

300

socks	kaos kaki
camp stove	kompor lapangan
sunglasses	kacamata hitam, sunglas
tshirt	kaos dalam
uniform	seragam
web gear	dragrim

GENERAL VOCABULARY

AAA	Arhanud / meriam anti udara
academy	akademi
accurate	jitu
address (v), call	panggil
adjust	mengatur
advance, go forward	maju
after action report	laporan kemudian tindakan
air-to-air	antar udara
aircraft carrier	kapal induk
Air Attache	Atu, Atud (Attase udara)
Air Force	AU (ah-u) Angkatan Udara
Air Force Base (AFB)	pangkalan udara (Lanud)
alert (n)	siaga
antenna	antena
area of operations (AO)	daerah operasi (daop)
area of responsibility (AOR)	daerah tanggungjawab
armored	berlapis baja
Army	AD-Angkatan Darat
artillery	artileri
attache - military	Atmil (Attase militer)
attack (v, n)	mengenang, senang, peperangan
attention!	hormat!
attitude	sikap
attitude adjustment	memperbaiki sikap
at ease!	istirahat, gerak!
at will (fire at will!)	semau kamu
AWOL	pergi tanpa ijin
azimuth	azimut

barracks	barak, graha (militer, prajurit), asrama
barrage	brondongan
barricade	barikade
base	pangkalan, kesatrian
basic training	pelatihan dasar, PLP
battalion	batalion
bayonet	sangkur

be stationed	bertugas
bearing (degrees)	baringan
billet (v)	mengawakkan
billeting	penginapan, wisma tamu
briefing	penerangan ringkas
bunker	bunker
calm down!	tenang
camouflage	samaran, kamu
captain	kaptén
cargo, a load	muatan
carry out (an order, plan)	melaksanakan
carry out (an operation)	mengadakan
chain of command	rantai komando
checkpoint	pos pemeriksaan
citizen	warga
civil affairs	urusan sipil
civil defense	hansip
civilian	orang sipil
copy/clear/got it?	paham
close air support	rapat bantuan tembakan udara
code	sandi
combat	tempur
combat engineer	zeni tempur
combat training	PLP
command	komando
command & control	penguasaan dan pengawas
command post	pos komando (POSKO)
communications	perhubungan
company	kompi
conceal	menyembunyikan
concealed (hidden)	tersembunyi
copy (on radio)	ganti
corporal	korpral
corps	korps
(corps of) engineers	(korps) zéni
counterinsurgency/guerilla	contragerilya
counter measures	pengelak /alat pengelak
court martial n, (v)	mahmil(kan)
'cover me'	lindungi ku
crew, personnel	awak
cut off (communications)	terputus

deck (of ship)	geladak
defense	pertahanan
degrees (5 degrees right)	sudut (5 kanan)
demolitions	demolisi
Department of Defense	Departemén Pertahanan
desertion	desérsi
destroy	hancurkan
detached to another unit	(men)détasir, ditasering
detachment	détasemén
dig	menggali
direction	arah
discipline	disiplin
dismissed/fall out!	bubar!
dive/go under water	menyelam, selam
division	divisi
drill	baris, barisan
drill leader	pengaba
duty	tugas
enemy	musuh
engineer	zéni
enlisted ranks	tamtam
EOD	Jihandak, EOD
esprit de corps	semangat korp, semangat militer
fall back on (a spot)	kembali
fire!	témbak!
fire support	bantuan tembakan
flag	bendéra
flag ceremony	upacara bendéra
flak	témbakan penangkis udara
forces	pasukan
formation	barisan, jajaran
foxhole	lubang
frequency	frékuénsi
friendly (allied) forces	pasukan sekutu
front line	garis delapan
FTX	latihan medan
garrison	garnisun
general	jenderal
get back/stay back!	mundur!
get down! (on ground)	tiarap!
get down (on your knees)!	berlutut!
get off!/out! (the truck)	turun!

303

get out/quit/get a discharge	berhentikan
give a briefing	memberi taklimat
go to/adopt an alert condition	menerapkan
guard (n., v.)	jaga, menjaga
Guard/Reserves, (part-timer)	pasukan cadangan, (bertugas paruh waktu)
hard-ass, a tough SOB	keras kepala, bréngsék tangguh
heavy weapons	senapan otomatis
high explosive	berdaya ledak tinggi
hold out (against an attack)	tahan, bertahan
high ranking officer	pati (perwira tinggi)
honor	kehormatan
honorably discharged	diberhentikan dengan hormat
housing-military/family	perumahan militer
HQ (Headquarters)	marbes (Markas Besar)
Indonesian Military	TNI
in charge (of)	pimpin
infantry	infanteri
insignia	tanda
inspection	pemeriksaan
instructions, orders	juklak (petunjuk pelaksana)
intelligence	intelijen
interrogation	interogasi
join (the military)	masuk militer
joint forces	pasukan gabungan
joint training	latihan gabungan
jump (paratrooper) school	Sekolah Para
kill	membunuh
land (a plane)	mendaratkan
landing strip	landas udara
launch (v, n)	luncur, peluncuran
launch pad	landas peluncuran
leave (furlough)	cuti
be on leave	sedang cuti
shore leave	cuti darat
liaison	penghubung
lieutenant	letnan
lieutenant colonel	letnan kolonel/letkol
light weapons	senjata ringan
located	berada

major	mayor
march (n, v)	baris, berbaris
Marine Corps	Korps Marinir
martial law	UU darurat (emergency law)
MEDCAP	Program Keséhatan (sipil)
medic/Team Medic	médik/Bintara Keséhatan
member	anggota
mercenary	prajurit bayaran (lit. soldier for hire)
military academy	Akmil
(military) exercise	latihan (militer)
military leave	cuti
military parade	paradé militer
mine (landmine)	ranjau
sweep/clear mines	bersihkan ranjau
miss (a target)	luput
missile	rudal, misil
mission	misi
mobilization	mobilisasi
Morse code	sandi Morse
MOS/Job Specialty	spesialisasi jabatan militer
move! (out of the way)	minggir!
Navy	AL (Angkutan Laut)
NCO	bintara tinggi, sersan
observation	peninjauan
observation post, tower	rangun, tempat peninjauan
obstacle course	PKT
occupy	menduduki
officer	prawira, perwira
operations	operasi
orders (printed copy)	surat perintah
orders (on drill field)	aba-aba
orienteering/orientation	orientasi, 'wide games'
'over' (on radio)	ganti
part-timer in Guard, Reserves	prajurit paruh waktu pasukan cadangan
pass (n) (an overnight pass)	izin malam (overnight), izin keluar (day)
pavilion	balai
pilot	pilot
plane	kapal terbang
platoon	platon
position (n, v)	stéling
post (guard post)	pos

post, station, barracks	markas
POW	tawanan
power, energy	daya
power, force, staff	tenaga
promotion	kenaikan pangkat
provisions	bekal
psychological operations	operasi psikologis
pull-ups (n. – chin up)	restok (mantap)
push ups (n. – give me 10..)	tolak angkat
qualified	memenuhi syarat
quarantine (v., n.)	membarak, karantina
quarters	tangsi
radar	radar
raft	rakit
raid (v./n.)	penggerebakan
rank	pangkat
ranks (rank and file)	barisan
range (100 meters)	jarak (100 meter)
ready, readiness	(ke)samapta(an)
readiness test	uji kesiapan
rebel	pemberontak
rebellion, uprising	pemberontakan
reconnaissance	pengintaian
reception (radio)	penerimaan
regiment	résimén
report	laporan
Reserve (Forces) (& Guard)	(pasukan) cadangan
rescue (v.)	menyelamatkan, menolong
retire(ment)	pénsiun
retreat (v)	mundur
retreat ceremony	aubadé, penurunan bendéra
reveille	pengibaran bendéra
review (pass in -)	défilé, berparade
rogue elements in military	oknum-oknum militer
roll call	apél
round (of ammo)	butir
safety	aman
safety (on rifle)	pengaman
'safeties on'	tuas pengaman dipasang
sailor	pelaut
salute	berhormat
SAR	SAR (same pronunciation)

schedule	jadwal
scout (n)	séko, pengintai
senior NCO	bintara
sergeant	sersan
search	mencari-cari
security	keamanan
secured area (safe & secure)	di amankan, 'aman dan tenteram'
seize, take, capture	merebut
self discipline	disiplin diri
send	kirim
shelter	perlindungan
shrapnel	serpihan bom
sight (on weapon)	pembidik
signal	sinyal
signal corps	korps penghubung
signal strength (QSA, QRK)	kuatan sinyal
signal is good, clear	sinyal terang
SOI, SOP	SOP (es oh pé)
soldier	tentara, prajurit, serdadu
Special Forces	Pasukun khusus
Special Forces Indonesia	Kopassus
special warfare	peperangan khusus
squad	regu
squadron	skuadron
staff meeting	rapat staf
static (radio)	gangguan (udara)
strategy	stratégi
submarine	kapal selam
supervisor	penyelia
supplies	pasokan
surrender (v)	menyerah
surrounded	dikepung
surveillance	pengawasan
survival training	pelatihan ketahanan/bertahan hidup
switch, knob	tombol
tactical	taktis
take off (a plane)	lepas landas, keberangkatan
take prisoners	menangani tawanan
tank	tank
taps, retreat	taptu, aubadé
target	sasaran
task force	satgas (satuan tugas)
TDY	(di)-BKO-(kan) / penugasan sementara, detaséring

tent	ténda
tough (person)	tangguh
tracers	cahaya peluru
transmission (signal)	transmisi
transport	pengangkut
trench	parit
trigger	pemicu
tube	tabung
UCMJ	UU TNI
unit	(ke)satuan
volume (radio)	suara
keep watch, stay alert	menjaga, tetap waspada
watch (n: chief of watch)	pengawas
watch out!	awas!
weapon	senjata
win hearts and minds	merebut hati dan perhatian
wing	sayap
wings	wing (on uniform)

Language & Culture Notes

1. PDL stands for *Pakaian Dinas Lapangan*, literally battle dress uniform. For the fatigue uniform, a 'T' for *Tropis* - Tropical is added (PDLT). Sometimes, soldiers refer to BDUs/camo uniforms as PDLT as well, in which case the 'T' can mean "Tiger stripe." To date, the TNI still uses the 'tiger stripe' camouflage pattern, more common to Asian militaries. PKL stands for Pakaian Kebesaran Lengkap.

2. As in the U.S., there are two common paths to becoming an officer (*perwira/prawira*) in the *TNI*: ROTC - *Perwira Prajurit Karier*, or by attending military academy (*Akmil*). Most officers attend military academy.

3. All officer candidates attend 4 years of military academy before being commissioned as 2nd Lieutenants (*Letda*). Regardless of branch of service, all cadets attend the army's military academy (*Akmil*) in Magelang the first year. Army cadets continue there for 3 more years; the AF and Navy cadets move on to their respective academies (*AAU* in Yogya, *AAL* in Surabaya) for 3 years. Currently, they are not awarded degrees for education received at academy.

4. Over the course of their careers, officers will attend 5 schools: (1) military academy, (2) company commander course at branch school, (3) their respective branch Staff and Command School (*Sesko*) as majors or Lt. colonels, (4) Joint Senior Staff College (*Sesko TNI*) in Bandung as colonels, and finally (5) the National Resilience/Defense Institute (*Lemhannas*) in Jakarta as senior colonels or generals.

5. One of the best high schools in Indonesia is the military high school *SMA Taruna Nusantara*, located near *Akmil* in Magelang. Top middle school students from all over Indonesia are admitted. The educational demands of the school and close relationship with the military academies ensure that any student who wants to attend military academy and become an officer in one of the branches of TNI, or attend the police academy and become a member of *Polri*, will have an excellent chance at doing so. About 1/3 students at the school choose this course of action, others attend prestigious universities in Indonesia or go to school overseas.

6. A good way to learn Indonesian language pertinent to military operations is to watch one of the many older (often 'B-grade') Hollywood military/action movies that play nightly on Indonesian TV networks such as Global TV or Trans TV. Reading the Indonesian subtitles will substantially increase your vocabulary. (Although some of the subtitling is inaccurate, most of it is correct.)

7. In conversation 3 about a haircut, notice that the barber starts to give the customer a neck and shoulder massage at the end; not every barbershop will do this, but it is common, as it is throughout Asia. If you don't want the massage, simply do as the customer in the conversation does and politely decline.

Indonesian Conversations

1. Visit and Speech by an Air Force Sergeant

A USAF Sgt gives some opening remarks at a joint exercise/training event

Selamat siang. Hari ini saya mau memperkenalkan diri dulu, lalu bicara sedikit saja tentang kesatuan kami. Pangkat saya 'Master sergeant dalam bahasa Inggris. Itu seperti Sersan Satu – Sertu di AU Indonesia. Sebegai sersan, saya melakukan hal-hal yang biasanya dilakukan oleh sersan, seperti latihan keprajuritan, membuat rencana, mengawasi operasi harian, menyiapkan presentasi – seperti sekarang ini – kepada prawira tamu, memberi penerangan ringkas kepada awak pesawat tempur dan hal hal lainya.

Tanpa sersan, prawira tidak tahu apa pun yang harus mereka lakukan. Mungkin itu yang sebenarnya terjadi pada militer RI, sama seperti yang terjadi juga pada militer AS.

Kesatuan kami adalah kesatuan dengan prajurit yg ahli dalam hal logistik dan transportasi udara. Kami mengadakan operasi taktis di daerah Asia menggunakan sebanyak mungkin kapal terbang C-130. Kita bangga dengan kenyataan bahwa bilang kita bisa terbang di mana pun, kapan pun, dan kondisi apa pun. Saya sering pergi ke luar negeri, tapi tidak biasanya ke Indonesia. Jadi, saya tidak sabar bekerja bersama kalian semua di AU Indonesia dan saya juga berharap kita bisa belajar dari masing-masing, dan juga menikmati waktu yang ada bersama. Saya yakin bahwa latihan gabungan ini akan sukses. Terima kasih.

2. Two soldiers on Base

An Indonesian soldier talks to an American Sergeant, who is off-duty and in civies, on base. The Indonesian is also a Sgt.

Sersan RI: Halo. Tatonya bagus Mister.

Sersan AS: Terima kasih. Yang ini udah lama.

RI: Dapatnya di mana?

AS: Yang ini, di Thailand. Sekitar enam tahun lalu.

RI: Ada yang lainnya? Ma'af namaku Wisnu.
               Siapa nama Mister?

AS: Kenalkan. Nama saya Don. Ada ini juga (pulls up
               sleeve to show other tattoos). Yang ini, di Filipina,
               lebih baru lagi, kira-kira hanya 3 tahun yang lalu.
               Apa Mas juga punya tato?

RI: Tidak mungkin, Mister. Agama saya Islam. Ngak boleh.
               Mister, udah lama di Indonesia?

AS: Tidak. Saya datang sini beberapa kali. Sekarang ini cuma
               satu minggu lamanya membantu latihan tentara Indonesia.

RI: Pangkat Mister apa?

AS: Saya sersan.

RI: Aku juga. Kita sama.

AS: Sudah berapa lama Mas masuk militer?

RI: Sepuluh tahun.

AS: Mau terus ada di militer?

RI: Ya, sampai pensiun.

AS: Masih berapa tahun lagi?

RI: Dua puluh tahun.

AS: Lama ya.

RI: Ya, Ini Mister mau pergi ke mana?

AS: Sekarang mau ke kantin.

RI: Tidak énak Mister. Ada warung makan yang enak di luar
          pangkalan. Kebetulan, saya mau pergi ke luar sekarang.
          Mau ikut?

AS: Terima kasih tapi saya belum makan hari ini. Kalo tidak
          enak, tidak apa-apa. Mau yang dekat, pilih yang cepat aja.
          Lagian saya juga tidak ada banyak waktu. Ada janji temu
          dengan prawira segera.

RI: Oh begitu. Kalo mau kantin, terus aja, sampai gedung
          besar itu, lalu belok kanan.

AS: Terimah kasih banyak. Sampai jumpa lagi.

RI: Hati-hati.

3. Getting A Haircut

Pemangkas: (Silahkan) duduk. (Waves Mister into chair.)
Potong seperti apa, Mister?

Mister: Péndék sekali, sama seperti marinir. Di sekeliling telinga sini (shows with hands), pakai cukur langsung supaya tinggal kulit ya. Lalu, pakai cukur nomer satu di bagian belakang dan sisi, sampai atas (shows where with hands). Atasnya lebih panjang lagi, jadi potong sedikit aja, pakai gunting aja.

Pemangkas: Bagian depannya?

Mister: Potong sedikit aja juga, begini (shows with hands).

Pemangkas: (As he's finishing haircut): Bagaimana? Sudah cukup?

Mister: Ya, tapi lebih sedikit diratakan di sini, supaya tidak ada lapis.

Pemangkas: Baik. (Uses clippers to blend in/taper the cut more.)
Mau dikerik?

Mister: Mau. Lagi, sedikit lebih pendek di depan (points to bangs).

Pemangkas: (Cuts bangs, finishes shave around ears and neck.)

Mister: Ya, bagus.

Pemangkas: (Begins to rub Mister's shoulders or temples.)

Mister: Tidak usah Mas. Sudah. Tidak perlu dipijat. (Gets out of chair.) Berapa?

Pemangkas: Sepuluh.

Mister: Ini Mas. (Hands barber 11.000 rup.) Terima kasih.

Pemangkas: Sama-sama Mister.

4. First Aid Training

Pelatihan: Hari ini, kita meninjau pelajaran kita yang kemarin, yaitu tentang lagi Pe tiga ka (PPPK) dasar, lalu cara menyadarkan orang, atau CPR. Baik, pertama, kita berpasang-pasangan.

Pasukan: (All soldiers pair up with each other.)

Pelatihan: Baik. Coba saya cék pengetahuan kalian tentang bagaimana cara menangani luka dulu. Kalau ada orang yang terluka oleh pisau atau benda tajam, apa yang harus dilakukan?

Prajurit: (Raises his hand.)

Pelatihan   Ya, silahkan jawab.

Prajurit: Membersihkan luka dengan air.

Pelatihan: Kalau lukanya kecil, ya, lebih baik kalau begitu dulu. Pastikan airnya bersih. Ketika membersihkannya, periksa seberapa serius luka itu. Lalu, pakailah plester atau lap yang bersih untuk menutupnya. Oke, tapi kalau luka cukup besar sekali dan banyak keluar darah bagaimana?

Prajurit: Lukanya ditutup ya?

Pelatihan: Benar. Pakai ditekan ya? Tekanan langsung, atau 'Direct Pressure.' Kalau di dekatnya, ada kotak PPPK, pakai perban yang bersih, tapi kalo gak ada pakai kain apa pun yang ada. Atau, jika tidak ada, cukup pakai tangan aja, begini (demonstrates on a nearby soldier). Oke, kita latihan seperti itu beberapa menit ke depan.

(First Aid Training continues, to include splints, moving injured personnel safely, and CPR.)

Javanese Conversations

The Indonesian conversations in this unit have not been translated into Javanese for the simple reason that they are unlikely to occur in Javanese in the real world. However, it would make for good practice to translate them into Javanese, and once completed, have an Indonesian friend or teacher check them and correct any mistakes . . .

TNI – The Indonesian military – is ethnically diverse, made up of recruits from all over the archipelago. By necessity, Indonesian is the common language of communication.

For conversations that may well occur in Javanese in military-related situations in the real world, check the Table of Contents and see the appropriate units of this text: Village Life, Medical, Mechanical Things, NGO Life, Terrorists & Separatists. The text Indonesian for Military Training & Operations, contains a large number of conversations about various military operations.

Reading Sample: Newspaper Article about a SAR Effort

Evakuasi Terhambat Cuaca Buruk

JAYAPURA (KR): Lokasi jatuhnya pesawaat Mimika Air di Gunung Gergaji Kabupaten Puncak Papua, Minggu (19/4) berhasil dicapai Tim SAR yang berjumlah enam orang. Namun tim belum dapat melakukan evakuasi akibat cuaca yang berubah memburuk, meski telah menemukan lima jenazah dalam pesawat.

Wakil Bupati Puncak Jaya Hanock Ibo membenarkan keenam anggota tim saat ini sudah di lokasi, namun evakuasi belum dapat dilakukan akibat cuaca yang berubah memburuk.

"Selain enam anggota tim SAR, helikopter milik PT Freeport Indonesia juga ada di lokasi," ujarnya seperti dikutip *Antara*.

Untuk menunjang upaya evakuasi, lanjut Hanock Ibo, saat ini tercatat enam pesawat berbadan kecil yang siap sewaktu-waktu digunakan. Pesawat Mimika Air yang dipiloti Nan Linn Aung warga negara Myanmar dana Makmur yang merupakan WNI itu membawa sembilan penumpang dari Ilaga (ibu kota kabupaten Puncak) menuju Mulia (ibukota Kabupaten Puncak Jaya) serta membawa berita acara hasil pemilu.

Sebelumnya, sabtu (18/4) sekitar pukul 09.25 WIT Tim SAR berhasil menemukan puing pesawat Mimika Air di sekitar Gunung Gergaji dengan ketinggian sekitar 1.200 feet di atas permukaan air laut.

Penemuan puing pesawat naas itu dilaporkan pilot Gustav yang membawa pesawat Primair saat melintas di kawasan itu. Bahkan pilot Gustav juga melaporkan masih melihat asap yang mengepul di sekitar bangkai pesawat.

Vocabulary from Article:

evakuasi	evacuation, 'recovery' of bodies
jenazah	corpse (respectful)
Bupati	head of Kabupaten, like a mayor
ujarnya seperti dikutip	was quoted as saying
Antara	name of news agency, similar to AP, which is the source of lots of stories
WNI	Warga Negara Indonesia- an Indonesian citizen
upaya	evacuation efforts (work to do), operation
tercatat	listed, on stand-by, ready to go
asap	smoke
bangkai	the remains (for things, animals, or people)
puing	wreckage, debris

316

Kronologi Jatuhnya Hercules

① Jakarta
Pada ketinggian 1000 meter. Sayap kiri pesawat terbakar dan akhirnya lepas

Lokasi jatuhnya pesawat
Semarang Magetan
Bandung
DIY Surabaya

② Sesaat kemudian pesawat menabrak tiga rumah warga Desa Geplak, Karas, Magetan

③ Akhirnya menghantam pepohonan, terbakar hebat dan hancur di sawah

● Grafis : SiBhe

TENTANG HERCULES C-130

● **Produksi :** Lockheed Ac Co, Amerika Serikat
● **Fungsi :** Angkutan militer/sipil (pasukan, barang, kendaraan)
● **Kapasitas muatan :** 33.000 kg
● **Berat maksimum** (saat lepas landas) **:** 70.300 kg
● **Berat kosong :** 38.000 kg
● **Panjang :** 29,8 m
● **Tinggi :** 11,6 m
● **Rentang sayap :** 40,4 m
● **Daya jelajah :** 3.800 km
● **Kecepatan maksimum :** 610 km/jam
● **Sumber tenaga :** 4 buah mesin turboprop Allison T56-A-15

● Indonesia mulai menggunakan pesawat Hercules pada tahun 1960, ditandai penyambutan Hercules C-130B dengan pilot Letkol (Udara) Tjokrodirejo di Lanud Kemayoran oleh KSAU Marsekal Suryadarma pada 1 Maret 1960.

● Saat ini sedikitnya ada 27 unit pesawat Hercules, terbagi dalam 2 (dua) skuadron yakni Skuadron 31 (pangkalan Lanud Abdulrachman Saleh, Malang) dan Skuadron 32 (pangkalan Lanud Halim Perdanakusuma, Jakarta).

DARI BERBAGAI SUMBER   GRAFIS JOS

21. English Translation of Conversations and Reading Samples

1. Visit and Speech by an Air Force Sergeant

Sgt: Good afternoon. Today I want to introduce myself first, then talk a little bit about our unit. My rank is Master Sergeant in English. That is like a 'Sersan Satu – Sertu – in the Indonesian Air Force. As a sergeant, I do the things that are usually done by sergeants, like train the troops, make plans, oversee daily operations, prepare presentations – like this one – for visiting officers, give briefings to combat air crews, and other things.

Without sergeants, officers wouldn't have a clue about what they should do. Maybe that's as true for the Indonesian military as it is for the American military.

Our unit is a unit with airmen that are experts in air logistics and transport. We conduct tactical operations in the Asian region using mostly C-130 planes. We are proud (of the fact) that they say we can fly anywhere, anytime, and in any conditions. I often go overseas, but not usually to Indonesia. So, I can't wait to work with all of you in the Indonesian military and I also hope we can learn from each other and enjoy the time we have together. I'm sure that this joint training will be a success. Thank you.

2. Two Soldiers on Base

Indonesian Sgt: Hello. Nice tattoo, Mister.

American Sgt: Thank you. I've had this one for a long time.

Indo Sgt: Where did you get it?

Am. Sgt: This one – in Thailand. Around 6 years ago.

Indo Sgt: Do you have any others? Excuse me, my name is Wisnu. What's your name?

Am. Sgt: Nice to meet you. My name is Don. I've got these too. This one – in the Philippines. It's newer – only about 3 years ago. Do you have any tattoos?

Indo Sgt: It's impossible. I'm Muslim. We can't have them. Have you been in Indonesia long?

Am. Sgt: No. I've been here a few times. This time only for one week helping train the Indonesian military.

Indo Sgt: What's your rank?

Am. Sgt:	I'm a sergeant.
Indo Sgt:	Me too. We're the same.
Am. Sgt:	How long have you been in the military?
Indo Sgt:	Ten years.
Am. Sgt:	Are you going to stay in?
Indo Sgt:	Yeah, until I retire.
Am. Sgt:	How many more years?
Indo Sgt:	Twenty years.
Am. Sgt:	That's a long time.
Indo Sgt:	Yeah. Where are you going to now?
Am Sgt:	Now, I'm going to the canteen.
Indo Sgt:	It's not good. There's an eating place that's better off-base/post. I happen to be going off-base now. Do you want to come along?
Am. Sgt:	Thank you, but I haven't eaten yet today. It's no big deal if the food's not good. I just want something close by that'll be quick. Besides, I also don't have much time. I'm scheduled to meet with an/our officer soon.
Indo Sgt:	Oh, I see. To get to the canteen, just go straight until that big building, then turn right.
Am. Sgt:	Thank you very much. See you later.
Indo Sgt:	Take care.

3. Getting a Haircut

Barber:	Have a seat. How do you want it?
Foreigner:	Really short, the same as a marine. Around the ears here, use the clippers without a guard so that it's skin, then use a number one on the back and sides, up to here (shows where with fingers.) Longer on top, so just take off a little with the scissors.
Barber:	How about the bangs?

Foreigner:	Just cut them a little shorter too, like this (shows him).
Barber:	(As he's finishing) How is it? Is it okay?
Foreigner:	Yeah, but even it out a little here, so there's no shelf.
Barber:	Okay. (Uses clippers and comb to blend in the cut.) Do you want a close shave with the razor blade around the ears and neck?
Foreigner:	Yes. Also, the bangs a little shorter.
Barber:	(Cuts bangs, finishes shave.)
Foreigner:	Yeah, that's good.
Barber:	(Starts to rub the foreigner's shoulders or temples.)
Foreigner:	Don't bother sir. That's good. I don't need a massage. (Gets out of the chair.) How much?
Barber:	Ten.
Foreigner:	Here you are. (Hands barber 11,000.) Thank you.
Barber:	You're welcome, Mister.

4. First Aid Training

Trainer:	Today, we're going to look at our training/lesson from yesterday – that is about basic first aid – again, then the way to revive someone, or CPR. Good. First, let's pair up.
Troops:	(Pair up with each other.)
Trainer:	Good. I'll check your knowledge about how to handle wounds first. If there is a person who is wounded by a knife or sharp object, what should you do?
Soldier:	(Raises hand.)
Trainer:	Yes, go ahead and answer.
Soldier:	Clean out the wound with water.

Trainer:	If the wound is small, yes, it's better if you do that first. Make Sure the water is clean. While you're cleaning it, check how serious the wound is. Then, use a bandage or clean cloth to cover it. Okay, but if the wound is rather large and there's a lot of bleeding, what should you do?
Soldier:	Cover the wound, right?
Trainer:	Right. Use pressure, okay. Direct pressure. If there's a first aid kit/box nearby, use a bandage that's clean, but if there isn't, use any cloth/material that there is (available). Or if there isn't any, it's enough just to use your hand, like this (demonstrates). Okay, we'll practice that for the next few minutes.

(First Aid Training continues, to include splints, moving the injured safely, CPR.)

Reading Sample: Newspaper Article about a SAR Effort

Recovery Hampered by Bad Weather

Jayapura (KR): The location of the Mimika Air plane crash on Saw(tooth) Mountain, Puncak District, Papua on Sunday (19 Apr) was successfully reached by a SAR team consisting of six people. However, the team hasn't been able to carry out the recovery yet due to deteriorating weather conditions, though they have discovered five bodies inside the plane.

Vice Mayor Hanock Ibo confirmed that six team members were on location at this time; however, the recovery (of the bodies) had not taken place due to worsening weather conditions.

"Besides the six-member SAR team, a helicopter belonging to Freeport Indonesia is also on location," was his statement as cited by Antara.

To support the evacuation efforts, continued Hanock Ibo, at this moment six small aircraft are on standby and ready to be used on a moment's notice. The Mimika Air plane piloted by Nan Linn Aung a Burmese citizen and (copiloted by) Makmur, who was apparently an Indonesian citizen, was carrying nine passengers, along with the official report of the election results, from Ilaga (the capital of Puncak District) to/bound for Mulia (the capital of Puncak Jaya District). Before that, on Saturday (18 Apr) around 0925 Western Indonesian Time, the SAR team succeeded in finding the remains of the Mimikar Air flight around Saw Mountain, with an elevation of around 1,200 feet above sea level.

The discovery of the wreckage of the ill-fated flight was reported by a pilot Gustav who was at the time taking his Primair plane across that border. In fact, Pilot Gustav also reported he still saw smoke billowing out from around the remains of the plane.

Chronology of the Hercules Crash

1. At an elevation of 1000 meters, a fire broke out on the left wing and eventually escaped	2. A moment later the plane crashed into 3 houses in Geplak Village, in Karak, Megatan.	3. Finally, it rammed into some trees, in flames, and was broken up in the rice paddies.

About the Hercules C-130

Manufacturer: Lockheed Ac Co., USA
Function/Use: Military/Civilian (troops, supplies, transport)
Load Capacity: 33,000 kg.
Maximum Weight: (at take-off) 70,300 kg.
Weight Empty: 38,000 kg.
Length: 29.8 m.
Height: 11.6 m.
Wingspan: 40.4 m.
Cruising limit: 3,800 km.
Maximum Speed: 610 km/hr
Power Source: 4 Allison T-56-A-15 turboprop engines

Indonesia began using the Hercules aircraft in 1960, marked in a C-130B reception with pilot Lt. Col (AF) Tjokrodirejo at Kemayoran Air Base by Air Force Chief of Staff Marsekal Suryadama on 1 March 1960.

At this time there are at least 27 Hercules aircraft (in service), divided into two squadrons, namely Squadron 31 (based at Abdulrachman Saleh AB, Malang) and Squadron 32 (based at Halim Perdanakusama AB, Jakarta).

22. RELIGION

Vocabulary – arranged alphabetically in Indonesian

abangan	a generally 'non-religious' person
adzan (azan)	call to prayer by mosque
al-hamdu lilah	'Praise/thanks to God'
alkitab	Bible
Al Quran	the Quran in Arabic
assalamu' alaikum	Arabic greeting
ashar	3rd daily prayer (3:00-3:45 pm)
azza wa jalla	to whom belongs glory and majesty (Allah)
Balinese 'Day of Silence'	Nyepi
Balinese 'New Year'	Ngembak Geni (the day after Nyepi)
berdoa	to pray
berguk*	'burka,' head to ankle dress for women
Buddha's birth/death day	Waisak
Buddhist	penganut Budai
bulan sabit	Islamic crescent moon symbol
beriman	faithful
dasasila	the 10 Commandments
Depag (Departemen Agama)	Department of Religion in government
doa	prayer (any kind)
dzikir (zikir)	religious chanting
dzuhur (zuhur)	2nd daily prayer (about noon)
fitrah	tithe in cash or rice, paid at end of Ramadan
FPI	Front Pembela Indonesia - a hardline Islamic group often involved in social unrest and attacks on Non-Muslims, esp. in Jakarta
Hadits	Hadith - stories of the Prophet Muhammed
haji	the haj-holy trip to Mecca
hari raya haji	same as Idul Adha (day haj ends)
Idul Fitri	Id al-fitr, holiday celebrating end of Ramadan similar to Christmas or New Year in function

imam	'leader,' the one who leads salat in mosque
Ibrahim	Abraham
Idul Adha	holiday celebrating Abraham's sacrifice, lamb or goat meat distributed through neighborhood
isya	5th daily prayer (about 7pm)
janabah	temporary impurity due to some act
jamaah	a group/congregation of Muslims
Jewish	Yahudi
jilbab	Muslim head scarf
jiwa	soul
juzamma	short sura (pl) used for prayers
kada	1) divine decree 2) make-up for missed prayer or fast day
kebatinan	spirituality, study of inner man
kepercayaan	faith, often used to refer to mysticism
keranda	Muslim casket, to display body in mosque
khotbah	sermon
kiblat	direction of Mecca
kitab kuning	Islamic books that contain procedures, guidelines, interpretations of the Koran and Hadith, etc. In Indonesia, members of NU organization use them.
kuil	Hindu shrine
kyai (pron. 'kiai')	recognized spiritual leader, knows about religion and has been on haji
madrasah	Islamic school
maghrib	4th daily prayer (about 6pm), 'dusk'
mandi keramas	full, thorough cleansing bath (Javanese), also same as *mandi wajib*
mandi wajib/besar	ritual cleansing after exposure to unclean thing, during menstruation, etc.
massa	Catholic mass
merapali	pray over someone (laying hands on them)
misionaris	missionary

MMI	'Majelis Mujahedeen Indonesia,' an umbrella Islamic group, which advocates sharia law.
Muhammidiyah	One of 2 largest Islamic organizations in Indonesia (NU is the other)
mukena	white robe + headscarf worn during *salat*
musholat	room for performing prayer
nyawa	the spirit (inside your body)
NU	Nahdatul Ulama - one of two largest Islamic organizations in Indonesia
pasantren	Islamic boarding school with dorms
peci	men's Muslim hat
pengajian	regular neighborhood study group-Muslim
perjamuan	communion, eucharist
perjanjian/kitab baru	New Testament
perjanjian tua	Old Testament
penghulu	Muslim priest who marries people
pindah agama	convert (verb or noun)
puasa	fasting, used as general term for Ramadan
putihan	pure one, who follows Islamic duties
Ramadan mubarak	'a blessed Ramadan to you'
roh	spirit
roh suci/kudus	Holy Spirit
rukuh	same as mukena
sajadah	prayer rug
serban	turban
sholat, shalat, salat	n. 5 daily Islamic prayers v. to perform one of them
salib	cross (n)
santét	black magic
santri	same as *putihan*
sembahyang	ritual prayer (any faith)
subuh	1st morning prayer (about 4:50), 'dawn'
suci	holy, pure
sujud	touch one's head to ground while on knees

sunat	circumcision
sura	books in the Quran
syukur Allah	'Thank God'
takwa	devotion, piety
tasbih	rosary/prayer beads (not an Arabic word)
umroh	religious trip, haj outside of season
ustadz	'guru' title for preacher/teacher
	recognized expert, knows some Arabic
utusan injil	missionary
wa'alaikum salam	return greeting for 'Assalamalaikum'

Language & Culture Notes

1. Although it is not technically correct in most of the Muslim world, in Indonesia, *jilbab* is the word used to refer to any Muslim head scarf.

2. *Juzamma* are kept in a separate book and children memorize the most commonly used ones, like a book of Psalms.

3. *Pasantren*, or 'Islamic boarding school,' consists of all levels: *Madrasah Ibtidaiyah* (elementary schools), *Madrasah Tsanawiya* (middle), and *Madrasah Aliyah* (high schools). Students usually go to public school in the morning, and return to the *Madrasah* in afternoon. Some poorer students live in the boarding school.

4. Many Indonesians do not know the word *berguk*, as it is extremely uncommon for a woman to wear a Burka. In private, some might even jokingly refer to such an outfit as a 'ninja costume' and reactions to seeing a woman wearing one on Java, for example, do not differ greatly than what you what expect in America - ranging from wondering what kind of extremist her husband might be, to feeling sorry for her for having to wear such restrictive clothing.

5. In the conversation, the driver yells out "Bubur" to attract passengers. The yelling out of destination to people standing on the side of the road is common for buses and *angkotan* in Indonesia, and often the place name is shortened.

6. The Ministry of Religion is tasked with promoting, overseeing, and protecting proper religion and the values it represents in society. It is headed by a Minister of Religion, who is appointed by the President, and has seven Director-Generals, one representing each of the 5 official religions of the state (Islam, Catholicism, Christianity, Buddhism, Hinduism), one in charge of Haji matters, and one who overseas Islamic Education. Some of the matters they oversee and either rule or give opinion on are controversial, like recent anti-pornography laws, or on what day/time exactly the fasting month will officially begin and end for Indonesians. Many foreigners or non-Muslims assume the Ministry promotes Islam, but based on its composition and rulings, it is more accurate to picture it as what it claims to be: an executive body that deals with all religious issues and promotes religion in general. It is the fact that government is directly involved in religion in this manner, and that the country carefully segregates the recognized religions, which seems strange (or wrong) to Westerners.

7. Officially, only 5 faiths are recognized as legal in the country (serving the political purpose of allowing Indonesia to be unified) and every citizen has to choose one (being 'spiritual, agnostic, atheist or no preference' are not official options). One can choose to be Muslim, Christian-Protestant, Catholic, Buddhist, or Hindu. It often strikes foreigners as strange that *Katolik* is a separate category from *Kristen* which means Protestant or any non-Catholic Christian. Due to influence of political, modern Islam, 'Jewish' is noticeably absent as a choice, as are many other popular world religions. From a Western viewpoint, the Indonesian categorization scheme leaves something to be desired in terms of accuracy and inclusiveness.

8. You are typically asked your religion (on forms or in-person) when moving into a house, opening a bank account, going to the hospital, etc. This is not for any sinister purposes. Rather, like much other info considered personal or private in the West, it is not considered so in most of Indonesia, and for administration purposes, those in charge consider it their business to collect information on religion as a matter of course. If you choose to leave the *agama* question on a form blank, the person behind the counter will usually fill-in *Kristen* or *Katolik* for any Westerner.

9. Active proselytizing by (Christian) missionaries is not allowed in Indonesia. Under the 2002 Child Protection Act, converting children under 17 from their religion is a crime. In general, any proselytizing is viewed by a majority of Indonesians as illegal and with suspicion, and there has been a history of local tensions, court cases, fights, vigilante justice, public unrest springing from proselytizing efforts. On the other hand, some Christian churches and organizations, like the LDS (Mormon) Church, Mission Aviation Fellowship, New Tribes Missions, etc. seem to have an active presence in Indonesia with few or no problems, and Christian schools and universities flourish.

10. The holy fasting month of Ramadan is often referred to simply as *puasa*, or 'fasting.' In Jakarta, one hardly notices *puasa*, as malls, fast food restaurants, and bars all remain open. Depending on the neighborhood, *warung* and small stores may close early and be closed in the afternoon, but overall, the impact of the month of Ramadan on foreigners and non-Muslims is minimal. In smaller cities and rural areas, however, the situation is different. Most neighborhoods are quiet and businesses closed from morning til the end of fast in the evening. Many bars or clubs close for part of *puasa* and then close early for the remainder of the month. Any evening classes or business will be interrupted for a time while everyone celebrates the end of the fast with special drinks and by socializing together. One golden bit of advice: it is unwise to get a haircut, transact business, or engage in any activity that requires an Indonesian to be attentive to detail in the late afternoon, as it is likely he/she has been fasting since 4am and the chance for mistakes to be made increases significantly...

11. If you are working for an Indonesian school, government agency, or business during Ramadan, you need not fear. While eating out options for lunch might be significantly fewer, there will be a number of employees, teachers, and students who are not fasting each day - either because they are not Muslim, or are ill, or for women, because it is that time of the month. A box lunch - consisting of chicken, fried snacks, rice, etc. is provided each day for those not fasting. As a foreigner, it will be expected that you will not be fasting, and you will be taken care of, along with the other employees who aren't fasting - they won't let you starve or expect you to fend for yourself.

12. Most Westerners would not acquaint Christmas time with anything negative, but every year in America, for example, there is a significant rise in crime (robbery, domestic disputes, assault, hate crimes, etc.) during the holiday season. Similarly, the month of Ramadan has a tragic side. Every year, during this time, there are a number of attacks on non-Muslim businesses and individuals. Some of these are spontaneous, usually by groups of young men who wrongly perceive they are defending the spirit of Ramadan by attacking or burning a neighborhood store which is selling food or liquor during the fasting period. Others are premeditated and planned attacks by hard-core extremist Islamic groups trying to stir up trouble and dissent. And still others are simply neighborhood disputes that have little to do with religion, but where a perceived violation of Ramadan provides a convenient excuse for violence. Such attacks on individuals or businesses are routinely treated as crimes by the police. However, many foreigners, non-Muslims and Muslims alike feel that since the motivation for such crimes is often religious, they deserve special consideration and that too often, these crimes are not adequately investigated and the perpetrators often remain at large or unpunished.

13. Traditional gift giving at the end of Ramadan ,during Idul Fitri, long ago fell prey to the massive corruption in the country, as influential patrons and corporations found it to be a convenient time to give expensive 'gifts,' including money, as bribes. In recent years, some government officials have called on all government workers to not accept any gifts for this reason.

14. During Idul Adha, lambs or goats are typically butchered, and the meat distributed to all members of a neighborhood for free. If you happen to be an animal lover or are squeamish about such things, you should probably stay indoors since cries of the animals being killed can be heard and the butchering seen outside the local mosque. Bloody body parts and inards are washed and cut up in canals and waterways around the neighborhood/village. For those of you who love meat, get your barbecue ready and enjoy the free meat!

Indonesian Conversations

1. Friday Prayers

Two young men are on their way to the mosque for Friday prayers.

Arman: Rin, ayo pergi ke jumatan.

Rinto :   Ya, sebentar aku harus mengambil peciku. Baiklah, ayo pergi.

Arman: Hm, siapa yang jadi imam hari ini ya?

Rinto: Oh, Pak Aminudin. Memangnya ada apa?

Arman: Oh, tidak, aku cuma kadang bosan dengan isi ceramah. Kalau bosan aku biasanya tidur.

Rinto: Wah, sebenarnya nggak boleh itu tidur ketika imam memberi ceramah. Tetapi kalau Pak Aminudin yang memberi ceramah biasanya menarik kok.

Arman: Iya, kalau isi ceramah Pak Aminudin memang biasanya bagus.

Rinto: Wah, ayo cepat itu sudah dengar suara adzan

Arman: Ayo..

2. Teaching Children How to do Sholat

Guru:	Anak-anak, hari ini Ibu akan mengajarkan cara melakukan sholat. Tetapi sebelumnya ibu akan bertanya kepada kalian dulu tentang sholat.
Murid:	Baik, Bu.
Guru:	Sholat wajib itu ada berapa?
Murid:	Ada lima, Bu Guru. Isya, Shubuh, Dhuhur, Ashar, dan Maghrib.
Guru:	Pintar. Kemudian sebelum sholat biasanya kita melakukan apa?
Murid:	Wudlu, Bu.
Guru:	Mengapa kita harus wudlu sebelum sholat?
Murid:	Agar kita suci dari najis, Bu.
Guru:	Kemudian kita harus apa setelah sholat?
Murid:	Mendoakan orang tua.
Guru:	Pintar. Kalau begitu, Ibu akan mulai mengajarkan cara melakukan sholat. Tetapi sebelum itu, anak-anak harus praktek wudlu di depan ibu dulu. Masih ingat cara melakukan wudhlu?
Murid:	Masih, Bu.

3. Getting Circumcised

Ayah: Bagaimana rasanya setelah disunat?

Mardi: Masih sedikit nyeri, Pak.

Ayah: Ya, semua pasti nyeri, tetapi nanti lama-lama tidak terasa kok.

Mardi: Iya.. Mengapa Mardi harus sunat?

Ayah: Ya, semua anak laki-laki yang sudah dewasa harus melakukan sunat. Itu hukumnya wajib bagi semua laki-laki muslim.

Mardi: Kalau nggak mau sunat bagaimana, Pak?

Ayah: Kalau nggak mau ya berarti tidak bisa dianggap déwasa. Selain itu kamu pasti berdosa karena sunat itu hukumnya wajib.

Mardi: Oh begitu ya, Pak?

Ayah: Iya, karena itu mulai sekarang Mardi nggak boléh malas lagi melakukan sholat wajib ya.

Mardi: Iya, Pak.

4. Christian Missionaries

Minah: Kamu tahu siapa yang mengontrak rumah baru itu?

Rianti: Setahuku orang-orang itu misionaris.

Minah: Misionaris itu apa, Mbak?

Rianti: Itu lho orang yang menyebarkan agama Kristen.

Minah: Berarti seperti pastur itu, ya?

Rianti:	Iya, tetapi misionaris datang ke rumah-rumah kemudian mengajak orang-orang untuk pindah agama.
Minah:	Seperti itu boléh ya, Mbak?
Rianti:	Sebenarnya nggak étis itu. Tapi ya itu tergantung sama orang-orang itu sendiri. Kalau imannya kuat ya nggak mungkin pindah agama begitu saja.
Minah:	Apa misionaris itu nggak sebaiknya ditindak saja ya Mbak?
Rianti:	Kalau sampai ditindak ya nggak perlu. Yang penting kita yakin saja dengan agama kita. Kalau seperti itu misionaris juga nggak bisa apa-apa kok.

5. On an Angkota

The driver talks with a foreigner, who is a lone passenger in his minivan, about religion.

Supir:	Mister, berbicara Indonesia?
Passenger:	Ya, bisa.
Supir:	Mau turun di mana, Mister?
Passenger:	Jl. Bambu Apus, sebelum Indomaret.
Supir:	Udah lama di Indonesia?
Passenger:	Ya, udah hampir empat tahun. Tapi di Jakarta tahun ini pertama kali.
Supir:	Sebelumnya, di Bali?
Passenger:	Tidak. Lebih dua tahun di Yogya, lalu setengah tahun di Magelang. Pak asalnya dari Jawa tengah kan?

Supir:	Ya, betul. Agama Mister apa?
Passenger:	Saya Kristen.
Supir:	Aku juga Kristen. Sama. Pergi ke geréja yang mana?
Passenger:	(Laughs) Tidak pernah ke geréja sejak murid SMA.
Supir:	Lho, kenapa? Mister, harus pergi ke geréja. Ada geréja Kristen baik di Kebayoran.
Passenger:	Oh, betul?
Supir:	Ya, itu gereja besar, Mister. Ada bulé pergi ke sana.
Passenger:	Oh ya?
Supir:	Harus cari Tuhan mister. Itu penting. Cari Tuhan Mister.
Passenger:	(Tries to be agreeable, although he has no intention of setting foot in a church.) Ya, ya, saya tahu.
Supir:	(Yells out destination to people standing on side of street.) Tamini! Bubur! (short for Cibubur)
	(Conversation stops as driver picks up another passenger.)
Passenger:	Kiri Pak. Ya, di sini. Jalan itu (points). (Driver slows down.)
	(Hands driver 2.000 rupiah and gets out.)

Javanese Conversations

1. Friday Prayers

Arman: Rin, ayo lunga menyang jumatan.

Rinto: Ya, kosék aku kudu jukuk kuplukku. Ya, ayo lunga.

Arman: Hm, sapa ya sing dadi imam dina iki ya?

Rinto: Oh, Pak Aminudin. Pancene ana apa?

Arman: Oh, ora, aku mung kala-kala bosen karo isi ceramah. Nék bosen aku biasane turu.

Rinto: Wah, sakjane ora oléh kuwi tuu pas imam ngenéhi ceramah. Nanging nek Pak Aminudin sing ngenehi ceramah biasane apik kok.

Arman: Iya, nek isi ceramahe Pak Aminudin pancen biasane apik.

Rinto: Wah, ayo lekas kuwi wis krungu suara adzan.

Arman: Ayo . . .

2. Teaching a Child how to Perform Sholat

Guru: Lare-lare, dintan punika Ibu badhé nuturi pacara nglajenganken sholat. Nanging sakdéréngipun Ibu badhe tanglet perihal sholat.

Murid: Inggih, Bu.

Guru: Sholat wajb menika wonten pinten?

Murid:	Wonten gangsal, Bu Guru. Isya, Shubuh, Duhur, Ashar, kaliyan Maghrib.
Guru:	Pinter. Lajeng sakdéréngipun sholat biasanipun kawula sedanten kedah ngelajengaken menapa?
Murid:	Wudlu, Bu.
Guru:	Kengén menapa kawula sedanten kedah wudlu sakderengipun sholat?
Murid:	Supaya kawula sedanten suci saking najis, Bu.
Guru:	Lajeng kawula sedanten kedah menapa saksampunipun sholat?
Murid:	Ndongaaken tiyang sepuh.
Guru:	Pinter. Menawai mekaten, Ibu badhe mulai nuturi picara nglajengaken sholat. Nanging sakderengipun menika, laré-laré kedah prakték wudlu ing ngajeng Ibu rumiyin. Taksih émut cara ngalajangaken wudlu?
Murid:	Taksih, Bu.

3. A Circumcision (Sunat)

Ayah:	Piye rasane sakwise disunat?
Mardi:	Taksih sekedhik nyeri, Pak.
Ayah:	Ya, kabéh mesti nyeri, nanging mengko suwe-suwe ora krasa kok.
Mardi:	Inggih.. Kengén menapa Mardi kedah sunat?

Ayah:	Ya, kabéh bocah lanang sing wis akil baligh kudu nglakoni sunat. Kuwi hukume wajib kanggo kabéh bocah Muslim.
Mardi:	Menawi mboten purun sunat kados pundi, Pak?
Ayah:	Nék ra gelem ya artine ora isa dianggep akil baligh. Sakliyane kuwi, kowe mesti dosa karena sunat kuwi hukume wajib.
Mardi:	Oh mekaten nggih, Pak?
Ayah:	Ya, sebab kuwi mulai saiki Mardi ora oléh males menéh nglakoni sholat wajib, ya.
Mardi:	Inggih, Pak.

4. Missionaries

Minah:	Kowe ngerti sapa sing ngontrak omah anyar kuwi?
Rianto:	Sakngertiku wong-wong kuwi misionaris.
Minah:	Misionaris kuwi apa, Mbak?
Rianti:	Kuwi lhu wong sing nyebarake agama Kristen.
Minah:	Berarti kaya rama pendeta kae ya?
Rianti:	Iya, tapi misionaris iki teka neng omah-omah njur ngajak wong-wong-wong kanggo pindah agama.
Minah:	Kaya ngono kuwi oléh ya, Mbak?
Rianti:	Sakjane ora étis kuwi. Tur ya kuwi tergantung karo wong-wonge dhéwé. Nék imane kuat ya ora mungkin gampang pindah agama ngono wae.

Minah:	Apa misionaris kuwi ora luwih becik ditindak wae ya Mbak?
Rianti:	Nék tekan ditindak ya ora perlu. Sing penting awa(k)édéwé yakin wae karo agama awakedhewe. Nek kaya ngono misionaris uga ira isa ngapa-ngapa kok.

5. In an Angkota

The conversation starts out in Indonesian rather than Javanese, in order to be more realistic – a driver would never start a conversation in Javanese with an unknown foreigner.

Supir:	Mau turun di mana, Mister?
Passenger:	Jl. Bambu Apus, sebelum Indomaret.
Supir:	Udah lama di Indonesia?
Passenger:	Ya, udah hampir empat tahun. Tapi di Jakarta tahun ini pertama kali.
Supir:	Sebelumnya, di Bali?
Passenger:	Tidak. Lebih dua tahun di Yogya, lalu setengah tahun di Magelang. Pak asalnya dari Jawa Tengah kan?
Supir:	Ya, betul. Mister ngendikan basa Jawi?
Passenger:	Iya, isa.
Supir:	Agamanipun Mister apa?
Passenger:	Aku Kristen.
Supir:	Kula ugi Kristen. Sami. Tindak dhateng geréja ing pundi, Mister?

Passenger:	Ora tau néng gereja két murid SMA.
Supir:	Lho, kengen menapa? Mister kedah tindak dhateng gereja. Wonten gereja Kristen sae ing Kebayoran.
Passenger:	Oh, betul?
Supir:	Nggih, gereja ageng, Mister. Wonten bule lunga neng kéné.
Passenger:	Oh betul?
Supir:	Kedah émat Tuhan, Mister. Menika penting.
Passenger:	(Trying to be agreeable.) Iya, aku ngerti.
Supir:	(Yells out destinations to potential passengers on the street.) Tamini! Bubur!

(Conversation stops as driver picks up another passenger.)

Passenger:	Kiwa Pak. Ya neng kene. Dalan kuwi.

22. English Translation of Conversations

1. Friday Prayers

Arman: Rin, c'mon let's go to Friday prayers.

Rinto: Okay, just a minute – I have to get my hat. Alright, let's go.

Arman: Hmm, I wonder who will be the Imam/prayer leader today?

Rinto: Oh, Mr. Aminudin. Why – what's up?/is there anything wrong?

Arman: Oh, no (nothing). Only sometimes, I'm bored with the sermon. If I'm bored, I usually fall asleep.

Rinto: Well, you really can't sleep when the Imam gives his sermon. But, when it's Mr. Aminudin who gives it, it's usually interesting.

Arman: Yeah, Mr. Aminudin's sermons are usually good.

Rinto: Hey, let's hurry up – I already hear the call to prayer.

Arman: C'mon...

2. Teaching Children how to Perform Sholat

Instructor: Children, today I'm going to teach you how to do the ritual prayer.

Students: Okay Mam.

I: How many compulsory/daily prayers are there?

S: There are five, teacher. Isya, Shubuh, Dhuhur, Ashar, and Maghrib.

I: Very good. And what do we usually do before praying?

S: (Ritual) washing Mam.

I: Why should we wash ourselves before daily prayer?

S: So we are clean from dirt, Mam.

I: And what should we do after daily prayers?

S: Pray for our parents.

I:	Very good. In that case, I will begin teaching you how to do the daily prayers. But before that, you children have to practice washing in front of me first. Do you still remember how to do the washing?
S:	We do Mam.

3. Planning a Circumcision

Father:	How do you feel after being circumcised?
Mardi:	Still a little sore.
Father:	Yes, it will definitely hurt all over, but later after a while you won't feel it.
Mardi:	Yeah... why did I have to get circumcised?
Father:	Well, all boys, when they become adults have to get circumcised. It's a commandment for all Muslim men.
Mardi:	What if you don't want to be circumcised, Dad?
Father:	If someone doesn't want to it means they can't be considered a grown-up. Besides that, you would be committing a sin because circumcision is a commandment.
Mardi:	Oh, that's it?
Father:	Yes, and so from now on, you mustn't be lazy anymore in doing the (5) daily prayers, okay?
Mardi:	Okay Dad.

4. Missionaries

Minah:	Do you know who is renting that new house?
Rianti:	As far as I know, the people are missionaries.
Minah:	What is a missionary?
Rianti:	It's a person who spreads the Christian religion.
Minah:	You mean like a pastor, yeah?

Rianti:	Yes, but missionaries come to people's homes and then encourage people to change religions.
Minah:	It's okay (for them) to do that?
Rianti:	Actually, it's not ethical. But you know it depends on the people themselves. If their faith is strong, it's not possible they'll change religions just like that.
Minah:	Wouldn't it be best to just take action/do something against these missionaries?
Rianti:	There's no need to take any action/go that far. What's important is that we are sure of our religion. And so, the missionaries can't do anything at all.

5. In a Public Minivan

Driver:	Mister, do you speak Indonesian?
Passenger:	Yes, I can.
Driver:	Where do you want off?
Passenger:	Bambu Apus Street, before Indomart.
Driver:	Have you been in Indonesia long?
Passenger:	Yeah, almost four years. But in Jakarta – this year is my first time.
Driver:	Before this (were you) in Bali?
Passenger:	No. Over two years in Jogja, then half a year in Magelang. You're from Central Java, aren't you?
Driver:	Yes, I am. What religion are you?
Passenger:	I'm Christian.
Driver:	I'm Christian too. The same. Which church do you go to?
Passenger:	(Laughs) I haven't been to church since I was a student in high school.
Driver:	Really? Why? Mister, you should go to church. There's a Christian church in Kebayoran.

Passenger: Oh, really.

Driver: Yes, it's a good church, Mister. There are foreigners who go there.

Passenger: Oh yeah?

Driver: You need to find God, Mister. It's important. Find God.

Passenger: Yeah, yeah, I know.

Driver: Taman-Mini, Cibubur!

Passenger: Okay, pull over. Yeah, right here. That street. (Pays, gets out.)

23. TERRORISTS AND SEPARATISTS

Basic Vocabulary

Aceh Security Disturbance Movement   *GPK
agencies (police/govt.)   *aparat (from apparatus)
Al Qaida   Al Kaida/Al Qaida
Area Military Command   *Kodam
ATA (Anti-Terrorism Assistance)   *ATA (ah-té-ah)
ambush, attack on, capture of   penyergapan
arrest (v)   menangkap
Australian Federal Police   *Polisi Federal Australia

background   latar belakang
blow up (a building)   meledakkan
bomb (n)   bom
bomb (v)   membom

capture of/attack on posts   penyergapan
catch   tangkap
caught   ditangkap
cease-fire agreement   gencatan senjata
break a cease-fire   melanggar

dead   tewas
Defenders of Islam Front   *FPI - Front Pembela Islam
Defenders of the Truth (one of   *PEMKA - Pembela Kembenaran
main commands of Free Papua)
Defense Cooperation Agreement   *pertahanan keamanan
(with Australia)

explode   meledak
explosion   ledakan
exposed, uncovered   terbongkar

Free Aceh Movement   *GAM - Gerakan Aceh Merdeka
Free Papua Movement   *OPM - Organisasi Papua Merdeka

handcuffs   borgol, belenggu
hostage   sandera
hunt for, pursue   memburu

Indonesian National Police   Polri
infiltrate   merémbés

informant	informan
injured (in bombing)	terluka
interrogate	*menanyai
Islamic boarding school	*pesantren
Islamic law	*syariat
Israel	*Israel
Jemaah Islamiyah	Jemaah Islamiyah
Jew	Yahudi
kidnap	menculik
Laskar Jihad	Laskar Jihad
murder (v)	membunuh
murderer	pembunuh
network	jaringan, jejaring
Palestine	*Palestina
place in custody	mengamankan
put down a rebellion	memadamkan pemberontakan
raid	gerebak
rebellion/uprising	pemberontakan
refugee camp	kamp pengungsi
safehouse (hideout)	rumah/tempat persembunyian
secret agent/undercover informant	agen rahasia
shooting	tembakan
slaughter (v), n	(mem)bantai
South Maluku Republic	*RMS - Republik Maluku Selatan
storm a building	menggempur, menyerang
suicide bomber	pengebom benuh diri
support (v, n)	menyokong, sokongan/bantuan
surround	kepung
suspected of	dicurigai
taken and held prisoner	ditawan
terrorism	térorismé
terrorist	téroris
torture (v, n)	siksaan, penyiksaan
track a person	melacak
tribe, ethnic group	suku
undercover	rahasia

Military Units with Anti-Terrorism/Separatist Missions

Denjaka (Detasemen Jala Mangkara)	TNI AL
Densus 88 (Detasemen Khusus 88)	POLRI
Detasemen Bravo 90	TNI AU
Gegana	POLRI/Brimob
Kopaska (Komando Pasukan Katak)	TNI AL
Sat 81 (Satuan 81 Gultor)	TNI AD
Yon IPAM/Yontaifib (Batalyon Intai Para Amfibi)	Korps Marinir

Language & Culture Notes

1. GPK was the name given to the Acehnese Independent movement early on, by the government. The term GAM or Aceh Merdeka is more popular.

2. The term *aparat* appears frequently in the news, such as *aparat polisi*, to mean various levels/units of the police. In the USA, this would be the same as saying "state and local police," or "the FBI along with local police..."

3. ATA is money appropriated by the U.S. Congress thru NADR: Nonproliferation, Anti-Terrorism, Demining and Related Programs.

4. Notice that the root of *menanyai* - interrogate is *tanya*, as in question. *Pentanya* is an interrogator, and *pentanyaan* is interrogation/questioning.

5. There isn't a good, single word for the English noun 'suspect.' Usually, the phrase '*orang yang dicurigai*' is used instead. Often when someone has been called in for questioning, whether they are actually only a witness or in fact a suspect, they are 'called in as a witness' - *dipanggil sebagai saksi*. To the public and to the authorities, this is perceived as being a 'suspect'. After being called in, the 'witness' often endures many hours or days of questioning, before either being let go or arrested.

6. All separatist organizations and activities are considered terrorist in nature and treasonous by the Indonesian government and military. Given the diverse and widespread nature of Indonesia's geography and ethnical make-up, along with its modern history, this is not surprising. Indeed, the unity of Indonesia as one nation is fairly precarious, and the government/military cannot afford to take chances.

7. Indonesia had been under various bans on U.S. military assistance from the Clinton Administration and U.S. Congress since 1992, stemming from human rights violations in East Timor. In 2006, nearly all were lifted and massive assistance resumed.

8. Detachment 88 was created in response to the 2002 Bali bombing, has since become very famous in Indonesia, and is the recipient of Australian and U.S. (ATA) money.

9. The Defense Cooperation Agreement was finalized in 2009 and was the formalization of a close working relationship between the Australian Federal Police and POLRI, resulting from the Bali bombings and the subsequent joint effort to track down the perpetrators.

10. There are several factors contributing to the Acehnese problem: a strong ethnic identity, which is tied up with a stronger Islamic identity and practice of sharia, the feeling that the Javanese have stolen resources from the province, not invested in the region, except to give jobs to transplanted Javanese, and the history of counterinsurgency efforts - a legacy of crackdowns by TNI on insurgents, which has resulted in civilian casualties. In this way, the problem with Aceh is similar in many ways to the problems with the Islamic provinces of Mindanao, in the Philippines and the provinces in southernmost Thailand.

11. Papua was officially 'Irian Jaya,' until 2002, when the name became Papua.

12. Grievances of Papuans who want independence include: the fact that the province was not originally part of the Indonesian state, but became so in 1969 as the result of an 'unfair and illegitimate' referendum after many years of 'harassment' and 'infiltration' by Indonesian forces, and also that the people are ethnically and culturally very different from Indonesians. Other grievances, like human rights abuses coming from counterinsurgency efforts, and perceptions that Java has stolen natural resources but given little in return, are the same as Acehnese grievances.

13. Like Muslims worldwide, many Indonesians are extremely interested in the Palestinian question and feel an affinity for the Palestinians, based solely on a shared religion. Most consider the Palestinians to be the victims and Israel the aggressors or terrorists, but among the general public this sentiment does not often include the kind of zionist conspiracies which are commonly found in the Middle East. Only a small percent of the population seems to subscribe to or talk about such Jewish conspiracy theories, although they seem to have become more popular in recent years among younger, devout Muslims.

14. Gegana is the Indonesian Police special response unit. This unit was formed in 1976 as a detachment. Later in 1995, with the expansion of Brimob, the Gegana Detachment was expanded to become the 2nd Regiment BRIMOB. Its duties are anti-terror, dealing with armed criminals, close protection, search and rescue (SAR), and explosive disposal operations in urban settings.

15. Laskar Jihad was officially created in a stadium gathering in Yogyakarta, in 2000, in response to Muslim-versus-Christian violence, which was ongoing in Maluku province (capital: Ambon). Thousands of volunteers were given military training in Bogor, and sent to Ambon, to 'protect Muslims,' but in reality, stirred up unrest, were actively involved in the continuing violence, and hindered efforts by locals at bringing peace to the region.

16. The RMS declared an independent Maluku from the Republic of Indonesia during the country's war of Independence against the Dutch (1945-1949). This was one of several separatist movements during the time, which were all opposed to the idea of being dominated by Java and in the case of the RMS, also by a Muslim-majority culture. Because of this, the Maluku region is still often portrayed as traitorous and untrustworthy in Indonesian history texts/classes, which has played into the periodic Muslim-Christian violence there since 2000.

Indonesian Conversations

1. I'm Being Stationed in Papua !

Letnan Siregar: Duduk sebentar sayang. Aku punya kabar untuk kamu.

Isteri: Apa itu? Kita harus pindah lagi kan?
             Kok cepat ya rasanya?

Letnan: Iya, betul.

Isteri: Ke mana?

Letnan: Papua.

Isteri: Papua? Aduh! Ngapain harus ke Papua?

Letnan: Itu biasa bagi Prawira muda Kopassus. Kadang-kadang
             masih ada pemberontakan yang harus dipadamkan ya,
             dan ..

Isteri:	Pemberontakan? Ada téroris dan suku asli gila yang membunuh orang dengan panah di Papua. Waduh, Aku takut.
Letnan:	Tidak apa-apa. Di sana cukup aman kok. Lagian hanya dua tahun, lalu setelah itu bisa pilih tempat bagus di Sumatra.
Isteri:	Dua tahun?

2. Office Conversation - They caught a Terrorist

Pekerja 1:	Udah lihat kabar di koran?
Pekerja 2:	Kabar apa?
Pekerja 1:	Polisi tangkap téroris penting dekat dari sini...
Pekerja 2:	Siapa dia?
Pekerja 1:	Katanya dia petinggi J I punya hubungan dengan Al Kaida.
Pekerja 2:	Di mana?
Pekerja1:	Sebentar... ini... Désa Sukamaju.
Pekerja 2:	Di mana itu?
Pekerja 1:	Di Jawa Tengah, goblok. It kurang 50 kilo dari sini.
Pekerja 2:	Ya udah. Bagaimana kejadiannya? Dénsus 88 kan?
Pekerja 1:	Nggak tau. Katanya Polres.

Pekerja 2:   Ngapain téroris mau sembunyi di desa kecil di
              Jawa Tengah?

Pekerja 1:   Mungkin dia pikir warga desa lebih mudah dipengaruhi.

3. Those Poor Palestinians

Sari: Kamu sudah baca koran hari ini?

Tuti: Belum, ada apa sih?

Sari: Sepertinya Jalur Gaza rusuh lagi. Tentara Israel menyerbu
         perkampungan Palestina.

Tuti: Hah, yang benar? Bukannya baru beberapa minggu yang lalu
         Tentara Israel berjanji tidak akan masuk ke daerah
         perkampungan?

Sari: Ya itu sebelum tentara itu curiga kalau ada gerakan Hamas di
         perkampungan itu.

Tuti: Aduh, lalu apa yang tentara-tentara itu lakukan?

Sari: Ya tentara itu masuk ke perkampungan itu dengan artileri berat.
         Banyak rumah-rumah rusak.

Tuti: Banyak korban tidak?

Sari: Di beritanya sih mémang terjadi perlawanan dari warga
         perkampungan itu, tetapi sepertinya tidak banyak korban
         meninggal.

Tuti: Oh, syukurlah jika tidak ada banyak korban meninggal. Tapi
         sebenarnya kasihan juga rakyat Palestina selalu ketakutan seperti
         ini.

Sari: Iya, tetapi yang namanya perang memang menyengsarakan
         banyak orang.

Reading Samples: Terrorists Caught

The following are excerpts from several newspaper articles about the capture of terrorists, which is a common occurrence in Indonesia.

1. News Posted by Temanggung city on Internet

August 7, 2009

Suara tembakan terdengar berasal dari dalam rumah Rumah Mohzahri yang berada di Desa Beji, RT 01 RW 07, Kelurahan Kedu, Kecamatan Kedu, Temanggung, Jawa Tengah . . .

Selain itu, polisi juga mengamankan Mohzahri, yang merupakan pemilik rumah itu. Hendra dan Aris merupakan keponakan Mohzahri, 70, pemilik rumah yang digerebek Densus 88 dan aparat kepolisian.

Rumah Mohzahri dikepung oleh tim Densus 88 dan aparat kepolisian sejak pukul 15.45 WIB dan sekitar pukul 16.00 WIB mulai terdengar tembakan sampai pukul 22.45 WIB...

Meski sudah dikepung selama empat jam, teroris yang diduga jaringan Noor Din M. Top tak kunjung menyerah. Malah beberapa menit lalu terjadi baku tembak. Menurut saksi mata di Desa Beji, Kecamatan Kedu, Kabupaten Temanggung, pukul 21.50 orang-orang yang ada di dalam rumah yang dikepung menembaki polisi sebanyak tiga kali. Detasemen Khusus 88 Antiteror lalu membalasnya dengan tembakan sebanyak tujuh kali...

Pasukan Densus 88 ini datang dengan tiga mobil dan beberapa sepeda motor. Hingga malam, mereka mengepung rumah tersebut. Lampu mobil dinyalakan untuk menerangi persawahan di sisi timur rumah Moh Zahri.

Aksi pengepungan ini sempat memunculkan isu bahwa Noor Din M. Top, dalang teror bom di Indonesia, ada di rumah itu. Stasiun TV Al Jazeera malah memberitakan bahwa lelaki mirip Noor Din telah tertangkap . . .

Densus 88 dikabarkan melakukan pengepungan rumah itu setelah mereka menangkap dua lelaki bernama Indra (35) dan Aris (38) di Pasar Parakan Temanggung, Jawa Tengah (Jateng). Kedua orang ini konon sepupu pria bernama Tatag, yang sudah ditangkap Densus 88 Mabes Polri 3 tahun lalu.

Menurut Ketua RW setempat, Moh Khoil, Moh Zahri adalah sehari-hari bekerja sebagai petani dan guru SMP swasta di daerah itu. Moh Zahri telah tinggal di rumah itu sejak enam tahun lalu.

Rumah yang digerebek Densus 88 Mabes Polri di Kedu Temanggung, diduga dihuni oleh kelompok Teroris Noordin M. Top. Selain Noordin M Top, di rumah itu diduga ada murid Dr. Azahari, yang piawai merakit bom, bernama Reno alias Tedy, alias Mubarok.

info dari berbagai media

2. Polda Jateng Berhasil Menangkap 'Calon Pengantin' Noordin

WIKIBERITA.COM-BERITA: Jajaran Polda Jawa Tengah menangkap seorang pria yang diduga sebagai anggota teroris jaringan Noordin M. Top dengan inisial ZA. Berita ini disampaikan Kapolda Jawa Tengah Irjen Pol Alex Bambang Riatmojo di sela-sela acara pengarahan kepada seluruh kepala desa dan Irah se-Solo Raya di Diamond Convention Center Solo, siang kemarin (23/7).

Ditambahkan, penangkapan ZA dilakukan Rabu malam lalu (22/7) di daerah Cilacap.

Dari hasil pemeriksaan sementara, lanjut Kapolda, diketahui bahwa ZA sudah menjadi anggota jaringan teroris Noordin sejak 2001. Dia, katanya, sengaja dipersiapkan menjadi pelaku bom bunuh diri di beberapa lokasi berikutnya.

"Belum diketahui, ZA ini berasal dari kelompok mana dan daerah mana yang akan dijadikan target sasaran berikutnya. Sebab, yang bersangkutan masih menjalani pemeriksaan," beber Kapolda.

ZA, lanjut Kapolda, sudah mendapatkan pembinaan khusus dari Noordin sejak 2001. Bersama beberapa anggota lain, ZA dipersiapkan sebagai pengantin (sebutan untuk pelaku bom bunuh diri).

[Story Continues]

3. Polisi tangkap istri Noordin M Top

Diperbaharui Jumat Juli 24, 2009 5:27pm AEST

Istri Noordin M Top yang ditahan Rabu pagi di Cilacap mengaku mengenal suaminya dengan nama lain dan mengira bahwa ia adalah seorang guru.

Wanita berusia 25 tahun tersebut ditahan polisi anti teror bersama dua orang anaknya.

Namun menurut pengacaranya, ia sama sekali tidak tahu bahwa ia bersuamikan teroris paling dicari di Asia Tenggara.

Arina Rochmah ditahan berdasarkan undang-undang anti-terorisme Indonesia dan diwakili secara hukum oleh Achmad Michdan, pengacara yang juga mewakili pelaku bom Bali.

Menurut Michdan, kliennya tidak mengetahui bahwa suaminya yang ia kenal sebagai seorang guru bernama Abdul Halim sebenarnya adalah Noordin M Top.

Menurutnya, suaminya jarang di rumah karena mengajar di sebuah pesantren di Sulawesi Selatan.

(Radio Australia)

Javanese Conversations

1. Stationed in Papua

Lt. Siregar: Lungguh kéné sedhilit. Aku duwe kabar nggo kowe.

Isteri: Apa kuwi? Awa(k)édhéwé kudu pindah manéh to? Kok cepet ya rasane?

Letnan: Iya, bener.

Isteri: Néng endi?

Letnan: Papua.

Isteri: Papua? Aduh! Ngapa kudu neng Papua?

Letnan: Kuwi biasa kanggo Prawira Muda Kopassus. Kadangkala isih ana pemberontakan sing kudu dipadamke, lan...

Isteri: Pemberontakan? Ana téroris lan suku asli édan sing maténi wong nganggo panah neng Papua? Waduh aku wedi.

Letnan:	Ora apa-apa. Neng kana cukup aman kok. Lagian mung rong taun, njur setelah kuwi isa milih panggon apik neng Sumatera.
Isteri:	Rong taun?

2. Office Conversation - They Caught a Terrorist

Pekerja 1:	Wis ndelok kabar néng koran?
Pekerja 2:	Kabar apa?
Pekerja 1:	Polisi nangkep téroris penting cedhak saka kéné
Pekerja 2:	Sapa dhéwé(k)é?
Pekerja 1:	Jarene dheweke petinggi JI, nduwe hubungan karo Al Kaida.
Pekerja 2:	Neng endi?
Pekerja 1:	Sedhilit, iki Desa Sukamaju.
Pekerja2:	Neng endi kuwi?
pekerja 1:	Neng Jawa Tengah, goblok, kuwi kurang 50 kilo saka kene.
Pekerja 2:	Ya wis. Piye kedadiane? Densus 88, ta?
Pekerja 1:	Ra ngerti. Jarene Polres.
Pekerja 2:	Ngapa téroris gelem ndelik néng desa cilik neng Jawa Tengah?
Pekerja 1:	Mungkin dheweke mikir warga desa luwih gampang dipengaruhi.

353

3. Those Poor Palestinians

Sari: Kowe wis maca koran dina iki?

Tuti: Durung, ana apa ta?

Sari: Kayane Jalur Gaza rusuh manéh. Prajurit Israel nyerbu
             perkampungan Palestina.

Tuti: Hah, sing bener kuwi? Nék ora salah pirang minggu
             kepungkur prajurit Israel janji ora arep melbu néng daerah
             perkampungan?

Sari :   Ya kuwi sakdurunge tentara kuwi curiga nek ana gerakan
             Hamas neng perkampungan kuwi.

Tuti: Aduh, trus tentara kuwi padha ngapa wae?

Sari: Ya tentara kuwi melbu neng perkampungan karo artileri
             berat. Akéh omah-omah padha rusak.

Tuti: Akeh korban apa ora?

Sari: Neng beritane sih pancén ana perlawanan saka warga
             perkampungan kuwi, tur kayane ora akéh korban sing
             seda.

Tuti: Oh, syukur nék ora akéh korban sing seda. Tur sakjane
             mesakake uga ya rakyat Palestina kuwi mesti kewedhén
             kayu ngéné.

Sari: Iya, tur ya sing jenenge perang pancén gawe sengsara
             wong akéh.

23. English Translations of Conversations and Readings

1. I'm Being Stationed in Papua!

Lt. Siregar: Sit down a minute honey. I have some news for you.

Wife: What is it? We have to move again, don't we? It's going to be right away?

Lt.:   Yes, that's right.

Wife: To where?

Lt: Papua.

Wife: Papua! Oh no! What do we have to go to Papua for?

Lt.:   It's normal for new special forces officers. Sometimes, there are still uprisings that have to be put down, and…

Wife: Uprisings? There are terrorists and crazy native tribes who kill people with bows and arrows. I'm really scared.

Lt.:   It'll be fine. It's safe enough there. Besides, it's only two years, then after that I can pick a nice place/assignment in Sumatra.

Wife: Two years?

2. Office Conversation

Worker 1:   Have you seen the news in the paper?

Worker 2:   What news?

W1:   The police caught an important terrorist near here.

W2:   Who is he?

W1:   They say he's a (high-level) leader of JI (Jemaah Islamaya) and has connections to Al Qaida.

W2:   Where?

W1:   Just a minute… here… Sukamaju Village.

W2:   Where's that?

W1:	In Central Java, idiot. It's less than 50 km from here.
W2:	Yeah, okay. How did it happen? It was Densus 88 right?
W1:	I don't know. It says local police.
W2:	Why do terrorists want to hide out in small villages in Central Java?
W1:	Maybe they think the villagers are more easily fooled.

3. Poor Palestinians

Sari:	Have you read the paper today?
Tuti:	Not yet. What's in it?
Sari:	It seems the Gaza Strip is in unrest again. Israeli forces attacked a Palestinian camp.
Tuti:	Huh, it's true? Wasn't it just a few weeks ago that the Israeli military promised they weren't going to enter the camps?
Sari:	Yeah, that was before the military suspected there was a Hamas movement inside the camp.
Tuti:	Oh no, and what did the soldiers do then?
Sari:	They entered the camp with heavy artillery. Lots of homes were destroyed.
Tuti:	Aren't there a lot of casualties?
Sari:	In the story it says there was a lot of opposition from people in the camp, but apparently not many victims died.
Tuti:	Oh, thank God that there aren't many casualties. But I really feel bad for the poor Palestinians always living in fear like this.
Sari:	Yeah, but this so-called war is certainly causing so many people to suffer.

English Translation of Readings

1. News Posted by Temanggung City on Internet

August 7, 2009

The sound of gunfire could be heard coming from the house of Mohzahri located in Beji Village, RT 01 RW 07, Kedu area, Kedu Subdistrict, Temanggung, Central Java (province).

In addition, police took Mohzahri, who is allegedly the owner of the house, into custody. Hendra and Aris, were apparently nephews of Mohzahri (70), the owner of the house which was raided by Densus 88 with federal and local police.

Mohzahri's house was surrounded by the Densus 88 team and federal and local police from 1545 Western Indonesian Time and around 1600, the sound of gunfire began to be heard, until 2245.

Though surrounded for four hours, the terrorists who were presumably in Noor Din M. Top's network, never surrendered. On the contrary, a few minutes later a gunfight/an exchange of gunfire occurred. According to eyewitnesses in Beji Village, Kedu Sub-district, Temmanggung District, at 2150 the people who were inside the house which was surrounded, fired at the police as many as three times. Special Anti-terror Detachment 88 then returned fire on as many as seven occasions.

The members of Densus 88 came in three cars and on several motorcycles. Until night, they surrounded the house in question. Headlights were turned on to illuminate the rice paddies along the east side of Moh Zahri's house.

The action of surrounding the house allowed opportunity for rumors to spread that Noor Din M. Top, mastermind of terrorist bombings in Indonesia, was in the house.

TV station Al Jazeera in fact reported that a man resembling Noor Din had been caught...

Densus 88 reportedly completed the surrounding of the house after they arrested two men named Indra (35) and Aris (38) in Parakan Market, Temanggung, Central Java. These two men purportedly were cousins of a man named Tatag, who had already been caught by Densus 88 HQ, Republic of Indonesia Police, three years ago.

According to the Area Chief (RW), Moh Khoil, Moh Zahri was working day by day as a farmer and a teacher at a private middle school in the area. Moh Zahri had been living in the house for 6 years.

The house raided by Densus 88 Indonesian Police HQ in Kedu Temanggung, was seemingly occupied by Terrorist Noordin M. Top's cell. Besides Noordin M. Top, occupants of the house included his follower Dr. Azahari, who is a bomb-making expert named Reno, alias Teddy, alias Mubaruk.

Info from various media

2. Local Police Succeed in Arresting Noordin's "Potential Bridegroom"

News from Wikiberita (Wikinews).com: The Central Java police arrested a man who was presumed to be a member of Noordin M. Top's terrorist network, with the initials Z.A. This news was released by the Central Java Chief of Police, Inspector General Alex Bambang Riatmojo at a series of briefings for all village and section heads in the greater Solo area at the Diamond Convention Center, Solo, yesterday afternoon (23/7).

It was added that, the arrest of Z.A. took place the previous Wednesday night (22/7) in the Cilacap area.

Based on the tentative investigation, continued the Chief of Police, we know that Z.A. had been a member of Noordin's terrorist network since 2001. He said that he (ZA) had intentionally been prepared to be a suicide bomber at several of the following locations.

"Before he was detected, ZA came from gatherings and areas that were going to be targets in the future. Due to this, the involved are still undergoing investigation," revealed the Chief of Police.

ZA, continued the Chief, had received special cultivation from Noordin since 2001. Together with a few other members, ZA was prepared as a bridegroom (an expression for a suicide bomber).

3. Police Arrest the Wife of Noordin M Top

Updated Friday July 24, 2009 5:27pm AEST

Noordin M Top's wife who was detained Wednesday morning in Cilacap knew her husband under a different name and thought that he was a teacher.

The 25 year old woman was detained by anti-terrorist police with her two children.

However, according to her lawyer, she had no idea that she was married to the most wanted terrorist in Southeast Asia.

Arina Rochman was detained under Indonesian anti-terrorism laws and legally represented by Achmad Michdan, the lawyer who also represented the Bali bombers.

According to Michdan, his client did not know that her husband, who she knew as a teacher named Abdul Halim, was actually Noordin M. Top.

According to her, her husband was rarely at home because he taught at a *pesantren* (Islamic boarding school) in South Sulawesi.

(Radio Australia)

Pancasila

Pancasila is the founding political philosophy of the modern state of Indonesia. It consists of 5 principles, which are spelled out in the preamble of its constitution. Pancasila is a Sanskrit word, rather than a modern Indonesian or Javanese one: panca means 'principles,' and sila means 'five.'

Here are the 5 principles. The English translation is my own and differs only slightly from most found online or in other texts:

1. *Ketuhanan Yang Maha Esa* – (Belief in) God, the Almighty.

2. *Kemanusiaan Yang Adil dan Beradab* – Humanity that is just and civilized.

3. *Persatuan Indonesia* – the Unity of Indonesia.

4. *Kerakyatan yang Dipimpin oleh Hikmat Kebijaksanaan dalam Permusyawaratan/Perwakilan* – Democracy guided by the astute wisdom/strength of wisdom found in deliberation and representation.

5. *Keadilan Sosial bagi Seluruh Rakyat Indonesia* – Social justice for all the people of Indonesia.

The Constitution (UUD 45)

The Undang-Undang Dasar Republik Indonesia 1945 is made up of several parts. The preamble includes a justification for independence, much like the preamble to the U.S. Declaration of Independence, followed by the 5 principles of Pancasila. The preamble is followed by 16 chapters or 'Sections,' organized by topic. It is divided further into a total of approximately 40 articles, which often include sub articles (36, 36A, 36B, 36C). A single article commonly contains multiple provisions/rules.

The Constitution was first adopted August 18, 1945, then superseded 1949-1959, and restored in 1959. It has been amended 4 times – first in 1999, then in 2000, 2001, and finally again in 2002. The activity surrounding the amendments is related to the end of the Suharto era, and the beginning of a period of new democracy and the dramatic political changes that occurred within Indonesia during this time.

A few of the more interesting aspects of UUD 45 include:

Like the U.S. Constitution, it grants broad rights and power to local governments - in this case provincial (kabupaten) and city (kota) governments: 'regional administration shall exercise the broadest possible autonomy, except for matters of governance that are determined by law as the prerogative of the Central Government.' Relations between the central government and provinces 'are to be regulated by law with special regard for the specificity and diversity of each region.' (Article 18A.)

The right to make laws resides with the national and regional legislatures, or DPR - Dewan Perwakilan Rakyat and DPD - Dewan Perwakilan Daerah.

About the specific powers and procedures to be employed, it is flexible and non-specific in many instances, stating that these are to be 'regulated by law.'

As for rights, it states that: 'Each citizen shall be entitled to an occupation and an existence proper for a human being' and 'Each citizen shall have the right and the duty to participate in the defense of the nation.' (Article 27)

Section XA, which deals with human rights is surprisingly long and detailed. It includes approx. 30 specific rights granted to Indonesians, including freedom of assembly, religion and worship, medical care, schooling, a place to live, the right to possess and spread information via all channels, the right to own property, and for each Indonesian to 'develop himself as a dignified human being.'

The state is based on the worship of the One Almighty God, but each individual is free to choose his religion.

The state reserves the right to control economic production sectors that are vital and affect the livelihood of a large number of its people (Article 33).

A good online version of the Constitution with an excellent English translation can be found at:

http://www.humanrights.asia/countries/indonesia/laws/uud1945

National Song – 'Indonesia Raya'

Indonesia Tanah Airku,	Indonesia my homeland,
Tanah Tumpah Darahku,	Land of my fathers' blood,
Di sanalah aku berdiri,	Where I stand
Jadi pandu ibuku.	Watching over my motherland.
Indonesia kebangsaanku,	Indonesia is my nationality,
Bangsa dan tanah airku,	My people and my homeland.
Marilah kita berseru,	Let us all exclaim,
Indonesia bersatu.	Indonesia United!
Hiduplah tanahku,	Long live my land,
Hiduplah negeriku,	Long live my country,
Bangsaku, rakyatku, semuanya.	All of my nation and people,
Bangunlah jiwanya,	Rise up in spirit,
Bangunlah badannya,	Rise up in body,
Untuk Indonesia Raya.	For a Great Indonesia.
Indonesia Raya,	Indonesia the Great,
Merdeka, Merdeka	Free! Free! (Independent)
Tanahku, negeriku yang kucinta.	My land and country that I love.
Indonesia Raya,	Indonesia the Great,
Merdeka, Merdeka	Free, free! / and Independent.
Hiduplah Indonesia Raya.	Long live Indonesia the Great.
Indonesia Raya,	Indonesia the Great,
Merdeka, Merdeka	Free, free! (Free and independent)
Tanahku, negeriku yang kucinta.	My land and country that I love.
Indonesia Raya,	Indonesia the Great,
Merdeka, Merdeka	Free, free!
Hiduplah Indonesia Raya.	Long live Indonesia the Great.

Indonesian Society

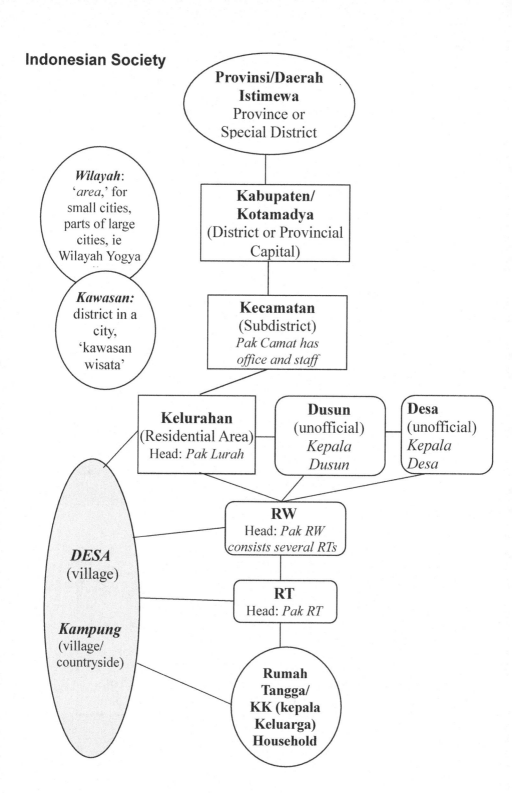

Provinsi/Daerah Istimewa
Province or Special District

Wilayah: 'area,' for small cities, parts of large cities, ie Wilayah Yogya

Kabupaten/ Kotamadya
(District or Provincial Capital)

Kawasan: district in a city, 'kawasan wisata'

Kecamatan
(Subdistrict)
Pak Camat has office and staff

Kelurahan
(Residential Area)
Head: *Pak Lurah*

Dusun
(unofficial)
Kepala Dusun

Desa
(unofficial)
Kepala Desa

RW
Head: *Pak RW*
consists several RTs

DESA
(village)

Kampung
(village/ countryside)

RT
Head: *Pak RT*

Rumah Tangga/ KK (kepala Keluarga)
Household

Organization of Police

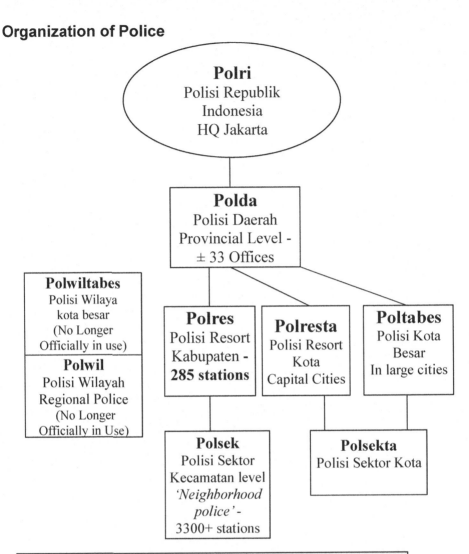

Polri
Polisi Republik
Indonesia
HQ Jakarta

Polda
Polisi Daerah
Provincial Level -
± 33 Offices

Polwiltabes
Polisi Wilaya
kota besar
(No Longer
Officially in use)

Polwil
Polisi Wilayah
Regional Police
(No Longer
Officially in Use)

Polres
Polisi Resort
Kabupaten -
285 stations

Polresta
Polisi Resort
Kota
Capital Cities

Poltabes
Polisi Kota
Besar
In large cities

Polsek
Polisi Sektor
Kecamatan level
*'Neighborhood
police'* -
3300+ stations

Polsekta
Polisi Sektor Kota

Polres is the basic operational unit in most of the country, which deals with day-to-day law and order. Above this level, most duties are administrative or specialized in nature.

Functionally, everything from Polres level down is divided into different divisions, which are:
(1) Intelpam- Intelligence & Security
(2) Reserse - Criminal Investigation, (3) Samapta - Patrol,
(4) Lantas - Traffic, and (5) Bimmas - Community Guidance.

Indonesian Calendars and Holidays

Four different calendar systems are used in Indonesia, and holidays and celebrations are based on all of them. The Gregorian (Western) calendar is the most often seen and officially used for many aspects of life in Indonesia, but the Islamic calendar is also used by the Indonesian government for deciding Islamic holidays, which are celebrated as official holidays by all the people. Throughout the island of Java, the Javanese calendar's *Pasaran* days of the week are found (in smaller print) on any common calendar you buy or see hanging from the wall. Other aspects of the Javanese calendar determine lucky days to hold important events like launching a business or getting married. The Sultan in Yogyakarta uses the Javanese calendar to determine when local festivals should be held. In Bali, where most people are Hindu, aspects of the Javanese calendar are similarly used to determine lucky days, Hindu celebrations, and for astrology. Finally, a Chinese calendar, also with various lucky, neutral, and unlucky days, is often found in Chinese-Indonesian homes and businesses. Official Indonesian holidays include Islamic, Christian, and Buddhist holidays, as well as Chinese New Year and secular government holidays like Independence Day.

Official Holidays 2011

Jan 1	Tahun Baru Masehi	New Year's Day
Feb 3	Tahun Baru Imlek	Chinese New Year
Feb 15	Maulid Nabi Muhammad SAW	Muhammad's Birthday
Mar 5	Hari Raya Nyepi/Tahun Baru Saka	Bali's Day of Silence
Apr 22	Wafat Isa Al-Masih /Jumat Agung	Good Friday
May 17	Hari Raya Waisak	Buddha's Birthday
Jun 2	Kenaikan Isa Al-Masih	Christ's Ascension
Jun 29	Isra Miraj Prophet Mohammad SAW	Muhammad's Journey to Heaven
Aug 17	Hari Kemerdekaan/17 Agustus	Independence Day
Aug 31	Hari Raya Idul Fitri/Lebaran	End of Ramadan
Nov 6-7*	Hari Raya Idul Adha/Haji	Feast of (Abraham's) Sacrifice/end of Haj
Nov 27-8*	Tahun Baru Hijriyah	Islamic New Year
Dec 25-6*	Hari Raya Natal	Christmas

*As in many countries, when a holiday falls on a Sunday, it is officially taken off by government, schools, and banks on the following Monday. All holidays based on the Islamic, Javanese, or Chinese calendars are lunar-based, and the date varies each year, just as Easter does in the West. For several of the Islamic holidays, the government sometimes does not officially come out and decree the day until the holiday is near, and large influential Islamic organizations do not agree on the exact date (within a day). *Idul Fitri* is the most important traveling holiday, when most Indonesians travel to their family's/grandparent's home. Workers generally take several days off work, so it is popular and beneficial when the official holiday falls so that this is possible.

Annual Indonesian Holidays (Dates = 2012)

Jan 1	Tahun Baru Masehi	New Year's Day
Jan 23	Tahun Baru Imlek	Chinese New Year
Feb 4	Maulid Nabi Muhammad SAW	Muhammad's Birthday
Mar 23	Hari Raya Nyepi/Tahun Baru Saka	Bali's Day of Silence
Apr 6	Wafat Isa Al-Masih /Jumat Agung	Good Friday
May 5	Hari Raya Waisak	Buddha's Birthday
May 17	Kenaikan Isa Al-Masih	Christ's Ascension
Jun 16	Isra al Miraj Muhammad	Muhammad's Journey to Heaven
Aug 17	Hari Kemerdekaan / 17 Agustus	Independence Day
Aug 19	Hari Raya Idul Fitri / Lebaran	End of Ramadan
Oct 26	Hari Raya Idul Adha/Korban/Haji	Feast of (Abraham's) Sacrifice/end of Haj
Nov 15	Tahun Baru Hijriyah	Islamic New Year
Dec 25	Hari Raya Natal	Christmas

The Javanese Calendar

The Javanese calendar was officially first put into use by Sultan Agung of Mataram in 1633. Prior to that, Javanese mainly used the Hindu Saka calendar. The Javanese calendar came to be used throughout most of the island of Java, but with notable exceptions in Batavia (present day Jakarta) and Banten. It is not surprising that the calendar combined features of the Islamic and Saka calendar, and even the Gregorian calendar used by the Dutch.

Here are the different ways of measuring time in the traditional Javanese calendar system, along with their designations/names:

- The 5-day week, or *Pasaran*
- The 7-day week, or *Dina Pitu*
- Combining the *Pasaran* days with the 7-day Gregorian calendar to create a 35 repeating cycle, or *Weton*
- Solar months, or *Mangsa*
- Lunar months, or *Wulan*
- Years, or *Tahun*
- 8-year cycles, or *Windu*

Pasaran

The *pasaran* comes from the word *pasar* – 'market.' It was based on a historical 5-day rotating/traveling market system. Here are the names of the days in *ngoko* (informal) Javanese. These can be found in smaller font on most Western/Gregorian calendars used on Java.

- Legi
- Pahing
- Pon
- Wagé
- Kliwon

Javanese considered these days to have a relation to colors and direction:

- Legi - white and East
- Pahing - red and South
- Pon - yellow and West
- Wage - black and North
- Kliwon - out of focus colors and 'center'

The Weton Cycle

Most Javanese astrology comes from combining the *pasaran* with the 7-day Gregorian calendar to make a 35-day repeating cycle. Individual characteristics and the future are divinable from this combination, and the resulting days are called **Weton/Wetonan**. *Weton* are important for certain celebrations, rites, commemorations and so on, which are all held on days considered lucky.

The combination of the *pasaran* day and the common day on a person's day of birth is like the Western Zodiac, and is believed by some people to indicate general characteristics of that person.

An example of the importance of holding an important event on an auspicious *weton* is Indonesia's Proclamation of Independence on August 17, 1945, which was purposely made on *Jumat Legi*. It was also the *Weton* for the birth and death of Sultan Agung, who as previously mentioned, is credited with the Javanese calendar. To this day, *Jumat Legi* is considered an important night for pilgrimage.

Solar Months – Mangsa

The solar year was traditionally divided into twelve periods (*mangsa*) of unequal length, and based on agricultural/weather patterns on Java. This was well-known by most Javanese in the late 1800s, but fell out of use after. In astrology, the *pranata mangsa* is used to predict personality traits in a similar way to sun signs in Western astrology. It is not widely used anymore for other purposes.

Lunar Months - Wulan

The lunar year (*tahun*) is divided into twelve *wulan*. Each is 29 or 30 days. This is adapted from and follows the lunar months of the Islamic calendar. The names of the months are given below:

Ngoko (informal) names of months

> Sura   30
> Sapar   29
> Mulud   30
> Bakda   29
> Jumadil Awal 30
> Jumadil Akhir 29
> Rejeb   30
> Ruwah   29
> Pasa   30
> Sawal   29
> Sela   30
> Besar   29 or 30* depending on the length of the year

The cycle of months is considered metaphorically to represent the cycle of human life. The first nine months represent time in the womb, while the tenth month represents the human in the world, the eleventh the end of his or her existence, and the twelfth death/the return to where he or she came from. The cycle goes from one phase of life (*rijal*) to another...

Just as the months of the year represent the human life cycle, so to do the individual dates/phases of the moon within the Javanese lunar months symbolize our life cycle:

The first of a Javanese month, when the moon is barely visible as a sliver is like a newborn baby; night by night it grows bigger. The 14th of a Javanese month on the full moon, is called *Purnama Sidhi*. It symbolizes an adult with a wife/husband. The 15th is called *Purnama* – it is still a full moon, but its brightness is diminishing. The 20th is *Panglong,* when a human begins to lose his memory.

The 25th is *Sumurup*, when one has to be taken care of by others, just like when he/she was a small child. The 26th is *Manjing*, representing a return to where we came from (death) and a spiritual consciousness/existence (*Rijal*). The remaining days of the month are the time when we will be reincarnated/born again as a new life in the world.

Windu

Eight *tahun* make a *windu*, much like ten years make a decade. A *windu* is 81 repetitions of the *weton* cycle, or 2,835 days. (The *tahun* are lunar years, and slightly shorter in length than Gregorian years.) Here are the names of the tahun (in krama/ngoko) that comprise a *windu*:

1. Purwana/Alip (354 days)
2. Karyana/Ehé (354 days)
3. Anama/Jemawal (355 days)
4. Lalana/Jé (354 days)
5. Ngawanga/Dal (355 days)
6. Pawaka/Bé (354 days)
7. Wasana/Wawu (354 days)
8. Swasana/Jimakir (355 days)

Very few Javanese take note of the *windu* anymore, but the passing of one is still often seen as a milestone of sorts, a reason to celebrate, and deserving of a *slametan,* or ritual feast.

'Noble Days'

Traditional Javanese who still practice traditional spiritual teachings or use the Javanese calendar consider the following to be noble days (*dino mulyo*):
- Satu Suro – the first of Sura or the New Year
- Hanggara Aish – Selasa Kliwon
- Dino Purnomo – Jumat Legi/Sukra Manis

Pawukon

Pawukon is a 210-day calendar, related to Hindu tradition. It is now only really used in Bali.

Javanese Astrology in Real-Life

In *weton*, each day has its own *jejer* (position), and *neptu/naktu*. *Neptu* is a value attached to the names of people and calendar units and a crucial element on which calculations are based for deciding lucky and unlucky days and times.

Friday (*Jumat*) is the most important day of the 7-day week and the Islamic Holy Day; it gets the first *jejer*. The seven-day week runs from Fri to Thur. In the *pasaran*, *Kliwon* is the most important day and starts the week's cycle.

Friday appears often on lists of good days. It is the day of *kemresik* (cleansing), a good time for weddings or other feasts during the months of *Mulud*, *Bakdomulud* and *Jumadilawal*. Friday is a fair day during *Sura* and *Sapar* and is unfavorable in *Jumadilakir*.

By using the *jejer*, *neptu*, and as in Western astrology, the position of major celestial bodies like the sun, moon, venus, etc., practitioners of Javanese astrology produce charts noting lucky, neutral, and unlucky days and times for holding various events or performing certain kinds of work or actions. A large number of Javanese pay some heed to these forecasts, and when it comes to really important events, most Javanese choose not to tempt fate by ignoring traditional wisdom or custom.

For such life-changing events like marriages or building a new home, the month itself is important too. Three months are good for marriage: *Raya Agung*, *Ruwah* and *Jumadil Akhir*. Four are good for building a home. Each month has its own consequence, good or bad. For example, getting married in *Sura* may lead to a broken marriage. Like days, months can be lucky, neutral, or unlucky for a certain endeavor. In the modern world, a couple can't always wait until a good time to get married, but they will still likely avoid the dangerous day (*raspati*) and choose a neutral one (*dina lowong*). *Raspati* occurs when the value of *naktu* of the particular month combined with the *naktu* of the day is either twelve or five.

*A SAMPLE JAVANESE CALENDAR'S MONTHS OF MAY AND JUNE
FOLLOW, WITH AUTHOR'S NOTES TO HELP YOU READ THEM**

Mei

Jumadilawal/Jumadilakhir 1432 H
Jumadilawal/Jumadilakhir 1944 Be

This typical desk calendar from Yogya combines aspects of the Gregorian, Javanese, and Islamic calendars. The months of the Islamic and Javanese calendars: Jumadilawal/Jumadilakhir (thru May 4) and Jumadilakhir (May 5 -), are at top left. 1432 H is the Islamic yr, counted from the Hijrah/Hegira, when Muhammad emigrated from Mecca to Medina. 1944 Be refers to the Javanese yr, officially created by Sultan Agung in 1633. Note also Tahun 2555 or year 2555 of the Buddhist calendar for Waisak Holiday on 17 May.

MINGGU	SENIN	SELASA	RABU	KAMIS	JUMAT	SABTU
24	25	26	27	28	29	30
1	2	3	4	5	6	7
27 WAGE	28 KLIWON	29 LEGI	30 PAHING	1 PON	2 WAGE	3 KLIWON
8	9	10	11	12	13	14
4 LEGI	5 PAHING	6 PON	7 WAGE	8 KLIWON	9 LEGI	10 PAHING
15	16	17	18	19	20	21
11 PON	12 WAGE	13 KLIWON	14 LEGI	15 PAHING	16 PON	17 WAGE
22	23	24	25	26	27	28
18 KLIWON	19 LEGI	20 PAHING	21 PON	22 WAGE	23 KLIWON	24 LEGI
29	30	31	1	2	3	4
25 PAHING	26 PON	27 WAGE				

17 MEI 2011 (SELASA): LIBUR HARI RAYA WAISAK TAHUN 2555

Pasaran days are in small print underneath each day. Notice Kliwon (the most important and 1st day of pasaran week) falls on Wed the 1st, Sun the 6th, and so on. To track the weton cycle, look at the previous month of Mei and find the Senin Kliwon on May 2nd. Now, find each consecutive Kliwon. There are 7 more (8 total) until Senin Kliwon repeats itself, on Jun 6th - 35 days later. This is what is meant by the 35-day repeating wetonan. Note that Jumat Legi, an important date for pilgrimage - or a slametan wishing someone a safe trip - occurs on Jumat Legi/Jun 17th. Arabic numerals give the dates on the Islamic calendar. The 2 holidays in Jun were Christ's Ascension and Muhammad's journey to Heaven (bottom).

Juni

Jumadilakhir/Rajab 1432 H
Jumadilakhir/Rejeb 1944 Dal

MINGGU	SENIN	SELASA	RABU	KAMIS	JUMAT	SABTU
29	30	31	1 28 KLIWON	2 29 LEGI	3 1 PAHING	4 2 PON
5 3 WAGE	6 4 KLIWON	7 5 LEGI	8 6 PAHING	9 7 PON	10 8 PON	11 9 KLIWON
12 10 LEGI	13 11 PAHING	14 12 PON	15 13 WAGE	16 14 KLIWON	17 15 PAHING	18 16 PAHING
19 17 PON	20 18 WAGE	21 19 KLIWON	22 20 LEGI	23 21 PAHING	24 22 PON	25 23 WAGE
26 24 KLIWON	27 25 LEGI	28 26 PAHING	29 27 PON	30 28 WAGE	1	2
3	4	5	6	7	8	9

2 JUNI 2011 (KAMIS): LIBUR KENAIKAN YESUS KRISTUS **29 JUNI 2011 (RABU):** LIBUR ISRA' MI'RAJ NABI MUHAMMAD SAW

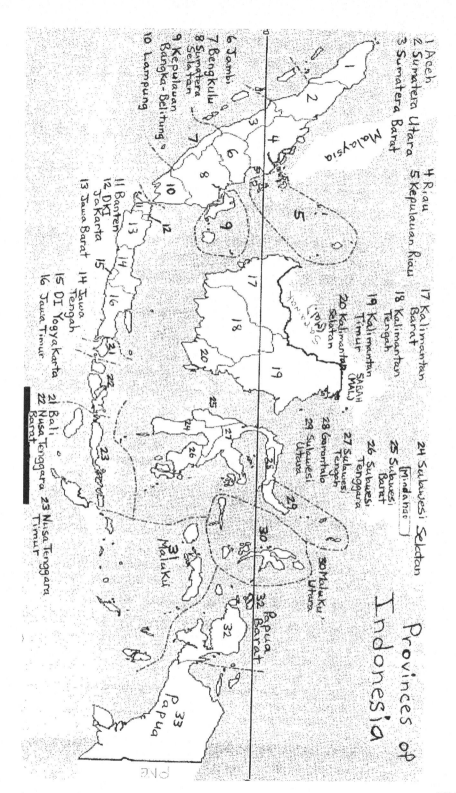

Provinces of Indonesia

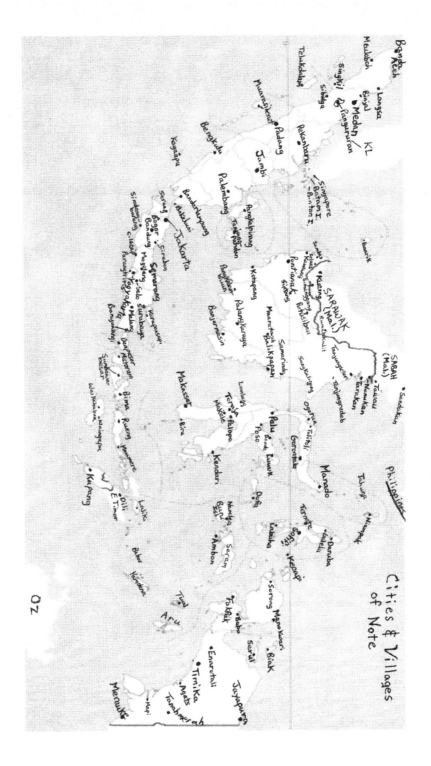

Cities & Villages of Note

375

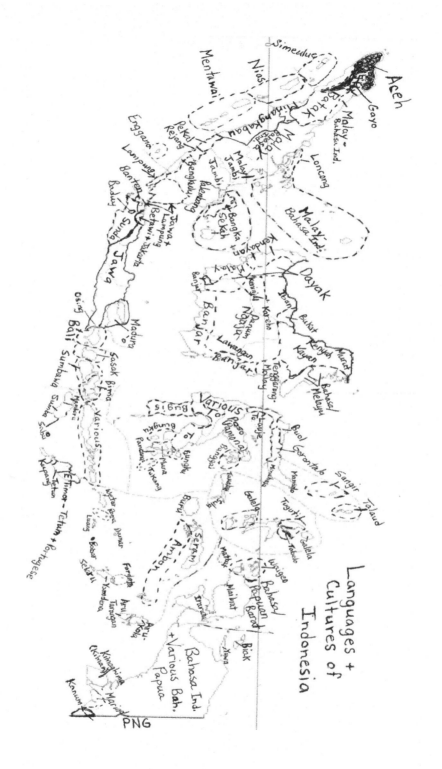

Languages + Cultures of Indonesia

376

Common Acronyms A – Z

Acronym	In Indonesian	In English
AAL	Akademi Angkatan Laut	Naval Academy - Surabaya
AAU	Akademi Angkatan Udara	Air Force Academy - Yogyakarta
ABG	Anak Baru Gedhe	'Young teen' aged 11-14
AD	Angkatan Darat	The Army
AKABRI	Anggkatan Bersenjata Republik Indonesia	The Armed Forces of Indonesia
AKMIL	Akademi Militer	Military Academy - in Magelang, Central Java
Allah SWT	Allah Subhanahu Wa-ta'ala	Allah the Creator
An Sendri	Atas Nama Sendiri	Sell by self, for sale by private owner
Angkota	Angkutan Kota	City transportation - the small vans running routes
APBN	Anggaran Pendepatan Belanja Negara	The National Budget
ART	Anggaran Rumah Tangga	Neighborhood rules
Askes	Asuransi Kesehatan	Health Insurance - for government employees
Askeskin	Asuransi Kesehatan Miskin	Health Insurance - for the poor
ASMI	Akademi Sekretaris Managmen Indo	Indonesian Secretarial & Management Academy
Atal	Atase Angkutan Laut	Naval Attache
Balita	Bawah Lima Tahun	children under 5 yrs old
BB	Bau Badan	Body odor
BBM	Bahan Bakar Minyak	Refined fuel oil
bc	buffalo color	Colored card paper
BEM	Badan Eksekutiv Mahasiswa	a university faculty organization
BEMU	Badan Eksekutiv Mahasiswa Umum	a university student organization
BH	Bust Holder	(a woman's) bra
BI	Bank of Indonesia	Bank of Indonesia
BII	Bank Internasional Indonesia	International Bank of Indonesia - one of the major banks

377

BKO	—	TDY - temporary duty, detached
BL	Barat Laut	NW
BOS	Bantuan Operasional Sekolah	School Assistance - a govt office in school, pays part cost
BPI	Badan Pembangunan Internasional	Int'l AID
BPK	Badan Pengawas Keunganan	Treasury Oversight Committee
BPKB	Bukti Pemilikan Kendaraan Bermotor	Motor vehicle 'blue book' proving ownership
BPOM	Badan Pengawas Obat dan Makanan	Food & Drug Administration (FDA), provides oversight
BRI	Bank Rakyat Indonesia	People's Bank of Indonesia - one of the major banks
BriMob	Brigade Mobil	SWAT - special Indonesian police sent to volatile situations
BS	Dutch - burgerlijke Stand	Office of civil registration, a civil marriage
BS	Bayar Sendiri	Go Dutch, pay own way on a date
BU	Butuh Uang	Need money
BUMN	Badan Usaha Milik Negara	any state-owned corporation
Capeg	calon pegawai	Candidate for civil service
Curanmor	Pencurian Kendaraan Bermotor	Theft of motor vehicle
Curhat	curahan hati	Outpouring of one's heart
CV	Commanditaire Venootschap	Limited Partnership
CW	Cat Warna	Color (cars or motorcycles)
D.	Danau	Lake
d.a.	dengan alamat	C/O - In Care of
D1	Diploma Satu	One yr diploma, from non-university/tech school
D2	Diploma Dua	Two-yr diploma, from non-university/tech school
D3	Diploma Tiga	Three-yr diploma, from a non-university/tech school
Danramil	Komdan Rayon Militer	Millitary commander at kecamatan level
Daop	Daerah Operasi	Area of Operations
DB	Drum Band	Marching band
DB	Denam Berdara	Dengue fever
Depag	Departemen Agama	Department of Religion

378

Deparlu	Departemen Luar Negeri	Ministry of Foreign Affairs / State Dept.
Depdag	Departemen Perdagangan	Department of Commerce
Depdagri	Departemen Dalam Negeri	Department of the Interior
Deperdag	Departemen Perdagangan	Dept of Commerce
Depkeh	Departemen Kehakiman	Dept of Justice
Depkes	Departemen Kesehatan	Dept of Health
Depkeu	Departemen Keuangan	Dept of Finance
Deplu	Departemen Luar Negeri	Ministry of Foreign Affairs / State Dept.
Depnaker	Departemen Tenaga Kerja	Dept of Labor
Deppen	Departemen Penerangan	Dept of Information
Depsos	Departemen Sosial	Dept of Social Services
DIP	Daftar Isian Proyek	Project Budget Proposal
Dirjen	Direktor Jenderal	Director General
Dirut	Direktor Utama	Managing Director
DIY	Daerah Istimewa Yogyakarta	Yogyakarta Special District
DKI	Daerah Kota Istimewa	Special District City = Jakarta
dll.	dan lain-lain	etc.
DPA	Dewan Pertimbangan Agung	Supreme Judicial Council - think tank with public influence
DPP	Dewan Pengurus Pusat	Board of Directors, Central Board of a company
DPP	Dewan Pimpinan Pusat	Leadership of daily ops of a political party (local level)
DPR	Dewan Perwakilan Rakyat	People's Representative Council - Parliament /Legislature
DPRD	Dawan Perwakilan Rakyat Daerah	Local government - Provincial/State Parliament/Legislature
DPT	Diphteri, Pertussis, Tetanus	Diptheria, Whooping cough, Tetanus vaccine
Dubes	Duta Besar	Ambassador
FH	Fakultas Hukum	Faculty/School of Law at university
FHPK	Fakultas Hukum dan Paengetauan Kemasyarakatan	Faculty/School of Law and Social Sciences at uni

FIPA	Fakultas Ilmu Pasti dan Alam	Faculty/School of Math and Physical Sciences at uni
FIPIA	Fakultas Ilmu Pasti dan Ilmu Alam	Faculty/School of Math and Physics at uni
FIS	Fakultas Ilmu Sosial	Faculty/School of Social Sciences
FK	Fakultuas Keguruan	School of Teacher Training/ Education Dept. at uni
FK	Fakultas Kedokteran	Faculty/School of Medicine at uni
FKIP	Fakultas Keguruan dan Ilmu Pendidikan	Normal School, Teacher's College/University
FPI	Front Pembela Islam	A hardline Islamic group often involved in social unrest
FPS	Fakultas Pasca Sarjana	Graduate School
FS	Fakultas Sastra	Faculty/School of Literature
G30S	Gerakan 30 September	The communist attempt to seize govt on 30 Sep, 1965
GAM	Gerakan Aceh Merdeka	Free Aceh (separatist) Movement
Golkar	Golongan Karya	A political party formed for govt workers w/ a long hist.
GR	Gotong Royong	Mutual Aid, ideology of helping neighbors
HAM	Hak Asasi Manusia	Human Rights
Hansip	Pertahanan Sipil	Civil Defense
HMI	Himpunan Mahasiswa Islam	Islamic Students Association
HPH	Hak Pengusahaan Hutan	A logging concession
Humas	Hubungan Masyarakat	Public Relations
HUT	Hari Ulang Tahun	Birthday
IAIN	Institut Agama Islam Negeri	National Institute of Islamic Studies
IB	Irian Barat	Papua / Irian Jaya
IKIP	Institut Keguruan Ilmu Pendidikan	Teachers' Training College/Institute
IP	Indeks Prestasi	GPA - grade point average
IPA	Ilmu Pasti Alam	Math and natural sciences
IPB	Institut Pertanian Bogor	Bogor Institute of Agriculture
IPDN	Institute Pemerintah Dalam Negeri	Civil Service Institute - academy for aspiring civil servants in Palembang, notorious for hazing incidents resulting in deaths
IPS	Ilmu Pengetahuan Sosial	Social Sciences

Ireda	Iuran Rehabilitasi Daerah	Regional Development Tax (on commercial property)
ITB	Institut Teknologi Bandung	Bandung Institute of Technology
Jabodetabek	Jak, Bogor, Depok, Tanggerang, Bekasi	Jakarta and surrounding areas
jadul	Jaman dulu	Old-fashioned
Jagung	Jaksa Agung	Attorney General
Jateng	Jawa Tengah	Central Java
Jatim	Jawa Timur	East Java
Jl.	Jalan	St. (street)
Kahumas	Kepala Hubungan Masyarakat	Head of PR, Spokesman
KAI	Kereta Api Indonesia	the Indonesian railway
Kalsel	Kalimantan Selatan	South Kalimantan
Kalut	Kalimantan Utara	North Kalimantan
Kanwil	Kantor Wilayah	Regional Office
karo	Kepala Biro	Dept/Division Head
Kasab	Kepala Staf Angkatan Bersenjata	Chief of Staff of Armed Forces
Kasad	Kepala Staf Angkatan Darat	Army Chief of Staff
Kasal	Kepala Staf Angkatan Laut	Navy Chief of Staff
KB	Keluarga Berencana	Family Planning
KBRI	Kedutaan Besar Republik Indonesia	Indonesian Embassy
Kedubes	Kedutaan Besar	Embassy
KIM	Kartu Izin Menetap	Residence Permit Card
KITAS	Kartu Izin Tinggal Terbatas	Limited Stay Permit - Immigration card
KJRI	Konsulat Jenderal Republik Indonesia	Indonesian Consulate General
KK	Kepala Keluarga	Head of Household
KKN	Kuliah Kerja Nyata	social rural internship for uni students (mandatory)
KKM	KK Minimal	minimum passing score (academic)
KKO	Korps Komando	Marine Corps
KM	Kapal Motor	Motorized boat, ship
Kodaeral	Komando Daerah Angkatan Laut	Regional Naval Command

KODAK	Komando Daerah Kepolisian	Area Police Command
KODAM	Komando Daerah Militer	Regional Military Command
KODAU	Komando Daerah Angkatan Udara	Regional Air Force Command
KOMNAS HAM	Komisi Nasional HAM	National Commission on Human Rights - Cabinet level
Konbes	Konperensi Besar	A large/major conference
KONI	Komite Olah Raga Nasional Indonesia	Indonesian National Sports Committee
KONJEN	Konsulat Jenderal	Consulate General
KOOPS	Komando Operasional	Operational Command
KOPASSUS	Komando Pasukan Khusus	Indonesian Special Forces
KORAMIL	Komando Rayon Militer	Sub-District/Ward Military Command - at Kecamatan level
KOREM	Komando Resort Militer	District Military Command - at the Kabupaten level
KORPRI	Korps Pegawai Republik Indonesia	Indonesian Civil Service Corps
KOWILHAN	Komando Wilayah Pertahanan	Territorial Defense Command
KPK	Komisi Pemberantasan Korupsi	Anti-corruption Commission - govt.
KPR	Kredit Pemilikan Rumah	A house loan
KPU	Komisi Pemilihan Umum	General Election Commission - preps ballots, counts votes
KRD	Kereta Rel Diesel	a diesel train
KRL	Kereta Rel Listrik	an electric train
KTP	Kartu Tanda Penduduk	Residence/National ID Card
KUD	Kooperasi Unit Desa	a farming co-op, found in only some villages
KUHAP	Kitab Undang-U. Hukum Acara Pidana	Criminal Code
KUUD	Kooperasia Unit Usaha Desa	Village (farm) Co-op Enterprise, in some villages
LABFOR	lab forensik	Forensic Lab
Lapas	Lembaga Pemasyarakatan	jail
LBH	Lembaga Bantuan Hukum	Legal Aid Services
Lemhanas	Lembaga Pertahanan Nasional	National Defense Institute - Jakarta, for generals sr. col.

382

Lemigas	Lembaga Minyak dan Gas Bumi	Petroleum and Natural Gas Institute
Ling Asri	Kamling Asri	A good neighborhood (in house ads)
LKMD	Lembaga Ketahanan Masyarakat Desa	Villager's Restraint League - voluntary, solves problems between families in the village
LP	Lembaga Pemasyarakatan	jail
LSD	Lembaga Sosial Desa	Village Social Group
LSM	Lembaga Sosial M	NGO
MA	Mahkamah Agung	the Supreme Court
Mabes	Markas Besar	HQ - Headquarters
MBA	Married By Accident	a marriage due to unplanned pregnancy
Menagama	Menteri Agama	Minister of Religion
Mendagri	Menteri dalam Negeri	Minister for Internal Affairs/Dept of the Interior
Menhan	Menteri Pertahanan	Defense Minister
Menhankam	Menteri Pertahanan dan Keamanan	Minister of Defense (and Security)
Menhub	Menteri Perhubungan	Minister of Communication
Menkes	Menteri Kesehatan	Ministry of Health
Menkes	Menteri Kesehatan	Minister of Public Health
Menkesra	Menteri Kesejahteraan Rakyat	Minister of Public Welfare
Menkeu	Menteri Keuangan	Minister of Finance
Menkop	Menteri Koperasi	Minister of Cooperatives
Menlu	Menteri Luar Negeri	Foreign Minister
Menmud	Menteri Muda	Undersecretary (of X)
Menpen	Menteri Penerangan	Minister of Information
Menperdag	Menteri Perdagangan	Minister of Trade
Menpora	Menteri Negera Pemuda dan Olah Raga	State Minister of Youth and Sports
Mens	Menstruasi	Menstruation
Mentan	Menteri Pertanian	Ministry of Agriculture
Mgl ctk	Mungil, cantik	Small and pretty
Mhd.	Muhammad	Muhammad
MMI	Majelis Mujahadeen Indonesia	An Islamic umbrella organization, advocating Sharia
Monas	Monumen Nasional	The obelisk monument in Liberty Park in Jakarta

MPO	Menghitung Pajak Org	Sales tax
MPR	Majelis Permusyawara-tan Rakyat	People's Advisory Assembly - highest body in Congress
Mps.	Menurut pendapat saya	In my opinion,
MT	Madrasah Tsanawiyah	Islamic Boarding School - Junior High/Middle School
MU	Majelis Umum	General Assembly
Muh. SAW	Muhammad Sallalahu Alaihi Wassalam	Muhammad the last prophet
MUI	Majelis Ulama Indonesia	Indonesian Council of Islamic Scholars
Munas	Musyawarah Nasional	National Deliberative Council/ Deliberation
Muspida	Musyawarah Pimpinan Daerah	Provincial Government Council
Naker	Tenaga Kerja	manpower
Nekad	Negara, Ekonomi, Kea-manan, Aga-ma,Demokrasi	a Sukarno-era slogan which out-lined the stated goals/political policies of the government
NIP	Nomer Induk Pegawai	Civil Service Number
NKRI	Negara Kesatuan Repub-lik Indonesia	The ideology that Indonesia is a single, unified country
Nopol	Nomer Polisi	Vehicle registration number
NPWP	Nomer Pokok Wajib Pajak	Tax ID Number
NRI	Negara Republik Indone-sia	The Republic of Indonesia
NRP	Nomer Registrasi Pokok	Soldier's Registration Number
NTB	Nusa Tenggara Barat	Western Lesser Sunda Islands
NTR	Nika, Talak, Rujuk	Married, Divorced, and Recon-ciled
NTT	Nusa Tenggara Timur	Eastern Lesser Sunda Islands
NU	Nahdhatul Ulama	One of 2 largest Islamic Organi-zations in Indo. More conserva-tive than Muhhamidya. Runs *Pe-santren.*
Nusra	Nusa Tenggara	Lesser Sunda Islands
Nusrabar	Nusa Tenggara Barat	Western Lesser Sunda Islands
Nusratim	Nusa Tenggara Timur	Eastern Lesser Sunda Islands
OB	Office Boy	young man who works in office, runs errands, etc.
ONH	Ongkos Naik Haji	costs of going on the Haj

OPM	Organisasi Papua Merdeka	Free Papua Organization - separatist movement Papua
Opspek	Orientasi Program Pengenalan Kampus	New Student Campus Orientation - at universities
Opstib	Operasi Tertib	Anti-corruption operation
Opsus	Operasi Khusus	a special (intelligence) operation in military
OR	Olah Raga	Sports
Orkeb	Orginisasi Kebudayaan	Cultural organization
Orpol	Organisasi Politik	Any political organization
OSIS	Organisasi Siswa Intra Sekolah	promotes school events & extra-curricular - like Student Council
OTW	On the way	On the way (in texts, sms)
PAL	Penataran Angkatan Laut	Naval Base
PAM	Perusahaan Air Minum	City/Municipal Water Company
PAN	Partai Amanat Nasional	National Mandate Party - one of the major parties
Panwaslu	Panitia Pengawas Pemilu	Election Oversight Committee
Para	Paratrooper	Paratrooper
Paspal	Ilmu Pasti dan Pengatahuan Alam	Math and natural sciences
PBB	Perserikatan Bangsa-Bangsa	the UN
PBB	Pajak Bumi dan Bangunan	Property tax
PD	Pegang Dunia	WW - World War
PD	Pendidikan Jasmani	PE - Physical Education
PD & K	Pendidikan Dasar dan Kebudayaan	Department of Basic Education and Culture
PDI	Partai Demokrasi Indonesia	Indonesian Democratic Party
PDLT	Pakaian Dinas Lepangan Tropis/Tiger	Fatigues / BDUs
Pelatnas	Pemusatan Latihan Nasional	National Sports Training Center
Pelni	Pelayaran Nasional Indonesia	Indonesian Ferry Service - runs throughout all islands
Pemka	Pembela Kebenaran	Defenders of Truth - one of Free Papua commands
Pemkab	Pemerintah Kabupaten	Local government at Kabupaten level
Penad	Penerangan Angkatan Darat	Army Information Office

Penal	Penerangan Angkatan Laut	Navy Information Office
Pendam	Penerangan Daerah Militer	Provincial / Regional Military Information Office
Penpres	Penetapan Presiden	Presidential Directive or Decision
Perdatam	Perindustrian Dasar dan Pertambangan	Basic Industry and Mining Office
Permesta	Pemerintah Revolusioner Perjuangan Semesta	a rebellion in N. Sulawesi and Sumatera against the central govt in the late 1950s
Perpres	Peratuan Presiden	Presidential Regulation
Perum	Perusahaan Umum	Public Corporation
Perumnas	Perumahan Nasional	National Housing Authority
Perwari	Persatuan Wanita Republik Indonesia	Women of Indonesia Unit - women's club charity
Pilkada	Pemilihan Kepala Daerah	Election for Provincial Governor
PKK	Pendidikan Kesejahter-aan Keluarga	Family Education & Welfare - administers Posyandu programs, educates women in village about family welfare
PKL	Pedagang Kaki Lima	Food cart vendors
PKL	Pakaian Kebesaran Lengkap	Dress uniform
PKPN	Pusat Kooperasi Pegawai Negeri	Union of Civil Servants - repre-sents government workers
PKT	—	Obstacle course
PLBI	—	The Suharto era
PLN	Perusahaan Listrik Negera	State Electric Company
PLT	Pelaksana Tugas	The acting head
PLTA	Pembangkit Listrik Tenaga Air	Hydroelectric power
PLTD	Pembangkit Listrik Tenaga Diesel	Diesel power
PLTG	Pembangkit Listrik Tenaga Gas	Gas
PLTN	Pembangkit Listrik Ten-gaga Nuklir	Nuclear power plants
PLTU	Pembangkit Listrik Ten-gaga Uap	Geothermal power
PMB	Penerimaan Mahasiswa Baru	new student admissions (to university)

386

PNI	Partai Nasional Indonesia	Indonesian Nationalist Party
Polda	Polisi Daerah	Provincial/State Police
Polresta	Polisi Resort Kota	City Police - in provincial/state capital cities
Polri	Polisi Republik Indonesia	Indonesian federal/national police
Polsek	Polisi Sektor	Local/Neighborhood Police - at *Kecamatan* level
Poltabes	Polisi Kota Besar	City Police - in large cities
Pores	Polisi Resort	Local Police - at *Kabupaten* level (County/Municipality)
Posma	Pekan Orientasi dan Studi Mahasiswa	Freshman Orientation week at university
PP	Pengurus Pusat	Board of Directors, Executive Board
PPN	Pajak Pendapatan Nasional	National Income Tax
PPP	Partai Persatuan Pembangunan	United Development Party - a Muslim development party
PPPK	Pertolongan Pertama Pada Kecelakaan	First Aid Kit
PR	Pekerjaan Rumah	Homework
PRAMUKA	Praja Muda Karana	Boy Scouts
PSII	Partai Serikat Islam Indonesia	Islamic Party of Indonesia
PSPB	Pendidikan Sejarah Perjuangan Bangsa	taught as a history subject in school - History of Nat'l Struggle
PSSI	Persatuan Sepak Bola Seluruh Indonesia	Indonesian Football League
PT	Perseroan Terbatas	Incorporated, a company with stockholders
PT	Panglima Tertinggi	mil officer rank - Regional Supreme Commander, geographically based, like a governor
PT	Perguruan Tinggi	Academy, Institute of Higher Education
PTIK	Perguruan Tinggi Ilmu Kepolisian	Police Academy
PTN	Perguruan Tinggi Negeri	Public university
PTP	Pos, Telkom, Parawisata	Post office, Telecommunications, Tourism
PTS	Perguruan Tinggi Swasta	Private university

PU	Pejabat Utama	A high official
PU	Pembantu Utama	Secretary General of a govt ministry, dept.
PU	Pekerjaan Umum	Public Works
Pungli	Pungutan liar	Amount charged above actual price by a corrupt worker
Puskesmas	Pusat Kesehatan Masyarakat	People's Health Center - in villages and rural areas
PWI	Persatuan Wartawan Indonesia	Indonesian Journalists Association
RAB	Rencana Anggaran Belanja	budget plan
RAPBD	Rencana Anggaran Pendapatan Belanja Daerah	the regional/provincial budget
Repelita	Rencana Pembangunan Lima Tahun	5-Year Development Plan
Reskrim	Reserse Kriminal	Criminal Investigations (in police station)
RK	Rukun Kampung	village association or unoffiicial pol organization
RMS	Republik Maluku Selatan	S. Moluccan Republic - name used by Moluccan separatist movement in Moluccas in 1950s-60s.
Rp.	rupiah	rupiah - indonesian currency
RPKAD	Resimen Pasukan Komando Angkatan Darat	Army Commando Regiment/troops
RS	Rumah Sakit	Hospital
RSI	Rumah Sakit Islam	Islamic-run Hospital
RSU	Rumah Sakit Umum	General Hospital
RSUD	Rumah Sakit Umum Daerah	General Hospital - smaller than RSUs
RT	Rukun Tetangga	Neighborhood Association - lowest level of administration
RW	Rukun Warga	Citizen's Association - 2nd lowest level of administration
S1	Stratum Satu 'es satu'	Bachelor's degree
S2	Stratum dua 'es dua'	Master's degree
S3	Stratum tiga 'es tiga'	Doctorate, Ph.D.
SARA	Suku, agama, ras, antar golongan	Ethnic, religious, and race relations
Satpam	Satuan Pengamanan	Security guard

SD	Sekolah Dasar	Primary/Elementary School
sd	sampai dengan	until (on advertisements, products)
SE	Sarjana Ekonomi	A bachelor's degree in economics
Sembako	Sembilan Bahan Pokok	The 9 Basic Necessities - oil, rice, etc.
Sesko	Sekolah Staf Komando	Staff and Command School
Seskogab	Sekolah Staf Komando gabungan	Joint Staff and Command School - in Bandung
SGA	Sekolah Guru Atas	Advanced Teacher's College
SGB	Sekolah Guru Bawah	Teacher's College
SH	Sarjana Hukum	Master's degree in law
SIM	Surat Ijin Mengemudi	Driver's License
siskamling	sistim keamanan lingkungan	Neighborhood security system
SK	Surat Keputusan	A decree, Directive. Or, a license for health professionals
SKN	Staf Kemanan Nasional	National Security Staff
SKP	Sekolah Kepandaian Puteri	Home Economics School
SLTP	Sekolah Lanjutan Tingkat Pertama	Middle / Junior High School (new name)
SMA	Sekolah Menengah Atas	High School (former name)
SMK	Sekolah Menengah Kejuruan	Vocational School (high school level)
SMP	Sekolah Menengah Pertama	Middle/Junior High School (former name)
SMTA	Sekolah Menengah Tingkat Atas	High schools and vocational schools
SMU	Sekolah Menengah Umum	High School (new name)
sob	sobat	pal, friend, mate
SOP	Standard Operating Procedures	SOP
Sospol	Sosial dan Politik	Social and Political Sciences
SPI	Sumbangan Pengembangan Institusi	An organization that helps pay part of tuition or arrange payment plan for poor students at uni.
SPMB	Seleksi Penerimaan Mahasiswa Baru	New Student Admissions (to university)
SPP	S P Pendidikan	Tuition - paid monthly by students

SPT	Surat Pajak Tahunan	Tax form (filed yearly)
SSKD	Sekolah Staf dan Komando Angkatan Darat	Army Command and Staff School
SSS	suka sama suka	By mutual consent, agreement
SSTB	Surat Tanda Tamat Belajar	School diploma - primary, middle school
STMJ	Susu, Telur, Madu, Jahe	A virility drink of milk, eggs, honey, ginger
STNK	Surat Tanda Nomer Kendaraan	Vehicle registration
SU	Staf Umum	General Staff
Sulselra	Sulawesi Selatan dan Tenggara	S and SE Sulawesi
Sulut	Sulawesi Utara	N Sulawesi
Sulutteng	Sulawesi Utara dan Tengah	N and Central Sulawesi
Sumsel	Sumatera Selatan	South Sumatera
TB	Toko Bangunan	Hardware Store, Building Supply
Tgl pake	Tinggal pakai	It runs well, is ready to go
THR	Tunjangan Hari Raya	Holiday work bonus
THT	Telinga, Hidung, Tenggorokan	Ear, Nose, and throat specialist
Tibum	Ketertiban Umum	Public Order
tilang	bukti pelanggaran	A ticket (like a traffic ticket)
TK	Taman Kanak-Kanak	Kindergarten
TKI	Tenaga Kerja Indonesia	Overseas workers
TKP	Tempat Kejadian Perkara	A crime scene
TKW	Tenaga Kerja Wanita	Women workers
TNI	Tentara Nasional Indonesia	The Indonesian Military
TNI AD	Tentara Nasional Indo Anggkatan Darat	The Indonesian Army
TNI AL	Tentara Nas. Indo Anggkatan Laut	The Indonesian Navy
TNI AU	Tentara Nas. Indo Anggkatan Udara	The Indonesian Air Force
TPA	Test Potensi Akademik	University entrance exam. Each uni makes own test.
TSP	Toko Sandang Pangan	A shop selling clothing and food
tst/TST	Tahu Sama Tahu	Unspoken deal between 2 people
TT	Tukar tambah	A trade-in (cars or motorcycle)

TT	Timur Tengah	Middle East
Tt. / Ttd.	Tertanda	Signed,
TTM	Teman Tapi Mesrah	intimate friends, sex buddies, friends with benefits
TU	Tata Usaha	administration
TVRI	Televisi Republik Indonesia	Indonesian (govt) TV channel
Ub.	Untuk Beliau	Signed on behalf of'
UGM	Universitas Gadjah Mada	Gajah Mada University in Yogyakarta
UI	Universitas Indonesia	University of Indonesia - Jakarta
USDEK	UU 45, Sosialisme, Demokrasi, Ekonomi, Kepribadian	5 principles of Sukarno's govt after 1960
UU	Undang-Undang	Law(s)
UUD	Undang-Undang Dasar	the Constitution
Wamil	Wajib Militer	The draft, conscription
Wampa	Wakil Menteri Pertama	Deputy Chief Minister, Vice Minister
WAPRES	Wakil President	Vice President
Warnet	Warung Internet	Internet shop/café
Wartel	Warung Telcom	Public telephone shop - with international service
WC	Water Closet	Restroom (bathroom)
WIB	Waktu Indonesia Barat	Western Indonesian Time (zone) - includes Jakarta, Java
WIT	Waktu Indonesia Timur	East Indonesian Time Zone
WITA	Waktu Indonesia Tengah	Central Indonesian Time Zone
WNA	Warga Negara Asing	foreign citizen
WNI	Warga Negara Indonesia	an Indonesian citizen
YME	Yang Maha Esa	The Almighty God
Yth.	Yang Terhormat	The Honorable (on letters)

Made in the USA
Monee, IL
03 July 2021

72872124R10216